Pelican Books
Memory

Professor Ian Hunter, B.Sc., D.Phil., is
head of the Psychology Department at
the University of Keele, Staffordshire.
He was born and brought up in Scotland,
and while still at school became strongly
interested in natural science and animal
behaviour. He entered Edinburgh
University to read physics, but transferred
to the study of psychology. After
post-graduate work at Oxford, he
joined the staff of the Edinburgh
Psychology Department and remained
there until 1962 when he took up his
present post at Keele. Apart from
university teaching and editorial work
for scientific journals, his chief professional
interest has lain in the experimental
study of human behaviour and
experience. His researches have given
rise to numerous reports in technical
journals. They have concerned such topics
as visual perception, the development
of problem-solving activities in
children, and the organization of adult
thinking and language. He has written
about the history of psychology, has
lectured in Canada and in several
European countries, and has held office
in various learned societies.

Ian M. L. Hunter

Memory

Penguin Books

Penguin Books Ltd, Harmondsworth,
Middlesex, England·
Penguin Books Inc., 7110 Ambassador Road,
Baltimore, Maryland 21207, U.S.A.
Penguin Books Australia Ltd,
Ringwood, Victoria, Australia
Penguin Books Canada Ltd,
41 Steelcase Road West,
Markham, Ontario, Canada
Penguin Books (N.Z.) Ltd,
182–190 Wairau Road,
Auckland 10, New Zealand

First Published 1957
Reprinted 1958, 1961, 1962
Revised edition 1964
Reprinted 1966, 1968, 1970, 1972, 1973, 1974

Made and printed in Great Britain by
Cox & Wyman Ltd,
London, Reading and Fakenham
Set in Monotype Baskerville

To Grace Philp Hunter

Contents

Editorial Foreword

'How can I improve my memory?' There can be few questions more frequently asked by those who turn to psychologists for advice on enhancing the powers of their minds. It is indeed an odd fact that people are apt to worry more about their memory than they do about their intelligence. 'Oh, I'm not very brainy,' people will gaily say, accepting the fact with cheerful resignation. Not so with memory. A poor memory is not to be accepted with cheerful resignation. A modest IQ is something with which one has been endowed and nothing much can be done about it, but one's memory, it is felt, is something for which some responsibility must be accepted. So notice is taken of courses of memory training advertised in the papers. Then the question is asked: Is there anything in these systems of memory training? Now this is a question which anyone should be able to answer for himself after reading this book.

Until quite recently it was easy to get the impression that in psychology there is little that is firmly established, and that the subject consists in a tissue of highly speculative theories, all extremely controversial and affording little basis for confident application. This has long ceased to be true. For a time the science resembled a vast territory much of which was covered by a rank growth of exotic weeds but containing a number of clearings in which through good husbandry a number of useful herbs have been produced. Today there are many new clearings, older clearings have been enlarged, and the clearings are joining up to form an organized whole – the *Science* of Psychology.

Editorial Foreword

The experimental study of remembering and forgetting is a field which has been cultivated for more than half a century. This is a clearing from which good crops of very saleable produce have been obtained.

This book is a comprehensive review of the facts, set out in a lucid readable way. In the light of this review the author gives in his final chapter his answers to the hundred dollar question: 'How can I improve my memory?' The answer costs a few shillings.

C. A. Mace.

Acknowledgements

The author thanks the following for their courtesy in allowing him to quote from publications of which they hold the copyright; the Editor of the *American Journal of Psychology* for excerpts from papers in volumes 35 and 45 of that periodical; the American Psychological Association for quotations from the *Journal of Abnormal and Social Psychology* and the *Journal of Experimental Psychology*; the Cambridge University Press for an extract from F. C. Bartlett's *Remembering*; The Historical Association for an extract from *Common Errors in Scottish History*; Prentice-Hall, Inc., for an excerpt from H. L. Kingsley's *The Nature and Conditions of Learning*; the Editor of the *British Journal of Psychology* for quotations from papers in volumes 15 and 32 of that Journal; the Pergamon Press Limited and the author for an extract from Professor Luria's article in *Problems of Psychology*, No. 1; The Clarendon Press for an excerpt from W. R. Russell's *Brain, Memory, Learning*; Routledge & Kegan Paul Ltd., for an excerpt from Théodule Ribot's *Diseases of Memory*; the British Medical Journal and the author for an excerpt from Dr Barbizet's article in the Journal of *Neurology, Neurosurgery and Psychiatry*, vol. 26; and The Nuffield Foundation for an excerpt from A. T. Welford's *Ageing and Human Skill*.

The author also wishes to thank Miss Patricia Creyke of the Keele Psychology Department for valuable secretarial help.

I What is Memory?

1 The Word Memory

'Memory' is an abstraction. In everyday speech, we talk of
having a good memory, of having a poor memory, of having
a better memory for faces than for names, of having a
memory that is failing, and so on. We talk about a person
having lost his memory for speech when he has sustained the
kind of brain injury which makes him unable to speak
coherently; and when he recovers, we say he has regained
his memory for speech. Such talk suggests that memory is
an object, a thing which we possess in the same way as we
possess a head or a big toe. Yet it is true, although alarming,
to say that there is no such thing as memory. A big toe can
be seen and touched, but not so memory. Suppose a friend
says, 'I have an excellent memory'. How can we test his
claim? We must ask him to do something; ask him to
execute a performance of some kind. We might, for example,
let him read the page of a book, then have him close the
book and try to recite what he has just read. If he reels off
the page verbatim, we conclude that his claim is, at the
least, not without foundation. But we have not observed
anything which could be called a memory. We have given
him an opportunity to learn something and then to demonstrate how well he can remember it. We have not, in any
direct sense, examined anything which he has. We have
watched him *doing* something, namely, repeating or trying
to repeat the page he has read. In short, we have concerned
ourselves not with an object but with activity; not with his
memory but with his activities of learning and remembering.

So memory is an abstraction, a shorthand way of referring

to certain kinds of activities. Memory is also ambiguous in the sense that the word is used to refer to very different kinds of activities. For example, our friend with the excellent memory may object to the test proposed above. Reciting a page of print after only one reading does, indeed, indicate remarkable memory. But this may not be what he means. He may mean that he can readily supply a large and detailed amount of information about some topic. The topic might be wide or narrow (history or geography or chemistry or general knowledge or sport), but ask him questions about his special topic and he can answer most of them quickly and correctly. On the other hand, he may mean that he can still perform some skill which he acquired a long time before and has not practised recently; although he has neglected the skill for years, he may still be able, say, to use a typewriter, or play chess, or speak a foreign language, or drive a car. Then again, he may mean that he can recall many episodes from his early youth. Or he may be using the expression 'excellent memory' to describe something he is doing right now, for instance, vividly seeing in his mind's eye a painting which he had looked at in the past. And yet again, he may mean that he can recognize and name melodies played to him, or works of art shown to him, or perfumes given to him to sniff. These different meanings illustrate the diversity of ways in which the word 'memory' may be used. They indicate that memory is an ambiguous word.

2 The Past and Present

'Memory' is, then, both abstract and ambiguous. However, it contains one common thread of meaning, which is this: what the person does and experiences here and now is influenced by what he did and experienced at some time in his past. When we talk of a person's memory we are almost always drawing attention to relationships between his past and his present activities.

These relationships between past and present arise out of a fundamental characteristic of human beings, namely, the fact that each person undergoes profound biographical change. In the course of his lifetime, every person changes. At birth he is the most helpless of creatures. But as he proceeds through life, he changes, not only in bodily build but also in the way he functions. He learns to speak, picking up new words and modes of expression. He becomes familiar with his environment. He grows in knowledge and understanding. He develops techniques for gaining this or that purpose. He acquires likes, dislikes, attitudes and prejudices. His moment-by-moment experiences and actions do not, all of them, pass and leave no trace behind: they act cumulatively so that he gains familiarity with the world around him and builds up accomplishments of an increasingly complex kind. Man, more so than any other living being, modifies himself by his own activities. There is a very real sense in which each individual becomes a different person in consequence of his own activities and experiences. And to the extent that these activities and experiences are under his own control, he also becomes capable of directing the future course of his own biographical development. This intricate influence of his past on his present, and of his present on his future, is one of man's outstanding features.

In its most general and comprehensive sense, memory refers to this pervasive and many-sided characteristic of biographical change. It refers to the effects which a person's past can exert on his present activities. It refers to the relationships that exist between what a person is doing and experiencing, here and now, and what he did and experienced at some time in his past. It refers to the ways in which past experiences are utilized in present activity.

What is Memory?

Three Phases of Memory. Memory concerns biographical changes which stretch over time, that is, event sequences such as the following. A person sees an accident and, at some later time, describes this accident in a court of law. A person learns how to manipulate a new kind of tin-opener and, sometime later, he uses this implement again with none of his original fumbling. A person listens to a melody, and when it is played again he recognizes that he has heard it before. In each sequence of events, there are three main phases. The initial phase involves some experience or activity, i.e., seeing the accident, learning to operate the tin-opener, hearing the melody. The final phase involves some experience or activity which is clearly influenced, and indeed made possible by, the first phase, i.e., describing the accident, using the tin-opener skilfully, recognizing the melody. The intervening phase involves retaining, for the initial phase must have changed the person in ways which persist through time. These persisting changes need not show during the interval. There may be nothing in a man's behaviour to indicate that he has learned how to use a particular kind of tin-opener. Yet when he does use the implement with skill, we can safely infer that he must have learned how to use it, and that this learning has somehow been retained by him in the interval.

We must consider the three phases just mentioned whenever we attempt to answer any question about memory; but some of our questions concern one phase more than another. Let us be more specific and consider a sequence of events where the three phases can be called learning, retaining, and remembering. A schoolboy is given the task of learning a Shakespeare sonnet. He sits down for quarter of an hour in the afternoon and learns the sonnet until he can recite it through without error. Then he does other things, has tea, plays football, reads a book, goes to bed, sleeps, and so on. Next day, his teacher asks him to recite the poem, and he tries to do so. Here we have a sequence of events spanning some twenty-four hours, and the three phases of memory seem fairly distinct.

The initial phase is that of learning. The boy reads and re-reads the sonnet, extracts its sense and the sequence of its ideas, tries to recite to himself the exact words in their correct order, masters some lines rapidly and other lines only with great effort. Notice that his learning is neither simple nor passive. It requires time and involves a complex of activities which are themselves derived from previous learning. He brings to the task a repertoire of accomplishments, and the way in which he learns depends conspicuously on what these accomplishments are. Thus, he must be sufficiently familiar with English language to be able to read the words and, to some extent, comprehend their meaning. Again, if he has learned other poems previously, he will probably have developed some general procedures which will help him to learn this one: for example, he will start by reading the entire sonnet and get a preliminary overview of the whole before he attempts to memorize the exact sequence of words. Learning is never a matter of passive absorption or registration but, rather, a complex of activities which depend partly on what is being learned and partly on the accomplishments brought by the individual to the learning. In relation to memory, the important thing about this learning phase is that it is a necessary condition for subsequent remembering; if the boy does not learn the poem, he cannot be expected to be able to recite it on some future occasion.

The final phase is that of remembering. He is asked to recite the sonnet, and proceeds to try to do this. He may start off well and then fumble. He may pause now and then, unsure how to continue. He may say some words, then stop and correct himself. He may omit a portion, or substitute a phrase which is not that of the original although close to it in meaning. He may get all the lines correct but in a wrong order. At one point, he may remember the rhythm or rhyme or general sense of what comes next but may not remember the exact words; and so he may hesitate, or fill in with other words, or come to a stop until someone prompts him with a word or two. Remembering, like learning, involves a complex of activities whose execution is affected by various circumstances. One obvious source of influence is the previous phase of learning. Other influences derive from present conditions, for instance, he may remember less well if he is tired, or unwell, or nervous. It must be emphasized that remembering is something a person *does*. It comprises activities which take place in the present and which are affected by conditions prevailing at the present time.

The intervening phase is that of retaining. The interval between learning and remembering is occupied by many activities quite unconnected with the sonnet. But if at the end of this interval, the schoolboy can, to any extent, remember the sonnet then, to that extent, the effects of learning must have been retained. During this interval, the retained effects of learning are latent, that is, they do not show themselves either in what the boy does or experiences. Nevertheless, they must persist if the boy can, under appropriate circumstances, carry out the activities of remembering the sonnet. We do not yet know much about the physiological bases of retaining. But we have no reason to doubt that retaining is accomplished by modifications of the nervous system and, furthermore, that these modifications are of a structural kind whenever retaining persists for longer than a few minutes. However, for all practical purposes, retaining is unobservable and has to be inferred from the person's remembering activities.

At this point, a word should be said about forgetting. In so far as the schoolboy cannot, in class, remember the poem as well as he did at the end of the learning phase, we say that some forgetting has taken place. This forgetting may or may not imply a failure to retain the effects of learning. If there is failure to retain, then there must be forgetting, that is, inability to remember. But there may be forgetting without failure to retain. In school, the boy may try unsuccessfully to remember the last four lines of the sonnet; yet he may, without consulting the original, be able to recite these lines at some later time. We are all familiar with this fact, that we may be unable to remember something at one time and yet be able to remember it at a later time. So, inability to remember need not mean failure to retain the effects of learning. It may, rather, reflect the point already made that remembering is an activity which is influenced by various circumstances. Retaining the effects of learning is a necessary condition for remembering but is not, of itself, sufficient.

The Value and Varieties of Memory. Memory, in its most comprehensive sense, refers to the effects of a person's past on his present. The person is modified, changed by what he does and experiences. And these persisting modifications affect what he does and experiences on later occasions; they enable him to accomplish much which would otherwise be impossible. Now, the accomplishments made possible by the retained effects of past experience are many, varied, and of enormous value to the person. Their value lies in their enabling him to adjust to present circumstances in the light of past events. In a phrase, they enable him to profit by experience.

Try to consider what would happen if a person were left totally unchanged by his experiences and activities. It is almost impossible to imagine what he would be like. Every situation he encountered would be forever strange, unfamiliar, unpredictable. He would commit the same errors over and over again with no chance of their ever being eradicated. He would develop no new accomplishments. Language would be impossible, so would thinking, self-awareness, anticipation of the future, and all art and science.

What is Memory?

He would be bereft of possibly everything that makes him recognizable as a human being. So the accomplishments made possible by the retained effects of past experience are of conspicuous value to the person. They are also very pervasive and diverse, for it is true to say that almost anything a person does is influenced in some way by his past. Suppose he picks up a small object with his fingers: the intricate coordination of muscle movements is a product of learning. Suppose he listens to someone speaking: the succession of auditory stimuli give rise to comprehension because of previous experience. Suppose he is laying plans for the future: this is possible because he lives in a world made familiar and predictable by his past. Whatever he does and experiences, it is no exaggeration to say that it is almost always influenced in some fashion by his past.

These accomplishments are so pervasive and diverse that it seems pointless to attempt any systematic classification of them. Much will be said about these accomplishments in subsequent pages but, in this present chapter, we shall consider only the two kinds of accomplishment to which the word 'memory' is applied more often than to any others. The first is the accomplishment of recalling, that is, of reproducing in the present some absent event from the past. The second is recognizing, that is, identifying some present event as being familiar from the past.

3 Recalling

We all know from our everyday lives what it is to recall successfully. We recite a poem or we play a melody which once we learned. We are asked for a name which we encountered in the past and we supply it. We re-live the experiences of a bygone episode. We see in our mind's eye the absent scenes of childhood. In all such cases, we re-create, in the here and now, the salient features of some event, or experience, or piece of information from our past. We produce, from the retained effects of a past occurrence, a replica of that occurrence.

Successful recalling is commonplace. It plays its smoothly familiar role at many points in our everyday lives. And for this reason, it is easy to overlook the marvellous subtlety of its operations. Likewise, it is easy and convenient in every-day affairs to believe that recalling is exactly duplicative in nature; that it duplicates precisely our experiencing of some past event, or even duplicates the event itself. However, on closer examination, it is found that recalling is by no means a simple activity and that the common belief in its dupli-cativeness is, strictly speaking, illusory. The complexity and non-duplicativeness of recalling are fundamental points which are perhaps difficult to grasp and will not be fully elaborated here. But it is worth turning some consideration to these points; and this will be done by discussing episodes which most readily illustrate the selective and constructive and non-duplicative nature of recalling.

Exactly faithful reproduction belongs, if anywhere, to the realm of recording machines and never, it would seem, to the realm of living beings. When a man describes an accident he witnessed yesterday, he is obviously not recreating the accident itself; he does not in any literal sense make the accident happen over again. At best, he recreates his experiencing of the accident: but even here, there never seems to be complete duplication of his ex-periencing in all its minute detail. When the schoolboy recites a poem with every word correct, he is, in a sense, making the poem happen over again. But on closer con-sideration, we find that he is producing one version of the poem which differs in many details of intonation and timing from every other version of the poem, even those spoken by himself on other occasions. The best rehearsed actor never gives two performances which are identical in every respect. Nor does a person ever look back upon his past, except in a metaphorical sense. In short, when a person recalls he does not effect a perfect forgery of past occurrences; he characterizes these occurrences rather than duplicates them. To be sure, his characterization may often be sufficiently detailed to be described, for all practical purposes, as accurate reproduction. But to assume that recalling is ever strictly duplicative is to ignore the selective and constructive nature of psychological functioning. It is also to ignore intrinsic features of recalling which can be of real practical concern for everyday life.

The above comments concerning the non-duplicative nature of recalling may be illustrated by referring to a specific memory task.

Recalling an Array of Digits. A university student is shown an array of nine digits as in Figure 1. He is asked to learn the numbers, in any way he likes, so that he will be able to write them out from memory in exactly the arrangement shown.

Figure 1

After one minute for learning, the array is withdrawn and he listens to a lecture for about an hour. At the end of the lecture, he is asked to reproduce the array. And this he does successfully, writing down all the correct digits in their correct locations.

He does not, of course, duplicate the original printed array in all details. For example, the figures are in his own handwriting, and his drawing of the squares departs from the dimensions of the original. There are conspicuous differences between his reproduction and the original, but they are not differences which he or anyone else would regard as important. The distinguishing characteristics of the array are all present and, in this sense, his reproduction is accurate. Granting this elementary point, the student appears to have engaged in straightforward reproductive activity. However, if we ask him to tell us how he went about reproducing the array, we quickly discover that matters are less simple than they seem. Here is his report.

'I drew the three-by-three grid and remembered the pattern into which the digit sequence 3, 4, 5, 6 fitted. I remembered that this was a magic-square.' (A magic-square is such that if the digits in any row or column or diagonal are added together, the total is always the same. In this square the digits in every row, column, or diagonal add up to 15.) 'I checked that the recurring total was 15 by adding the 4, 5 and 6 in the diagonal. I then worked out the remaining digits and their locations. In the middle row, I already had 3 and 5, so the required digit must be 7.' (In other words, 3 plus 5 totals 8; but the total for the row must be 15, and so the missing digit has to be 7.) 'Similarly the last column must be completed by 2, and then the top row completed by 9. The bottom row then worked out at 8 in the corner and 1 in the middle. This completed the square.' For this student at least, recalling is a complex constructive activity. The reproduction of the array involves a devious succession of activities which he describes, in part, as 'remembering' and, in part, as 'working out'.

The writer has given this particular memory task to more than two hundred students. They find it fairly easy. With only one minute spent in learning, some 90 per cent of students correctly reproduce the array one hour later.

What is Memory?

When students are asked afterwards to report as much as they can about what they did while learning and remembering the array, their reports strikingly bring out three points relevant to the constructive nature of recalling.

The first point concerns individual differences. There is great diversity in how students set about the tasks of learning and reproducing the array. In learning, a very few students proceed by what appears to be sheer rote repetition, that is, they repeat the nine digits over and over again, e.g., a student may recite 4, 9, 2; 3, 5, 7; 8, 1, 6, over and over as often as time allows. But the great majority, even though they use repetition, do not recite digits without noting relationships between them. In some cases, these noted relations are simple, e.g., that 3, 5, 7 is an odd-numbered sequence, or that 4, 9, 2 are the last three digits of the year in which Columbus landed in America. In other cases, these relations are more complex, e.g., the even sequence 2, 4, 6, 8 fills up the four corners in the order top-to-bottom and right-to-left, while the odd sequence 1, 3, 5, 7, 9 fills up the remaining gaps in the order bottom-to-top and left-to-right. Some students note that the array is a magic-square; some do not. The main point is that, even in this simple learning task, hardly any two students carry through their learning activity in quite the same fashion. This point warns us against assuming that when two people learn the same lesson they necessarily learn it in the same way.

The second point which emerges from the reports concerns *effort after meaning*. Despite individual differences between one student and the next, no learner passively absorbs the array. Rather, he proceeds by, so to speak, making of the material what sense he can. He attempts to impose pattern, to interpret the array in terms of relationships which are already familiar to him, to recast the material into familiar moulds. He elaborates relationships which coordinate one part of the array with another: a few examples of such relationships were cited above. Sometimes a student is acutely aware of seeking out these relationships, sometimes they 'just happen'. However, when he elaborates coordinating relations which are compact, familiar, and adequate to the array, then the material makes sense to him and his learning is felt to become much easier. When he does not elaborate coordinates of a familiar kind, then he relates component digits together by repetition. He repeats the digits in some appropriate order until he can run through the digits sequence without prompting himself by looking at the original. So learning is not a matter of passive registration. It is active and selective, and effort after meaning plays a conspicuous part. The reports also reveal that the particular coordinating relationships elaborated during learning later play a role in subsequent recall. And this brings us to the third, and last, point brought out by the reports.

The third point directly concerns the constructive characterization of past events. Each individual student shows similarity between the way he went about learning the array and the way he goes about reproducing it. His learning and his reproducing share the same individualistic coordinating relationships. In recall, he does not reproduce the array all in one passive instant. He constructs the array by deploying various coordinating characteristics which he elaborated during learning. Some of these characteristics are general, e.g., the array is a three-by-three square: some are particular, e.g., 4 occurs in the top-left corner. Whatever the characteristics, he deploys several of them so as to lead, eventually, to the construction of the total array. This constructiveness is evident in the report quoted earlier from the student who 'remembered' so much and 'worked out' so much. Constructiveness is also evident in the following report from another student. 'I remembered the square arrangement and simply filled it in by bringing to mind the jingle 438, 951, 276, inserting these three numbers (of three digits each) vertically and working from left to right.' Both of these students reproduced the original accurately by constructing a new array containing the characteristics they had noted as being salient in the original.

The reports of the above students testify that their learning is not a simple matter of taking the array passively into store, nor is their recalling a matter of merely withdrawing the array from storage. It would be nearer the mark to summarize their activities as follows. Learning is the working out of the characteristics of the array and the coordination of these characteristics into an interlocking pattern. Recalling is the re-employment of these general characteristics and the fitting of them together to create a new array which corresponds to the noted features of the original. Lastly, even though all students recall the array accurately, they are likely to do this by employing a pattern of characteristics which varies from one student to the next.

Recalling a Name. While a person is recalling, he is essentially engaged in selectively constructing the salient characteristics of the original event. This is evident in the situation just described. It is evident too whenever the original occurrence is especially complex, e.g., a story or a sequence of happenings. It is also evident whenever the original occurrence is difficult to recall. Consider the recalling of a person's name. To be sure, we often recall a required name rapidly and apparently without effort. We feel the name to follow instantly on its being sought and we have nothing to report about our activity except that the name was wanted and it came. Such instances tempt us to overlook the selective and constructive nature of our recalling. However, there are other occasions when we are aware of attempting to characterize the name. We must all have experienced those occasions when we try to recall a name and cannot do so until after an appreciable lapse of time during which we are aware of 'casting around' for it.

In attempting to achieve recall, we are aware of some of the name's characteristics, for example, its rhythm or its length or its first letter, or that it savours of some particular nationality, or that it is the same as that of a famous artist – if only we could specify which. We may proceed to fill out some of these characteristics by recalling a few names and we hope that we may recognize one of these as being the required name or, at least, that one of them may suggest the required name to us. We may proceed to recall events related to the elusive name and its possessor, for example, the person's appearance, his mannerisms, the circumstances in which we met him, the people whose company he keeps. There are times when we feel we are 'nearly there' and times when we feel we are 'caught in a rut', that is, we are proceeding in terms of inappropriate characteristics. Throughout all this, we are not only engaged in activity of a constructive kind but we are also aware of it. We are aware, as very often we are not, that recalling is no simple matter, that it is an active selecting and combining together of those characteristics which serve to specify the wanted past occasion and no other.

Localization in the Personal Past. Special mention should now be made of two further characteristics involved in many recalled occasions. One is that the person localizes the occasion, with greater or less precision, in past time: he constructs a historical context for it. The other is that he feels, with greater or less certainty, that he has actually witnessed the occasion: he gives it the warm intimacy of personal experience. When the recalled occasion involves both of these characteristics in marked degree, we have that especially rich and personal form of recalling which is termed *recollecting*. Recollecting is referred to colloquially as 're-living the past', 'thinking over old times', 'remembering when', or, more simply, as 'reminiscing' or 'having memories'. It involves more than recalling

27

an autobiographical fact: thus most people can recall the date and place of their birth but no one recollects this occasion. It involves the person in nothing less than recalling an occasion as being located in past time, and as having been experienced by himself at first hand. The recalled occasion is localized in his uniquely personal past experience. For anyone to be able to characterize an occasion as being localized in the context of his personal past is a truly remarkable achievement. Indeed it is one of the most subtly refined accomplishments made possible by the cumulative retained effects of past experience.

Much has been written, of a descriptive and introspective kind, about the phenomena of recollection, especially by the Scottish psychologists of the eighteenth and nineteenth centuries. But here, only three general points will be briefly made, each illustrated by a quotation from the French psychologist Théodule Ribot (1835–1916), whose important book *Diseases of Memory* appeared in English translation in 1885.

(1) Localization in the personal past can vary through every degree of precision. At one extreme, the occasion may be pin-pointed to the very year, month, day and hour. At the other extreme, there may be only a vague feeling of pastness, of the occurrence having been witnessed at some unspecified past time. Recollection may also be unexpectedly wanting.

'An instance is recorded by Macaulay in his essay on Wycherley, whose memory, he tells us, was "at once preternaturally strong and preternaturally weak" in his declining years. If anything was read to him at night, he awoke the next morning with a mind overflowing with the thoughts and expressions heard the night before; and he wrote them down with the best faith in the world, nothing doubting that they were his own' (pp. 56–7).

(2) Localization is achieved by selective and often conspicuously constructive activity. We are often aware of

having to construct a temporal context for the recalled occasion. We do not do this by performing a cumbersome progress from the present time backwards through our remembered past to the occasion in question. We proceed by relating the recalled occasion to some of those other occasions whose habitually precise localizations are the focal reference points of our remembered personal past.

'Our way is facilitated by the use of reference points. I will cite a familiar instance. On the 30th of November I am looking for a book of which I have great need. It is coming from a distance, and its transportation will require at least twenty days. Did I send for it in time? After a little hesitation I remember that my order was given on the eve of a short journey, whose date I can fix in a precise manner as Sunday, the 9th of November. With this, recollection is complete. In analysing this case, we observe that the principal state of consciousness – the order for the book – is first thrown into the past in an indeterminate manner. It arouses secondary states, compares them, and places itself before or after. After a number of oscillations, more or less extended, it finds its place; it is fixed, remembered. In this example the recollection of the journey is what I designate as a reference point' (pp. 50–1).

(3) Personal past, as a person represents it to himself, is often distorted relative to objective time. (For a recent and not too technical review, see *The Psychology of Time* by the French psychologist P. Fraisse. Published by Harper & Row, 1963.) The passing of time as experienced and as measured by a clock are often at variance: thus a clock-hour spent with agreeable companions is felt to pass more quickly than a clock-hour spent in unpleasant suspense. Likewise, the duration of a segment of time as recollected is often at variance with the clock-duration of the original period.

'If I represent the past ten years of my life by a line one metre long, the last year would extend over three or four decimetres; the fifth, very eventful, would occupy two decimetres; and the other eight would be compressed into the remaining space' (p. 60).

Automatization. This is a convenient point at which to make brief mention of a further, and very important, feature of recalling. So far, we have emphasized that recalling is a complex interaction of activities directed towards representing, in the present, the salient characteristics of a past occurrence. Discussion has dwelt on these recall episodes where we can experience for ourselves something of the selectiveness and constructiveness of our own recalling; that is, recall episodes in which we are aware of activities going on between the moment when we start trying to recall and the moment when recall is successfully accomplished. Now, it is noteworthy that the more often we are required to recall a particular occurrence, the easier does our recall become. On successive attempts, recall is carried through more rapidly and with progressively less involvement of conscious experience. With practice, the occasion is brought more readily and directly to mind. Recalling becomes progressively more 'automatic' or, to use the technical term, *automatized*.

The automatization of recalling is very conspicuously encountered in the school classroom. It is also familiar in everyday life, and examples are easy to cite. Suppose we are asked about an incident which we witnessed a month ago: suppose we reconstruct the incident with much difficulty, we fumble, correct ourselves, laboriously work out its characteristics by fitting together this fragment with that: if next day, we are asked again about the incident, we can recollect it more easily and directly. Suppose we learn a person's name by means of some mnemonic device: if we have frequent cause to recall the name, we no longer need to use this device, and with practice, the name comes 'automatically'. Suppose we are learning to touch-type: at the outset we have to think out the location of the key we want; but as practice continues, our finger seems almost to fly of its own accord to the correct place on the key-board. Suppose we are attempting to master the vocabulary of a foreign language: in the early stages we may have to recall a word by devious activities, including recollection of the time we first encountered the word: but after we have recalled the word several times, it 'just comes' when needed.

Automatization of recalling is, then, a familiar phenomenon. It is also important in several respects and more will be said about it later. Here, it is sufficient to describe its main features. By repeatedly attempting to recall the same occasion, we learn how to recall it with economy of time and effort. In the early stages, we often have to proceed deviously by recalling and recollecting other occasions that might serve as reference points. But with practice, these devious procedures become unnecessary and, by a kind of natural selection, cease to be involved in recall. Eventually, we attain that rapid, automatized and depersonalized recalling which is typical for material that, as we say, we know well.

4 Recognizing

We show someone a photograph. Does he recognize the photograph as a photograph rather than, say, a painting? Does he recognize the figure in the photograph as a woman rather than, say, a bush or a man? Does he recognize the woman as someone he has ever met before, or not? Does he recognize her as someone he has met within the past week, or not? Does he recognize her as one of his colleagues at work, or not? Does he recognize her personal identity, for example, is she Mrs X? Again, we let someone hear a musical composition. Can he recognize its identity, its authorship, or its style? A young school child is said to be able to recognize the letters of the alphabet when, on being shown individual letters, he names each correctly.

In these recognition tasks, there are three essential features. First, an event is present in the here and now. For example, the photograph, the piece of music, the letter of the alphabet. Secondly, the person supplies some character- istic of that event. For example, he identifies the photo- graph as a likeness of Mrs X; he is aware that he has heard the melody before; or he identifies the melody as a national anthem. Thirdly, this characterizing is made possible by the retained effects of his past experience. For example, he could not identify Mrs X without having retained some effects from having seen her at some past time. In recognizing, the person supplies some characteristic which is, in a strict sense, not present in the event con- fronting him. This characterization may be of many different kinds and may vary all the way from the extremely precise ('This is Mrs X') to the extremely imprecise ('I've seen this person before but I don't know where or when').

Preparedness for Recognizing. If we are expectantly waiting for the telephone to ring, we quickly recognize the bell when it does ring. But if we are not expecting a call, it may take us some moments to identify that strange ringing noise. Again, we quickly recognize our next-door neighbour when we meet him near our house. But when we encounter the same man unexpectedly in a distant town, we take longer to recognize his identity. These examples illustrate a general rule: an expected event is more easily recognized than an unexpected event.

Consider a further illustration of this rule. We tell a person that we are going to show him a single letter of the alphabet and that his task will be to recognize it and tell us its name. We make this task difficult for him by flashing the letter on to a screen for only a fraction of a second. Now, we can carry out this experiment under two conditions. In one condition we make use of only two letters. Each time a letter is flashed on the screen, it is either A or B. Each exposure shows one of only two possible letters: and the person is told this beforehand. In short, his task is to recognize which, out of two possible letters, is shown. In the other condition, each exposure shows one of the twenty-six letters of the alphabet: and he is told that any letter may appear. His task is, then, to recognize which, out of twenty-six possible letters, is shown. When he does these two tasks, we find that his recognizing is more successful under the first condition. Indeed, we can arrange a constant exposure value so that he is almost always successful in the 2-letter condition and almost always unsuccessful in the 26-letter condition. In other words, whenever the letter A is exposed while he is prepared for two possibilities, he usually recognizes it: but whenever A is exposed while he is prepared for twenty-six possibilities, he usually fails to recognize it. The exposures are the same under the two conditions: the difference lies in his state of preparedness. His recognizing is influenced not only by what *is* exposed but also by what *could* have been exposed.

In this experiment, we also find that the time he requires to name the letter is shorter in the 2-letter condition. We can arrange a constant value of exposure so that he always recognizes the letter shown under either condition: we can also arrange to measure very closely the time which elapses between the onset of exposure and the start of his naming the letter. If we do this, we find that the time to recognize correctly is measurably shorter in the 2-letter condition.

The results of this experiment illustrate, yet again, that a person recognizes an event more rapidly and correctly when he is prepared for the occurrence of that event. Furthermore, the results illustrate that preparedness is not an all-or-none affair but a matter of degree, which is related to the number of different events he expects may occur. For example, recognition becomes, on average, progressively more difficult as he passes from a 2-letter to an 8-letter to a 26-letter condition. He is better prepared to recognize the letter A if it is one of two likely events than if it is one of twenty-six. In the 2-letter condition, the event is more closely characterized beforehand. He does not, of course, know which event will occur; but the possibilities are limited to two. And so, when the event does occur, he has less to do in order to complete its unique specification, that is, to characterize it as the letter A and no other. In brief, the more narrowly a person is prepared for the occurrence of a particular event, the more rapidly and successfully will he be able to characterize that event when it arrives. (Several experimental studies have established quantitative relationships between recognition performance and the number of possible events. But such studies are of a rather technical nature and will not be considered here. For a survey, see W. R. Garner's excellent but difficult book *Uncertainty and Structure as Psychological Concepts*, 1962.)

Consider now another experiment which is slightly different from that just described. This time, it is a word which is flashed briefly on the screen each time, and there are three conditions of preparedness. In one condition, the person expects the word to be the name of an animal. In another condition, he expects the name of a flower. And in the third condition, he is merely told to expect a word without being told what kind of word to prepare for. Now suppose the word exposed is ZEBRA. Other things equal, he recognizes this word more quickly and accurately when he is prepared for an animal word rather than just any word. But his recognition is poorest when he is prepared for a flower word. This illustrates that preparedness facilitates and also impedes subsequent recognition. It facilitates recognizing an event of the kind expected but, at the same time, it impedes recognizing an event which is not of the kind expected. Being prepared in, so to speak, the wrong direction is worse than being relatively unprepared.

The above observations are summarized in the following general rule. The more narrowly prepared a person is to recognize one kind of event, the more rapidly and correctly will he recognize this kind of event when it occurs; and the more slowly and incorrectly will he recognize an event of another kind.

This is one of those general rules which is pervasively exemplified in human activities. Especially so if we include those more persistent states of preparedness which go by such names as disposition, interest, and prejudice. Only a few illustrations need be given. It is easier to recognize a spoken phrase when it occurs as part of connected discourse rather than by itself in isolation. Why? Because what is said at any moment in discourse is determined by what has gone before, and so we are, in some degree, prepared to recognize the phrase now being uttered: in isolation, this same phrase lacks the facilitation of preparedness. It is notoriously difficult to proof-read printed matter. Why? Because we are habitually prepared to read print for its sense and, indeed, to ignore printing errors: this impedes our recognizing these errors, even when we want to be able to do so. When research scientists talk about their methods of working, they frequently testify to the effects of their preparedness in making them fail to recognize some 'obvious' phenomenon. In the field of human relations, preparedness for recognizing is also important. What we recognize in a foreigner's behaviour is often strongly determined by our stereotype of his nation's characteristics. Likewise, what we recognize in any person's actions, say selfishness or selflessness, is influenced by what we are prepared to recognize in him. The aim of social propaganda, like that of the stage magician, is to prepare people to recognize events in some ways and not in others.

Preparedness Induced by Hypnosis. There are many ways in

which a person may become prepared to recognize some particular kind of event. The state may be established by explicit verbal instructions, as in the letter experiments reported above. The state may be established by the person's encountering a succession of events which all call for recognizing a similar kind of characteristic, as in the schoolboy ruse involving the word 'machines'. How, he asks his victim, do you pronounce this word? M-A-C-G-R-E-G-O-R. And this? M-A-C-H-U-G-H. And this? M-A-C-H-I-N-E-S. The first two tasks prepare the victim to recognize Scottish surnames beginning with M A C, and the ruse works if the familiar word 'machines' is recognized as being yet another surname of this kind. States of preparedness may also be established by the procedures known as hypnosis. In hypnosis, one person gradually induces in another a state of extreme suggestibility and cooperativeness in which the subject becomes unusually prepared to accept instructions given to him by the hypnotist. The subject progressively relinquishes more and more of his independence of action and increasingly subjugates himself to being controlled by the hypnotist's instructions. Once a moderate degree of hypnotic suggestibility has been established, the subject will readily accept instructions concerning what he will and will not recognize. This may be illustrated by outlining an experiment conducted in 1941 by two Cambridge psychologists, H. Bannister and O. L. Zangwill.

Five adults agreed to serve as subjects, and the critical part of the experiment fell into three stages, each stage on a separate day. In stage one, on the first day, a subject was simply asked to examine six photographs for about half a minute each. The photographs depicted scenes, objects, and little-known paintings. The subject was not hypnotized at this stage. In stage two, on the second day, the subject went through a similar procedure with a new set of six cards. There was, however, one important difference. This time, the subject was hypnotized before being shown the cards.

When a moderate degree of suggestibility had been established, he was told that he would be shown several cards, one at a time, and would look carefully at each card for half a minute. Then he was given the first card to scrutinize. This card was removed after thirty seconds and he was given the following suggestion. 'After you wake up, you will have forgotten all about this card, and you will *not* be able to recognize it if it is shown to you tomorrow.' He then examined the remaining cards, one after the other, and the above suggestion was repeated after each showing. At the end of the series of cards, the subject was restored to his normal unhypnotized state.

Stage three of the experiment took place on the third and last day. The subject, in his normal state, was shown cards and was asked to comment on them. He was shown all the photographs used on the two preceding days, together with some completely new ones. As each card was presented, he was asked to describe whatever came to mind in connexion with it; what it was like, what it suggested, whether he had seen it before, whether he liked it, and so on. Now, it would be expected that the cards shown on the first day would be recognized as having been seen on that day; and that the cards shown for the first time today would not be recognized as having been seen before. In effect, this is what happened. But how would the subject react to those cards which he had been shown under hypnosis and been instructed to forget? If the suggestion were completely effective, these cards would be seen as for the first time. If the suggestion were completely ineffective, he would recognize the cards as having been seen before: the hypnotic state, as such, would not prevent him from remembering what he had experienced.

What actually happened was that the suggestion to forget was not completely effective in any of the five subjects. Three of the subjects recognized the cards which had been presented on the second day. However, two subjects showed interesting near-failures to recognize. For example, one subject responded to one of the cards as follows. 'I have the impression ... I have the impression that I have seen that before ...' Here he pauses and the experimenter asks if he can remember where he saw it or anything about it. 'I have a feeling I should like to tell you, but why can't I say it? I have the same feeling as I had ... I know exactly ... There is something in my mind which is making continual efforts to tell you but my tongue won't get on with the job. Now where did I? I am just saying to myself now: "Come on, don't be so dumb! You know you have seen it before!" ... It's like making up one's mind to jump over one of those walls that give way under you – those dry walls in Yorkshire – I simply can't give you the answer. It's a very tiring process too.' This subject was certain that he had seen the card before but could not specify either where or when: he was able to characterize the card as having been witnessed by himself in the past, but unable to characterize it more closely by localizing this previous experience in his personal past. This minimal recognizing of a card as having been witnessed before was found to be accompanied by strenuous efforts at trying to recollect the circumstances of the original experience. The person tried hard to construct a personal historical context for it. These efforts were felt to be unpleasant, bewildering and tiring. And they sometimes led to the construction of a fabricated context, that is, the subject constructed a past encounter with the card which, although objectively fictitious, was accepted by him as genuine recollection.

This experiment, then, demonstrates two things. First, hypnotic suggestion can be used to establish a state of preparedness *not* to recognize an event as having been witnessed before. Secondly, it demonstrates how people deal with minimal recognition. It reveals the uneasy attempts to establish a closer specification of the event in relation to personal past experience; and to achieve such specification by means of that unwitting fabrication about which more will be said in later chapters. Before leaving this experiment, it should be mentioned that the degree of hypnotic suggestibility employed was relatively slight. With stronger hypnotic suggestion, subjects can be made to fail in recognizing events which are very familiar to them: they can also be made to fail in recalling familiar events. Conversely, they can be made to behave as though they recognized and recalled events they had never witnessed. They can also be primed to recall long past events which normally they cannot recall: events which have seemed forgotten can sometimes be genuinely recalled by means of procedures (hypnotic and otherwise) that establish in the person a strongly adequate state of preparedness for recalling these events. Such findings reaffirm the extent to which remembering, whether by recall or recognition, is actively constructive in nature.

Paradoxical Recognition. The experience known as *déjà vu* (literally 'already seen') involves two features which, under the majority of circumstances, are contradictory. On the one hand, a present event is recognized as having been witnessed before. On the other hand, there is certainty that this event has not been witnessed before. A description of this self-contradictory recognizing is given by the novelist, Charles Dickens, who is well known for his accurate delineations of the unusual and pathological in human functioning. The following passage occurs in his novel *David Copperfield.*

'If you had not assured us, my dear Copperfield, on the occasion of that agreeable afternoon we had the happiness of passing with you, that D was your favourite letter,' said Mr. Micawber, 'I should unquestionably have supposed that A had been so.' On hearing these words, Copperfield suddenly experienced the illusory recognition, which he described with an almost scientific exactitude as follows: 'We have all some experience of a feeling, that comes over us occasionally, of what we are saying and doing having been said and done before, in a remote time – of our having been surrounded dim ages ago, by the same faces, objects and circumstances – of our knowing perfectly what will be said next, as if we suddenly remembered it! I never had this mysterious impression more strongly in my life, than before he uttered those words.'

In its strongest form, *déjà vu* saturates all present experience with recollective familiarity. The person feels that he has already experienced all that is happening at this moment and all that is going to happen in the next. It is rather like witnessing a second showing of the same cinefilm, except that the person knows he has not experienced the present events before. When this experience takes place, it usually lasts, at most, for a minute or two. But in that brief time, the activities of recognizing are, as it were, out of hand so that everything which occurs is reacted to as having been witnessed previously. There is a tendency for this strong form of *déjà vu* to occur in people who suffer from a certain kind of brain dysfunction. In these people there is, from time to time, a period of spontaneous neural discharge from the temporal lobe region of the brain. During the temporal-lobe fits, the person experiences, without necessarily either fear or pleasure, this intense feeling that everything around him has happened in the same way before. He may come to know *déjà vu* well as a symptom of his fits. Now it must be emphasized that the occurrence of *déjà vu*, even in its strongest form, is not confined to people with brain dysfunction. Indeed many people, especially those who are sensitive to their own states of conscious awareness, have experienced this paradoxical recognizing at one time or another. Many people have also experienced the other kind of paradoxical recognizing known as 'alienation': here, there is a brief period in which intimately known situations and persons are experienced as being strange and unfamiliar. In normally healthy people, these experiences of paradoxical recognition are infrequent and their cause is not easy to discover.

In its weakest form, *déjà vu* involves mild puzzlement over unaccountable familiarity. It may be experienced while we are visiting some town for the first time. We have never been there before yet, to our surprise, the street where we stand looks familiar and, when we turn the corner, the scene we encounter is somehow not unexpected. In such cases, there may well be an environmental basis for our recognition: after all, some new towns have characteristics which are strongly similar to towns we already know. If we are able to specify such characteristics, we may simply remark how alike this town is to some other. If we cannot specify these characteristics, we may yet recognize them vaguely and be unable to account for our feeling of familiarity. Likewise in weak forms of alienation, we are perplexed by unaccountable lack of familiarity. We may return to a room we know well: all seems familiar yet strangely unfamiliar – until at last we specify the cause. Some piece of furniture has been changed since we saw the room last. We had vaguely recognized some change but, without being able to characterize the nature of the change more closely, we were left with the puzzlement of un-accountable unfamiliarity.

Recall and Recognition Compared. There are many instances in which it is conspicuously easier to recognize than to recall. For example, people often observe that they cannot remember (recall) a particular name or fact but would know it if they heard it or saw it (that is, they would recognize it as the name or fact required). Again, it is often remarked, 'I have a poor memory for people's names but never forget a face.' This remark usually seems to mean that, when a person is met, he can readily be recognized but his name is difficult to recall. Yet again, in their use of language, people can understand (recognize) far more words in the speech of others than they use (recall) in their own speech: and likewise their reading vocabulary is much larger than their writing vocabulary. Lastly, it is almost always easier to be successful in a short-answer test involving recognition as opposed to recall-type questions. In such tests, a recall task would be of the following kind. 'In what year was the battle of Hastings fought?' By contrast, a recognition task might be as follows. 'Was the battle of Hastings fought in 1149, or 1066, or 1035, or 988?' It is common experience that the second kind of question can often be answered successfully when the first kind cannot.

Now, why should it be the case that recognizing is so often easier to accomplish successfully than recalling? There would seem to be a number of different factors at work, depending on the particular situation. But in all situations, there is one underlying factor, which can be illustrated by considering the multiple-choice recognition task. If it is assumed, as it usually is, that one of those dates is correct, then it is apparent that, from the outset, the person's freedom of choice is closely restricted. The required date is already characterized for him as being one of four alternatives: a measure of characterization is supplied which, in recall, he would have to supply for himself. Furthermore, it is possible for him to specify the correct alternative by means of characteristics which would be insufficient for successful recall. For example, he might be able to characterize the date as being 'ten-something-with-a-double-digit-at-the-end'. Such general characterization is insufficient for successful recall but is sufficient to specify which of the four given dates is correct. In brief, the recognition task is easier than the recall task in that it enables the person to restrict himself to a smaller number of alternatives and to narrow down those alternatives by means of characteristics which may be insufficient for purposes of recalling.

Recall, then, is typically a more severe test of a person's ability to supply the characteristics of a required item. In recall, he must supply all those characteristics which are necessary to distinguish the item from all other similar items, e.g., to distinguish the date from all other historical dates. In recognition, he need only be able to supply those characteristics which suffice to distinguish the item from the alternatives presented to him. Notice that we can increase the demands of the recognition task by increasing the number of alternatives we present to the person. This is what is done by police when they arrange an identification parade rather than asking a witness whether or not he identifies a single suspect. We can also increase the demands of the recognition task by letting the person know that the correct item might not be one of the alternatives presented. This is what is done in multiple-choice tests which ask the following kind of question. 'Was the battle of Hastings fought in 1149, or 1066, or 1035, or 988, or none of these years?'

How Different Are Recall and Recognition? When we are exploring phenomena as complex and as varied as those of human functioning, we find that our classifications of these phenomena are often rather arbitrary. They are useful for some purposes but not for others. Such is the case with the distinction between recalling and recognizing. There are circumstances in which it is of value to distinguish between these two kinds of accomplishment. We need think only of the difference between recall and recognition examination questions. But there are other circumstances where it is impossible to draw any dividing line between recall and recognition, and where it is pointless to try to do so. Such circumstances generally arise as soon as we begin to explore closely what a person is actually doing in recall or recognition tasks. For example, when we ask a person to recall, we provide him with some characteristics of an event by saying, 'That man who drives the green car', and require him to supply some further characteristics of the event by asking, 'What is his name?' Similarly, when we ask a person to recognize, we provide him with some characteristics by getting him to look at the man in question, and we require him to supply some further characteristics by asking, 'Have you seen him before?' In both cases, certain characteristics are supplied and the person must supplement them by further characteristics derived from his past experience. What these supplementary characteristics are, and how the person produces them are details in the study of which we soon lose sight of the distinction between recall and recognition. Suffice it to say that this distinction is of value when we are considering, in relatively general terms, the kind of memory task a person is undertaking: but it may be of little or no value when we are considering, in close detail, the activities by means of which the memory task is being accomplished. It is probably wise to regard recalling and recognizing as being, at basis, the same complex type of process which utilizes the retained effects of past experience to supplement activity in the present.

5 The Cumulative Effects of Past Experience

It has already become clear that, as a person develops from infancy through adulthood, his experiences and activities become more and more influenced by the retained effects of his previous experiences and activities. These influences are cumulative. One accomplishment builds upon earlier accomplishments and, in its turn, lays the foundation for yet further accomplishments of ever-increasing variety and complexity. This cumulative building up of progressively higher-order accomplishments is perhaps most conspicuous during the childhood years. But it also occurs in adulthood, as can be illustrated by briefly considering the acquisition of skill in telegraphy.

The Cumulative Effects of Past Experience

The Development of Skill. Telegraphy involves the transmission of messages by means of a special language whose units are a short auditory click (a dot), a long auditory click (a dash) and pauses of varying length. The acquisition of this language presupposes familiarity with a verbal language, say, English; for each English letter is represented by a pattern of clicks. In sending a message by telegraphy, the task is to translate an English message into its telegraphic equivalent and send this by pressing a key once for each click. In receiving, the task is to listen to the incoming sequence of auditory signals, translate them into English and, very often, type out this translation as it is made. Now, the accomplishments of an expert telegraphist are impressive. In sending, he transmits something like 140 letters, say 400 clicks, every minute. In receiving, he types out clean copy at an average rate of perhaps eighty to eighty-five words a minute. He does this hour after hour: any slight mistakes made by the sender are corrected as they come in: any telegraphic abbreviations are translated out in full: the entire English message is typed complete with appropriate punctuation.

Telegraphic expertise of this order is not acquired rapidly. It is built up progressively over years of practice, and involves the successive mastery of increasingly more complex accomplishments. In brief and over-simplified terms, the sequence of development in receiving runs as follows. The beginner starts by learning to recognize the auditory pattern of clicks which represents each individual letter. With practice, his recognizing becomes automatized and he begins to recognize as a single pattern the longer sequences of signals which represent frequently occurring runs of letters, for example, 'the' and 'is'. As practice proceeds, he comes to recognize more and more auditory patterns as unitary and distinctive representations of whole words. By degrees, he comes to recognize as a single auditory pattern the telegraphic representation of progressively longer word sequences, phrases, and short sentences. These auditory patterns come to have, for him, the same unitary distinctiveness as spoken phrases have for us. In short, as he progresses, the retained effects of his previous experience enable him to accomplish a rapid identification of progressively more and longer sequences of auditory signals.

Alongside this cumulative enlargement of recognition-units there is a progressive development of copying behind, that is, he lets a longer and longer sequence of signals come in before he starts to type the translation of this sequence. The beginner must type a letter as soon as he hears its representation: otherwise he will soon 'get lost', forget what has already come in. In contrast, if the expert is dealing with straightforward messages, he prefers to let a sequence of some six to twelve words come in before he starts to type it. Such delay is, of course, an economy of effort. It enables him to operate in terms of his large recognition-units, and this means that he is able to take in a long message by making a few large-scale identifications rather than many small-scale identifications. Such delay also helps by setting each fragment of the message in the wider context of the fragments which follow it as well as of those which have gone before; and this means that a momentary ambiguity can be clarified in the light of what follows as well as what preceeded. Lastly, such delay gives the receiver a longer time to prepare the organization of his typing movements: the better prepared he is for a particular pattern of typing movements, the easier it is to execute this pattern both rapidly and correctly (and as an expert typist, he does not tap each key as an isolated operation but, rather, taps a patterned sequence of keys as a unitary large-scale operation).

Yet another feature of telegraphic development is that, as people gain expertise they develop individual styles of sending which other experts can readily recognize. An accomplished receiver can tell, after listening to a few words,

either who is sending the message or that the sender is unknown to him. Beginners cannot, of course, recognize these
individualistic styles of sending. As with learning any new
language, there must be long experience before a person can
recognize either dialects or those even more subtle variations
which make every person's expression different from that
of everyone else.

This brief sketch of the development of skill in telegraphic
language shows that cumulative experience leads to the
emergence of progressively more complex, higher-order
accomplishments. It shows that the differences between the
expert and the novice do not merely concern speed and
accuracy, but also, and more basically, qualitative changes
in the way the person carries through the activities. Now,
what is true of the cumulative effects of experience with
telegraphy is also true of myriad other accomplishments
which are distinctively human. For example, the child's
long slow mastery of his native language; the acquisition of
competence in arithmetic or cookery; the development of
skill in human relations; the growth of the individual's
general knowledge. In each of these spheres of activity, the
cumulative effects of past experience give rise to accomplishments of a kind which develop out of earlier accomplishments and make possible the emergence of yet higher-order
accomplishments. This whole point about the intricate
cumulative effects of past experience is well expressed in the
following quotation. It comes from Alexander Bain (1818–
1903) the eminent Scottish philosopher–psychologist.

A professed dancer learning a new dance is in a very different
predicament from a beginner in the art. A musician learning a new
piece actually finds that nineteen-twentieths of all the sequences
to be acquired have been already formed through his previous
education. A naturalist reads the description of a newly discovered
animal: he possesses already, in his mind, the characters of the
known animals most nearly approaching to it; and, if he merely
give sufficient time and attention for the coherence of the points

that are absolutely new to him, he carries away and retains the whole. The judge, in listening to a law-pleading, hears little that is absolutely new; if he keeps that little in his memory, he stores up the whole case. When we read a book on a subject already familiar to us, we can reproduce the entire work, at the expense of labour requisite to remember the additions it makes to our previous stock of knowledge. So in Fine Art; an architect, a painter, or a poet, can easily carry away with him the total impression of a building, a picture, or a poem; for, instead of being acquisitions *de novo*, they are merely variations of effects already engrained in the artist's recollection. (*The Senses and the Intellect*, fourth edition, 1894, pp. 567–8.)

The Development of Remembering. It is always difficult for adults to appreciate how much of their everyday activities are, in a very real sense, achievements which owe their existence to a lengthy period of early learning. In this section, we shall be concerned with the development of the achievements of recognizing, recalling and recollecting. These accomplishments, so easily taken for granted in normal adults, are absent in young infants. For the infant, there is only a very brief past which he could remember – even if he were able to do so. When does the child begin to show these accomplishments of remembering? And how do these accomplishments develop? These are very broad questions to which only general answers can be given by drawing distinctions between several levels of accomplishment. It should be emphasized at once that these distinctions are not hard and fast. The different levels shade into each other and their separation represents nothing more than a convenient way of drawing attention to focal points in a continuous scale of ever-increasing complexity.

Consider a block of wood. A craftsman takes it and carves it to resemble a figure. He then stops carving, his knife rusts, and he himself ages and dies. But the effect of his carving persists because the wood is now of a different shape than it was before. Now, this is, in a very broad and primitive sense, an instance of remembering. In this sense, remembering means simply that the condition of the individual, at any moment, is influenced by previous occurrences which, although past, have not been altogether abolished with the past but continue to operate into the present. In this primitive sense of historical conditioning, remembering is, of course, not unique to human beings, since it occurs also in the lower animals, in plants, and in non-living objects. But primitive though this form of remembering is, it is far from being unimportant. Consider a young child of eight months or so. At this moment, he is what he is because of his past history. He is plump or emaciated in consequence of the quality and quantity of the food he has had; he is sunburnt or pale in consequence of having been in the sun or indoors; his eyes are blue or brown in consequence of his having this or that background or heredity. Any occurrence may leave behind effects which are very different in nature from that of the occurrence itself. But the effects are left none the less. Notice, however, that in this primitive form of remembering, there is no question of looking back into the past or (to express it more accurately) of constructing, out of the retained effects, the nature of the original occurrence. There is, at this level, only a past history which has vanished, leaving its accumulated effects on the present condition of the person, animal, plant, or object. The same is true when we turn to the lowlier forms of biographical change.

First Level: Anticipatory Reactions. What are the earliest indications that an infant's present activities are being influenced by the retained effects of his previous activities, that is, by learning? The earliest indications are probably those simple anticipatory reactions which the child begins to exhibit in his first few months of life. If, on several occasions, he has witnessed two events, the one following the other, then he may come to react to the occurrence of the first event as though he anticipated that the second is to follow. These simple preparatory reactions are, of course, the classical conditioned responses so intensively studied by the Russian physiologist, Ivan Pavlov (1848–1936). Their essence is that the first event is reacted to in such a way as to prepare the child to deal with the arrival of that second event which, in the past, has often followed the first. The child does not merely react to the first event but recognizes it as heralding the second event.

Consider again our 8-month-old child. Not only does he show the effects of previous nutrition, exposure to sunlight, and so on, but he shows the effects of his own previous activities, i.e., the effects of learning. For example, he recognizes certain people and objects as being familiar, he executes coordinated movements of which he was formerly incapable, and he has acquired some routine habits. He has, in short, profited much from his past experiences. Probably as early as his second month of life he would have begun to greet the appearance of his mother's face and voice with a faint smile. And around the third month he would have begun to react to strangers in one way and to members of the immediate family in another. Again, he would, for example, have developed a coordination between the use of his eyes and his hands and his mouth. According to the observations of Professor Jean Piaget, the Swiss psychologist, there is, by the third month, no reciprocal interaction between grasping, sucking and looking. The mouth sucks the hands but the hands do not try to carry to the mouth everything they grasp; nor do the hands attempt to grasp everything that the mouth sucks; and the eyes look at the hands, but the hands do not try to feel or to grasp everything the eyes see. Gradually, as a consequence of continual exploration and experimenting, the child achieves coordination between grasping and sucking. The hand grasps objects which it carries to the mouth and, reciprocally, the hand takes hold of objects which the mouth sucks. Looking is not yet coordinated with grasping, for the child grasps objects only when he touches them by chance. But soon he begins to grasp objects which he sees and not only those which he touches or sucks. However, he still only attempts to grasp when the hand and the object are together at the same time in his field of vision; neither the sight of the object alone nor of the hand alone leads to grasping. Somewhere around the age of six months, the child grasps what he sees without limitations relating to the position of the hand. An object presented to the eyes is now grasped even though the hands are not in his field of vision to start with: likewise an object discovered by the hand outside the visual field is brought into the field of vision. He has now developed a coordination between grasping, sucking, and looking which, however modest in comparison with the much greater achievements of the adult, is none the less a remarkable accomplishment.

A detailed observation of the activities of the 8-month-old child reveals that they are permeated through and through with the effects of his past activities. Not only does he recognize certain people and objects, and possess certain motor coordinations which he lacked before, but he has acquired certain routine habits and has even become sufficiently acquainted with the pattern of recurrent activities to be able to anticipate, in a rudimentary way, what is to follow. For example, starting at the age of three and a half months, an infant was given broth from a spoon once a day as she lay on her mother's lap. At first, it was difficult to get her to hold her face up and, after each spoonful, she turned her face to one side as she had been accustomed to do at her mother's breast. After four weeks, however, she had gradually adjusted to the new way of feeding, for she now held her head straight and often even parted her lips before the spoon actually touched them.

Thus we see that, even in the child of a few months, past experiences have already exerted a profound effect on his present activities. But all these effects are bound to the immediate present. In this respect, the child's remembering is, despite its greater complexity, on a level with the remembering of the carving by the block of wood, since neither he nor the wood show any indication of being able to reinstate vanished past occurrences. There is no indication that, while lying awake and alone in his perambulator, he pictures to himself his mother's face, or imagines the sound of her voice, the soothing feel of her hand, the appearance of his feeding-bottle or of his rattle. There is, in other words, no indication that he can reinstate in the here and now that which is not here and now. The child seems, as yet, to have no acquaintance with his past. He owes, it is true, all his knowledge and his capabilities to this past and its after-effects, but he cannot look back on it. Nor does it seem that he is able to represent, in the here and now, events from his past.

Second Level: Recall. The earliest signs of recalling occur sometime towards the end of the first year of life. The following illustrative examples have been taken from a book entitled *Psychology of Early Childhood*, by the German psychologist William Stern (1871–1938). The 1-year-old child has often been observed to leave a ball or toy lying out of sight in some unusual place, such as under a piece of furniture, and, perhaps as long as fifteen minutes later, make his way straight to where it is hidden on being asked to fetch it. Delayed performances of this sort suggest that recalling is involved. These early indications of recall are often prompted by environmental circumstances: the child finds himself once more in some situation which elicits recall of something which was previously a part of that situation but is now absent. Thus, Stern reports the case of a boy of nineteen months who once saw bacon being fried and called an onion which was thrown into the pan a 'ball'. Two weeks later, bacon was being fried again and the boy, on seeing the pan, exclaimed, 'Da, mama ball ba!' Another boy of twenty-three months recalled an experience which had occurred ten weeks before. He heard his sister mention 'board' and at once pointed to an easel-board and said 'wow-wow'. There was no dog drawn on the board but, ten weeks before, his mother had sketched there the large heads of a dog, a horse, and a cat, much to the boy's delight. To be sure that his remark was really a question of recall, his mother asked what else he had seen on the board, to which the boy replied 'gee-gee'. In the ten-week interval, there had been no drawings on the board and the boy had been away from home for a period. Such instances of recall are, however, by no means frequent even in the third year of life, and it still seems to be largely a question of 'out of sight out of mind'.

In the fourth year, recalling is more frequent and even occurs a year after the original experience. Infrequently recurring situations, such as summer holidays and Christmas parties, elicit recall of the same situation a year before. Thus, one boy of three years and three months went for his summer holidays to a mountain resort and recalled events which had taken place in this resort on the previous year. He recalled, for example, that an aunt had lived in a certain room, and that a man had jokingly threatened him in a particular restaurant because he would not eat. In the fifth year, recalling is more frequent still and there are several reported instances of some chance incident eliciting recall of an experience which occurred more than half a lifetime ago and which has never been repeated or even mentioned in the interval. At this age, it might be said that the child can recall the events of his youth. From now on his recalling becomes less exclusively dependent on redintegration. It becomes increasingly spontaneous in that he reinstates earlier experiences which are not associated with the situation he is in at the moment or with the questions he is now being asked. As he grows older, his recalling becomes increasingly facile and selective. He recalls those past experiences which will assist him in solving some present problem; he even combines the recalled experiences of events which happened at different times in very different places and produces out of them experiences which have no equivalent in direct perception of the real world. At this point, his activities of recalling merge into those of thinking and imagining and, in his mental life, he gains freedom from the restrictions of present time and space.

Third Level: Recollecting. The observations of Stern and others suggest that the performance of recalling is not achieved until early in the second year of life and does not appear with any great frequency until around the age of three. But even when experiences are recalled, there is little question of their being referred to any definite point of past time, for the simple reason that the child has yet to develop a clear notion of time. Even the 4-year-old has little more than an indefinite notion of 'long ago' and a broad distinction between 'earlier' and 'later'. He cannot refer an event to 'the day before yesterday' or to 'last week' with any probability of accuracy. And temporal localization in terms of months or years is more than the child's necessarily limited past experience will permit. Sometimes he can accurately locate a recalled experience as having happened 'today' or 'not today', but he can scarcely use 'yesterday' as a more exact location for experiences from the less immediate past. So far as he is capable of making temporal distinctions between his recollected experiences, he does so by reference to places: 'That was at so-and-so's house', or 'That was at such-and-such a town'. He may even give the impression of a definite time-index, as when he says that a certain event occurred at Christmas or on his birthday. But it seems unlikely that these expressions reflect any definite notion of temporal sequence. He simply seems to place one event in the context of a more outstanding event which is recollected without any clear reference to its location in a temporal order of events. It would appear that he is in much the same position regarding the days, weeks, and months as are most of us regarding the eras of prehistory. Certainly, it is not until later that the child develops even a sketchy notion of having left a portion of his life behind, and it is not until after the age of six years that he acquires an awareness of his own past as a historical sequence of events.

The main emphasis of this introductory chapter has been on the variety and the adaptive value of these everyday activities referred to by the abstract and ambiguous word 'memory'. This word, in its most comprehensive sense, refers to the effects of a person's past on his present. The person is modified by what he does and experiences; and these modifications, if they are retained, affect what he does and experiences on later occasions. The value of these persisting modifications is that they enable the person to adjust to present circumstances in the light of past experience. Perhaps the most important general point to be made is that these modifications are both complex and selective. Using the retained effects of past experience to adjust to present circumstances is a high biological achievement which, on examination, has little to do with the passive storing up of past events for later reduplication.

II Short-term Memory

This chapter is concerned with memory episodes in which the entire cycle of receiving, retaining, and using information occupies a few seconds. To illustrate the time-scale involved, consider the following episode. We want to telephone someone. We ask the exchange for the number: we are told the number, say 69528: we replace the receiver: we then pick it up again, and dial the number we received a moment ago. Only a few seconds elapse between the moment when we hear the first digit of the number and the moment we dial its last digit. The whole episode stretches through only a few seconds of time. Memory episodes of about this time order are of great practical importance because there are innumerable real-life situations where people must make delayed use of information received some seconds previously. Furthermore, the events which take place immediately after the intake of information are, so to speak, the beginning of the memory story. Let us start by considering the classical studies of immediate memory span.

1 Immediate Memory Span

'It is obvious that there is a limit to the power of reproducing sounds accurately. Anyone can say "Bo" after once hearing it: but few would catch the name of the Greek statesman M. Papamichalopoulos without the need of a repetition.'

Immediate Memory Span

In 1887, the British psychologist, J. Jacobs, used these words to introduce his report on the first experimental study of immediate memory span. His procedure was to read out to someone a random sequence of, say, digits at a steady rate; and as soon as the sequence was completed, the person had to report it back as best he could. He gave the same person sequences of different lengths, and the person's span was the longest sequence he could grasp, that is, successfully recall immediately after a single hearing. Using this procedure in a standardized way, Jacobs determined the spans of hundreds of people of various ages. And from his results, he drew some general conclusions which have been confirmed by subsequent investigations. The main findings on immediate memory span will be listed below, but first a word must be said about its measurement. For convenience, reference will be made largely to memory span for sequences of digits; but this is not of course the only, or even the most important, material to which our considerations apply.

There are two main points about the measurement of a person's span. Both arise from the fact that the length of sequence which he can repeat back is a matter which varies slightly according to circumstances, e.g., the particular digit sequence used, its rate of presentation. The first main point is that the value given for a person's span is an *average* value for that person. Suppose his span is six digits. This does not mean that he will always fail to repeat back any sequence longer than six, nor always succeed with any shorter sequence. Six represents the longest sequence which he can, on average, correctly repeat back after a single presentation. It means that if he is given a large number of trials with different sequences, all of six digits, then he will repeat them correctly on fifty per cent of trials. Sequences of less than six digits will be got right on most trials, and sequences of more than six digits will be got wrong on most trials. The second main point is that, in order to compare the spans of two different people, these spans must be determined under conditions which are as standardized as possible. A general procedure which is commonly used is as follows.

The investigator has a number of standard lists of digits which vary in length from two digits to ten digits, e.g., 39418 or 4538217069. There are two or three different lists of each length. The person is told: 'I am going to say numbers and, when I have finished, I want you to repeat the numbers in the same order.' The investigator then starts with one of the shorter lists. He reads it out at a steady rate which, by tradition, is one digit every second; and he is careful not to accentuate any of the digits or introduce rhythm. The reason for these precautions is that the span varies slightly with differences in rate of presentation and is usually slightly longer if the items are given in rhythmical groupings rather than at a steady rate. If the person succeeds in repeating this sequence back, he is given progressively longer sequences until a length is reached at which he fails completely. Under these conditions, the span is taken to be the number of items in the longest list ever repeated correctly. It is worth noting that memory spans determined in this quick way accord fairly closely with spans which are arrived at by more exhaustively adequate procedures. (These more exhaustive procedures allow the person some practice in memory span tasks and, because of this, the average value tends to be slightly higher than that obtained by quick procedures.)

The Main Findings. It has been found that memory span is influenced by a large variety of conditions. For example, it is lowered by fatigue, distractions, consumption of alcohol, and the smoking of tobacco (at least in people who are not accustomed to smoking). However, the main variables can be listed under four sections as follows.

(1) Span varies according to the type of material used. Here are some average values for University students:

Digits; 8·5 items. Consonants and differently coloured cards; 7·5 items. Common nouns and simple geometrical figures; 6 items. Pairs of common words, nonsense syllables, and short simple sentences; 3 items. It will be noticed that, despite their variations, all of these values are small.

(2) Span varies with the age of the person. On average, the span increases during childhood at a rate which parallels physical growth; it levels out at about the age of physical maturity and, at the age of about thirty years, it begins a slow decrease which continues throughout adult life. These conclusions are derived from the large-scale surveys involved in preparing tests of general intelligence. These tests, if they are to be of any value, must be standardized on thousands of people selected, at every age, to be representative of the population at large. And most of these tests include, as one of their many items, a test of digit span. According to the published norms of these tests, the average digit span is 2, 3, 4, 5, and 6 items at the ages of $2\frac{1}{2}$, 3, $4\frac{1}{2}$, 7, and 10 years respectively. The average span increases, more and more slowly, to level out at 7 items in the mid-teens. (Note that the average digit span for the population at large is about 1·5 items lower than that for university students.) Then somewhere about the age of thirty, the average span begins to decline slightly. The rate of decrease is nothing like so rapid as the rate of increase in the very early years of life. But a fall is clearly present and, by the middle fifties, the average span has shrunk to 6 digits, that is, to the level of the 10-year-old.

(3) Span varies with general intellectual ability. In Jacobs' original inquiry, he noticed that among school children 'as a rule, high span went with high place in form'. Statistical analysis of his data confirmed this relationship and led him to suggest that immediate memory span 'may serve as some indication of ability'. He mentioned this possibility to that remarkably versatile psychologist, Sir Francis Galton (1822–1911). Galton realized that, if this were true, then

feeble-minded people ought to have much shorter spans than the normal population. Galton undertook to check this expectation and Jacobs was able to cite his findings: memory span differs widely among feeble-minded people but few, if any, attain the normal digit span. From that time onwards, immediate memory span for digits has been part of most intelligence tests. Span has been found to relate, not completely but to a moderate degree, with overall assessment of a person's general intellectual abilities. (For those who understand the language of correlation – a mathematical device invented by Galton – the results can be tersely expressed. A typical correlation between memory span and the results of the remainder of the intelligence test is about 0·5, and is higher for children than for adults.)

(4) Performance on memory span tasks is notably vulnerable to distractions. If the presentation of the sequence is followed by distractions of any kind, then its recall is very liable to be impaired in such a way that the person can never repeat it: some parts of the sequence are lost permanently. This vulnerability of short-term memory is familiar in everyday dealings with telephone numbers. When a person has been presented with a number for the first time, he can dial it correctly a second or more later. But if, in those few seconds, he is asked a question which he attempts to answer, or if he is startled by an unexpected noise, or if he thinks about something other than the number; then he is likely to have forgotten the number. Furthermore, he is unlikely ever to be able to recall it correctly without having to be given it again. Distractions also arise when the person is required to perform some operation on the sequence just received. In his original investigation, Jacobs noticed that span was shorter by about one item if people had to write the items out rather than simply repeat them by word of mouth. He interpreted this as due to the distraction 'involved in translating sounds into their visual symbols'. Again, it is well known that the person may lose

Immediate Memory Span

some of the sequence if he attempts to repeat it in reverse order. Suppose he is told beforehand that, if given 1, 8, 3, he must repeat 3, 8, 1. Under these conditions his backward-span is about two digits shorter than his normal span, and many children are unable even to attempt this reversal. In other words, the activity of reversing the sequence impairs the retaining of the sequence itself. Notice that this vulnerability of short-term retaining is not shared by long-term retaining. For example, the alphabet is a well-learned sequence. If someone attempts to recite it backwards, he may find this difficult. But he does not, as a consequence, forget the forward sequence.

The Dynamics of Short-term Memory. When a person is presented with a sequence of digits which he must recall immediately afterwards, he engages in a dynamic inter-action of activities. He receives the digits, he retains them, he recalls them – and these are all active processes. But there are limits to the amount of activity which any person can carry through in any specified period of time. And so these activities of receiving, retaining, and recalling may, if each is sufficiently demanding, compete with and disrupt each other. Suppose the person is required to deal with a sequence of six digits. He takes in the first few and must then actively hold them while, at the same time, he is engaged in taking in the remaining digits and holding them also. By the end of the presentation, he must be retaining all six digits. When he starts to repeat back the first few digits, he must still hold the last few until they can also be recalled and the memory task is completed. Most adults can deal with the concurrent activities involved in the immediate recall of a sequence of six digits. But when the person is required to attempt progressively longer sequences, there soon comes a stage at which these concurrent activities begin to interfere with each other. His engagement in one activity deprives him of freedom to engage in another necessary activity. Suppose he is attempting a sequence of ten digits. By the time he has taken in seven or eight items, it is difficult for him to engage in retaining these while, at the same time, attempting to take in and retain the remaining few items. People often report that they 'cannot concentrate' on the last few items or, if they do, that they have to 'let the others go'. Even if the person does succeed in taking in and retaining all ten items, he may still have difficulty in holding the later members of the sequence while engaged in recalling the earlier items. He may confidently start to recite the sequence only to find, half-way through, that the last few items have 'vanished'. With this length of sequence, there are too many activities to be carried through all at once. And any such failure, wherever and whenever it occurs, means that the person is unable to repeat the entire sequence correctly. In other words, he has exceeded his immediate memory span.

In general terms then, immediate memory span is the outcome of competing activities within a person whose capacity for activity is limited. This general conclusion is supported by a host of detailed experimental studies concerned with timing human skills and exploring the limits of human capability. None of these experiments will be cited here. (For an overview, see the excellent but difficult book *Perception and Communication* by D. E. Broadbent, Pergamon Press, 1958.) Notice that one essential feature of this general conclusion concerns the active nature of short-term retaining. When a person receives information which he knows he will have to use a few seconds hence, his retaining of this information is not a passive matter. It requires some kind of continuing activity. This requirement restricts his ability to engage meanwhile in other activities: it also makes short-term retaining vulnerable to disruption by other activities. In this connexion, it is noteworthy that there is rarely any lasting retention of individual sequences presented. A person who is given a succession of memory span tasks is, at the end of the session, rarely able to recall the particular sequences which have been presented. He retains each sequence long enough to repeat it back immediately afterwards. Then he 'lets it go'.

The above considerations are among those which suggest the value of distinguishing, however roughly, between short-term and long-term retaining. Short-term retaining is an active, ongoing process which is vulnerable to disruption by other activities and is, so to speak, preoccupying. By contrast, long-term retaining does not seem to require activities of a kind which are readily disrupted by and disruptive of other activities. For example, a well-learned poem can still be recalled after many intervening activities quite unrelated to it; it can even be recalled after recovery from a state of general brain paralysis. Long-term retaining, whatever its undoubted complexity, seems to involve a more or less enduring pattern of brain modifications which are relatively stable.

Short-term Memory and Problem-solving. In solving problems, the retained effects of past experience make a two-fold contribution. First, past experiences with similar problems provide ways of proceeding with the present problem. If the person can recognize the new problem as being of a familiar type, say a multiplication problem, then he can at once proceed by familiar methods. These methods enable him to select out the critical features of the problem and deal with them in accustomed ways so as to arrive at a conclusion. Every school teacher knows that, when children are mastering arithmetic, one difficulty is to recognize the type to which new problems belong. Secondly, during the solving of the problem, short-term memory plays an important part. Almost anyone can demonstrate this for himself by trying to multiply in his head 87 by 73. For most people there is too much work involved in this problem for the answer to be attained all in one effortless go. Rather the answer is arrived at through a succession of stages.

Short-term Memory

Now if the person observes this succession of stages he will notice that short-term memory is evident in at least two ways. (a) As he proceeds from one stage to the next, he needs to keep remembering which particular stage he is at in the calculation as a whole. He needs to remember what the original problem was, and must not lose his way as he progresses from one stage of working to the next. (b) He often needs to remember the outcome of a previous stage which he completed a few moments before. That is, he has to carry out the following kind of activity sequence. He completes one stage; he lays the outcome aside; he completes a second stage; and then he recalls the first outcome to combine it with the second. In such an activity sequence, he must retain the first outcome during the time he is arriving at the second outcome. And in general, the more difficult it is for him to complete the second stage, the more likely he is to lose the outcome of the first stage.

In this multiplication problem, as in almost all problems and tasks, the role of short-term memory is both important and highly selective. Sometimes the necessity is to remember, sometimes to forget. There is clearly no need for the person to retain every detail of his ongoing, moment-by-moment activities. The value of some, indeed probably most, activities is only momentary. They serve to carry the subject forward towards the solution and, their fleeting purpose done, they are best forgotten. Any attempt to retain these events of momentary value would impede rather than aid subsequent progress. But there are other events whose value is not merely momentary, events which must be retained for use a short time later. Such events were exemplified above. If there are many of these events which must be retained, then the demands on short-term memory may exceed the person's capabilities, and he will fail to solve the problem. To avoid such failure, he may be able to devise new methods of mental working which lighten his reliance on short-term memory. Alternatively, he may proceed by keeping an external record of his working, e.g., by making notes on a piece of paper.

There are innumerable occasions on which a person's failure to solve a problem is chiefly due to over-heavy demands on short-term memory. There is, at some stage on the way to solution, a need to retain more than he can keep in mind. Many instances of this occur with young school-children whose short-term memory is, of course, more limited than that of most adults. An almost trivial instance will suffice to illustrate this point. A 5-year-old is asked to count up to twelve, that is, recite the number-words in order from one to twelve. He may fail this simple task because he forgets, in the course of his recital, how far he was asked to go. Limitations of short-term memory also raise difficulties for highly accomplished thinkers. The solving of a complex problem in, say, scientific research involves novel combinations of ideas, that is, the bringing together of various items of evidence into a unitary pattern of unaccustomed relationships. Now this coherent pattern may comprise a large number of component relationships which must, so to speak, all be brought to mind together and at nearly the same time. Such holding together of com-ponents – comprehending – requires the collective recalling of the components. In other words, the activity of com-prehending may well be limited by short-term memory.

Many distinguished thinkers have been aware that, to accomplish this collective recalling, the recall of each com-ponent must be easy in itself, that is, as nearly automatized as possible. Two quotations suffice to illustrate this point. The first comes from Hermann von Helmholtz (1821–94), the German who made immense contributions to physiology, physics and psychology and who must be ranked among the greatest scientists of all time. On the occasion of his seven-tieth birthday, he reported something of his methods of thinking and, at one point, said this. 'It is always necessary, first of all, that I should have turned my problem over on all sides to such an extent that I had all its angles and complexities "in my head" and could run through them freely without writing. To bring the matter to that point is usually impossible without long preliminary labour.' The second quotation is even more explicit about the role of automatized recall in lightening the demands made on short-term memory. The quotation is from René Descartes (1596–1650), the great philosopher and mathematician. 'If I have first found out by separate mental operations what the relation is between the magnitudes A and B, then that between B and C, between C and D, and finally between D and E, that does not entail my seeing what the relation is between A and E, nor can the truths previously learned give me a precise knowledge of it unless I recall them all. To remedy this, I would run them over from time to time, keeping the imagination moving continuously in such a way that while it is intuitively perceiving each fact it simultaneously passes on to the next; and this I would do until I had learned to pass from the first to the last so quickly, that no stage in the process was left to the care of memory, but I seemed to have the whole in intuition before me at the same time. This method will relieve the memory, diminish the sluggishness of our thinking and definitely enlarge our mental capacity.'

2 Lengthening the Memory Span

The Effects of Practice. In 1929, two American psychologists, P. R. Martin and S. W. Fernberger, undertook to find out whether digit span could be increased by means of daily practice. The procedure on each day followed the same pattern. Digits were read out at a rate slightly faster than one every second, and the person tried to say the sequence back. There were two sequences of five digits, two of six digits, two of seven, and so on, until a length was reached on which both sequences were failed. The score for the day was the longest sequence correctly recalled. This procedure was repeated with the same person each day for some fifty days (the actual digit sequences were, of course, different). The people who took this daily practice were two university students who may be referred to as K and R respectively. The main question was this. Would these students show any improved ability to repeat back a digit sequence heard only once? The answer is that they did improve. This can be seen from the data in Table 1. This table gives the average daily score made by each student over successive blocks of five days.

Table 1

Days of Practice	Student K	Student R
1–5	9·0	10·4
6–10	8·8	11·4
11–15	9·4	11·0
16–20	9·6	11·6
21–25	10·4	11·0
26–30	12·8	11·6
31–35	12·4	11·8
36–40	12·0	11·8
41–45	13·0	14·2
46–50	13·2	15·4
51–55	—	13·6

Now, how did this improvement come about? According to the daily testimony of the students themselves, it resulted from their trying to break the digit sequence into groups. R tried such grouping from the start and became proficient in grouping by fives. By the fiftieth day of practice, he was able to recall three groups of five digits each. His poorer performance over the final five days was due to his unsuccessful attempt at grouping the digits in sixes. K did not attempt grouping until after the twentieth day but, almost as soon as he started this grouping (by fives), his span increased. His span continued to increase slightly as he gained proficiency in the use of grouping by fives. However, he never reached the stage of being able to recall three such groups. These results indicate that, at least in adults, digit span can be increased by a modest extent. They indicate further that this increase results not so much from an enlargement of 'pure' memory span as from changed methods of dealing with the digits. By grouping the digits, the person manages to deal more effectively with the concurrent activities of receiving, retaining and recalling. And this grouping enables him, with practice, to increase his immediate memory span by nearly a half of its original length.

Group-labelling. With digit sequences, the effect of grouping is to increase the span by a modest amount. However, if it is possible to group items together in such a way that each group has a distinctive characteristic, then the span can be increased even further. The basic procedure is, first, to group the items, then to note the group's characteristic (its label, as it were), and then retain only this label. When time comes for recall, the label enables the person to re-create the whole group with all its component items. This procedure is clearly exemplified by the taking of shorthand notes. The person receives a segment of dictation, treats it as a group, and 'remembers' this group by writing down a single shorthand symbol which labels it. Later, these labels are translated back into English so as to produce once more the salient characteristics of the original dictation.

A more familiar example of group-labelling may be illustrated by considering memory span tasks involving letters of the alphabet. An adult is presented visually with a random succession of letters of the alphabet. If he is asked to write out the sequence, the longest sequence he can usually manage correctly is about seven items. However, if he is able to group the letters into words (such as thin, box, knife, surf), he is able to recall a sequence of about six such words, that is, a sequence of more than twenty letters. Here, he groups the individual letters together into short sequences. Because of his past linguistic experience, each sequence has, for him, a distinctive label – it is a word. He then retains, not the characteristics of the individual letters but the more summary characteristic of the word. In this way he manages to deal successfully with a letter sequence which is three or four times longer than he could manage without his group-labelling procedure.

This example of letters-and-words is so familiar that the importance of its underlying principle is perhaps easy to overlook. So let us consider a situation whose very unfamiliarity forces us to note the powerful effects of group-labelling. This particular situation was brought to notice in 1956 by Professor George Miller of Harvard University. (In a brilliant but difficult and closely-reasoned article entitled, 'The magical number seven, plus or minus two: some limits on our capacity for processing information', *The Psychological Review*, vol. 60, pp. 81–97.) Before describing it, two brief warnings should be given. First, our considerations demand some modest arithmetic. Secondly, the significance of the general findings should not be dismissed because they derive from what is, in fact, a mnemonic 'trick'.

Binary Digit Span. Binary digits are of two kinds only, for example, 0 and 1. If adults are given sequences of such digits (like that in the top row of Table 2 below), the longest sequence they can recall correctly after only one presentation is about nine. However, this span can be increased by using a group-labelling procedure. Consider the binary digits, not individually but in groups of two. Four different kinds of pair are possible, namely, 00, 01, 10, and 11. We now work out a code whereby each of these pairs is represented by a single label. This label might be a digit of the normal kind. Let us represent oo by the label o; oi by the label 1; 10 by the label 2; and 11 by the label 3. Once we have decided on our code, we learn it until we can use it automatically and without hesitation or error. We are now ready to use this code in dealing with sequences of binary digits. We listen for the first pair of digits, quickly label this pair and remember only the label. We do the same for the next pair, and the next, and so on. This procedure is represented in Table 2. The top row shows a succession of binary digits. The next row shows these digits grouped into pairs. The last row shows the label used to represent each

Table 2

Binary Digit Sequence	1 0	1 1	0 1	0 0	1 0
Groups of Pairs	10	11	01	00	10
Labels for Pairs	2	3	1	0	2

pair. By the time we have got to the end of the sequence, we are not holding the ten original items. Rather, we are holding five label-items which stand for them. To recall the original sequence, all we need do is to 'expand' each of the five labels.

Anyone who uses this procedure properly can effect a marked increase in his binary digit span. This is obviously because he has less to remember. He need only retain half as many items as there are in the sequence presented to him. But notice that he must pay a price for this gain. He must engage in what might be called translation work. He must expend effort in grouping the presented items and translating these groups into their code equivalents. However, the cost of this translation work is more than compensated for by the gain of having to remember fewer items. And the result, on balance, is an increased binary digit span.

In his 1956 paper, Miller reports an experiment by S. Smith who, using himself as subject, carried out repeated binary digit memory span tasks. Whenever he made no attempt at grouping, his span was 12 items. (Note that this value is higher than the average for adults.) But whenever he used the procedure outlined above, his span was 24 items. So by grouping and labelling pairs of items, he doubled the size of his memory span for binary digits. This is a noteworthy increase and prompts us to ask whether the span could be increased even further. What happens if he uses a similar procedure for labelling groups of three items? Smith tried this. First, he devised a suitable code. When binary digits are grouped in threes, eight different triplets are possible. And each of these eight has to be given a label. He gave 000 the label 0; 001 the label 1; 010 the label 2; and so on up to 111 with the label 7. He learned this code thoroughly until all the necessary translations could be done automatically. Then he used the code with sequences of binary digits, and achieved a span of 36 items. Notice that, with this code, he can retain a sequence of 36 items by means of only twelve labels.

Smith then went on to devise a code for dealing with binary digits in groups of four. The procedure is the same as before except that sixteen different quartets are possible. So the code must be longer. But after he had mastered this code, his span increased still further to 40 items. These 40 items represent only ten labels rather than the twelve labels which had previously been manageable. Clearly, the cost of the procedure is getting heavier and beginning to balance the gains. When Smith devised and learned a code of 32 items which would enable him to label groups of five binary digits, his span showed no further increase but remained at 40. These 40 items are represented by only eight labels.

So the group-labelling procedure yields diminishing returns as the size of the group exceeds 3 items. The reason for this is apparent if we consider in detail what is involved in working with groups of five. To start with, the necessary code is a long one. There must be thirty-two labels, one for each possible quintet. So it is laborious to learn this code to the high degree of automatization required. Furthermore, the actual use of the code makes heavy demands. First, he must wait for five binary digits to come. Then he must recognize which of the thirty-two possible groups this is. Then he must recall the group's label. And all this must be done so as not to interfere with his listening to the ongoing presentation of more binary digits. Obviously, the gains of the procedure are being won at heavy cost in terms of translation work. Indeed, it is doubtful if the span of 40 binary digits could be increased, or even maintained, if he went on to the ambitious procedure of labelling groups of six.

However, the presence of these diminishing returns must not obscure the fact that a binary digit span of 40 items is a most impressive accomplishment and, even more important, that it is an accomplishment made possible by the procedure of group-labelling. The value of this whole experiment lies in its clearly illustrating the properties of a group-labelling procedure.

The Commonness of Group-labelling. In later chapters we will see that group-labelling is not the only procedure which can be used to increase immediate memory span. There are other procedures (mnemonic systems) which enable a person to accomplish the specialized task of, say, listening once to a random sequence of a hundred words and then recalling the sequence correctly afterwards. It must be stressed that such mnemonic procedures are oddities only in so far as they enable their users to deal with memory tasks which most people, for whatever reason, do not even attempt in everyday life. But they are not oddities in the sense that they employ any basic procedures which are absent from everyday activities. They are merely specialized elaborations of normal memory activities. Part of their interest is that, by exaggerating and caricaturing the normal, they cast light on our study of the normal.

Now, what is true of mnemonic systems in general, is also

true of group-labelling in particular. This procedure underlies and makes possible a great many of our everyday accomplishments. It underlies the familiar, yet curious, fact that memory span varies from one kind of material to another. For example, an adult may be able to receive and retain for immediate recall three short sentences such as 'Jack and Jill ran up the hill'. These three sentences may involve him in reading and writing out some sixty letters of the alphabet. Yet if these letters are shown in random sequence, he cannot recall more than about six. The reason for this discrepancy is that, in the two situations, he is dealing with different kinds of grouping. In the random-letter situation, he must virtually treat each letter as a separate group. But in the sentence situation, he treats whole sequences of letters as distinctive groups. For anyone who has never learned to read English, a sentence is a lengthy succession of curious marks which quite exceed his capacities to take in and retain for even a short time. For anyone who has learned to read English, it is a single familiar sentence which can readily be taken in almost as a unit, and easily recalled afterwards. In short, his past experience with written English enables him to accomplish a feat which, for the illiterate person, seems almost superhuman.

To anyone who knows nothing of the game of chess, it seems incredible that a person could watch a game being played and then give a move-by-move account of the game. But an experienced chess player can accomplish this feat of recapitulation because, for him, the game is not a succession of independent moves but, rather, a developing pattern of themes-of-play. Likewise, to anyone who knows nothing of telegraphy, it seems incredible that a person should listen to some hundred or more auditory clicks before he starts to type out the beginning of the message being sent. But an experienced telegraphist has built up by long practice the ability to recognize lengthy sequences of auditory signals as unitary patterns with meaningful group characteristics.

Group-labelling, then, underlies many situations where recalling is made possible by the acquired meanings of the material involved. This will become even more apparent in the discussion of long-term recall of stories and episodes. For example, when we listen to a person telling a story, we do not treat each momentary complex of sound as a separate unit, nor very often each word or even sentence. Rather, we treat the incoming auditory events in terms of their meaning. As we listen, we build up themes and sub-themes, note climaxes and turning points in the story. We extract what, for us, are the essential characteristics of the story. We retain successive sound sequences only long enough to bring the essence of the story up to date, and then let the myriad details of the moment go. In short, when we listen, we group the auditory signals not merely into words but into those larger, more synoptic, units whose distinguishing labels are called ideas. And when we recall, it is these group characteristics, these ideas, which we reintroduce into the present and attempt, with more or less success, to expand out into a word-by-word retelling of the story.

3 Immediate-forgetting

When a person receives information which he must use a short time later, he must retain this information by active means. We have already seen examples of this fact. But now, let us consider it from another point of view. It means that, if he does not engage in active retaining, then the information will be rapidly forgotten. Unless he is, in some sense, free to mull the information over, then he is unable to recall it a second or so hence. This very rapid forgetting takes place in less than a couple of seconds or so and may be referred to as 'immediate-forgetting'. Such immediate-forgetting is a fact long known to those who have closely observed the flow of their everyday experiencing. They notice that a great part of experience does not survive the instant of its passing and is irretrievably forgotten the moment it is over. We saw above that, when we listen to a story being told, a great many details are forgotten the moment they are received and that what we retain is a kind of cumulative abstraction of what was taken in. Further everyday instances of immediate-forgetting will be mentioned later.

The taking in of an item involves a complex chain of events. Suppose the item is a spoken digit. What arrives are intricate patterns of sound waves which set up mechanical reactions in the ear. These, in turn, lead to patterns of nervous discharges which give rise to patterns of activity in the nervous tissues of the brain. This central nervous pattern persists for some brief time and then dies out as it is replaced by succeeding patterns of activity. It is this rapid dying out which is responsible for immediate-forgetting. If this pattern is not to die out, it must, in some fashion, be selectively maintained and re-established as a distinctive pattern. That is, the pattern must be, for some time at least, a recurring component of central nervous activity; and to some extent, this recurring pattern must preclude the formation and recurrence of alternative patterns.

An Experiment on Immediate-forgetting. For several decades, experiments have been performed in which visual material is shown to a person for a period of time so short that he cannot move his eyes across the material while it is being exposed. In practice, this means that the visual display is shown for something less than a fifth of a second. The typical procedure in these experiments is to tell the person to watch the screen where the visual material will appear and to report afterwards what he saw. The typical result is that the person cannot report a great deal under such conditions.

However, many people who take part in these experiments make a curious comment. They say that they see more than they can remember afterwards. Their difficulty seems to lie less in receiving the material than in retaining it long enough for recall immediately afterwards. Their curious comment implies immediate-forgetting. And this implication is confirmed by experiments such as that reported in 1960 by the American psychologist, G. Sperling, ('The information available in brief visual presentations', *Psychological Monographs*, whole number 498). Sperling conducted a lengthy series of experiments with the same five adult subjects throughout. The following brief account of these experiments does scant justice to their technical details but suffices to indicate the flavour of their findings.

The kind of material used is shown in Figure 2. In this example, there are twelve symbols arranged in three rows.

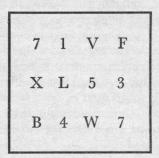

Figure 2

The first question to be asked is this. When the material is exposed for quarter of a second, how much can the subject correctly report? On each trial, the material was exposed, and the subject had to write out the symbols afterwards. The details of the material were, of course, varied from one trial to the next. The subject was given credit for each correct symbol written in its correct position. Under these conditions, the average number of symbols correctly recalled was 4·3. (Varying the exposure time between 0·015 seconds and 0·25 seconds made no difference to the recall score.) In summary so far, here we have a memory span situation where twelve visual symbols are shown simultaneously for quarter of a second or less; and the average number of symbols correctly written out in their correct positions is 4·3.

The next question is this. How much of this poor recall is due to immediate-forgetting? Sperling answered this question by asking the subject for only a partial report after each exposure. The display of symbols was shown, as before, but this time the subject was required to recall only some of them. On some trials he would be asked to recall the symbols in the top row; on other trials, he would be required to recall only the symbols in the middle row; on yet other trials, he was asked for the symbols in only the bottom row. However, he would not know until *after* the exposure which row he was to recall. He was told which row to recall by means of a tone that sounded shortly after the visual display was over: a high tone for the top row, a low tone for the bottom row, and a middle tone for the middle row. The delay between the end of the visual display and the start of the tone was varied between zero time and one second. In summary, the experimental procedure is as follows. The display of twelve symbols is exposed. When the exposure is past, a tone sounds which tells the subject to write down, say, only the symbols he can recall from the top row of the display. The subject then attempts to make this partial recall.

Now, what would we expect to happen under these conditions? Remember that, when the subject attempts to recall all twelve items in the display, he gets 4·3 correct on average. That is, he recalls just over a third of the items attempted. So if he is now attempting to recall only, say, the four items in the bottom row of the display, we might expect that, on average, he would recall about a third of these also. That is, we might expect that he would get an average recall score of about 1·4 items. This is what we would expect if his chief difficulty were the taking in of the items exposed. But this is not, in fact, what happens. If the tone sounds at the very moment when the exposure ends, the subject recalls an average of three items correct out of the four for which he is asked. Notice what this means. If he is asked to recall *any* one row of the display, he recalls three items on average. The very instant the display is over, he can recall three items from the top row, or three items from the middle row, or three items from the bottom row – whichever he is asked for. In other words, he is potentially able to recall a total of nine items from the display. But, as we have seen, when he tries to recall the entire display, he is in fact able to recall only 4·3 items. So, at the end of the exposure, he is potentially able to recall nine items, but by the time he has recalled some four of them, the remainder have been forgotten. This conclusion is confirmed by the fact that partial report is affected by the time delay between the end of the exposure and the start of the tone. As this time is lengthened from zero to 0·15 seconds, to 0·30 seconds, to 0·50 seconds, to 1 second, the average partial recall score drops progressively from three items to half that number. Notice that this last value is equivalent to a potential score of 4·6 items for the entire array. At a 1 second delay, the potential score (4·6 items) is very close to the actual score made in attempting to recall the entire display (4·3 items).

The main conclusion of this experiment is as follows. When the array of twelve items is exposed, it gives rise to patterns of central nervous activity which outlive the exposure itself. These patterns enable the person, potentially, to recall most of the twelve items. But they decay in fractions of a second. And by the time the person has recalled about four of the items, the decaying patterns no longer enable him to recall any further items. In other words, a large amount of information is taken in from the display but only a fraction of this can be retained for use even a second later.

Immediate-forgetting in Everyday Life. The above experiment shows that not all the information which is received can be retained for even a second. The information is taken in all right but, immediately thereafter, most of it is lost and cannot be recalled. Only a small part can be retained for future use. Now this immediate-forgetting is not an isolated phenomenon which occurs only in the psychological laboratory. It is, rather, the fate of most of the information which human beings are constantly receiving. Information is taken in, and the bulk of it vanishes within a second or so. On the whole, this immediate-forgetting is advantageous. Most of the information taken in during the daily round is of momentary value only. It serves to keep us abreast of the ever-changing relationships between ourselves and our environment and, this service rendered, its further retention would merely obstruct the ongoing flow of our activities. Suppose, for example, we are playing a fast ball-game. At each instant it is best to be informed about the detailed circumstances of that instant. But in the next instant, the circumstances of which we need to take account are different. It is not now necessary to retain every minute detail of immediately past circumstances; and indeed, if we did retain these details this would deprive us of freedom to consider the detailed requirements of the present moment. In all of life's activities, we take in, from one moment to the next, a great deal of information whose value is restricted to the moment of its intake. So it is altogether an economy that such information be forgotten immediately. It is an economy that what is selected for more lasting retention be only those minimal salient characteristics likely to be of future value.

It seems always to be the case that a feature of human functioning which is advantageous in general should, in some circumstances, be disadvantageous. Such is the case with immediate-forgetting. As we have already seen, it raises difficulties in problem-solving. It also raises difficulties when we attempt detailed comparisons between events which are separated in time. Only one illustration of this familiar difficulty need be given. Suppose we want to compare two strands of wool which are nearly the same colour. What do we do? If we can, we place the strands side by side so that we can look at both of them at the same time. We know that the further apart the strands are, the more difficult it is to compare them for small differences. Some of this difficulty could arise from the fact that, if the strands are apart, we may see them against different backgrounds: and of course, colours look different against different backgrounds. But the difficulty which is of interest at the moment is due to immediate-forgetting. We look at one strand, see its colour, and then move our eyes to the other strand some distance away. In the time it takes us to do this, we forget some of the detailed characteristics of the first strand, we are unable to retain a close specification of the colour. If we could retain this close specification, then the separation of the two strands would not impair our comparison. But as it is, immediate-forgetting of detailed characteristics makes us want to have the two strands as close together as possible.

It is, then, difficult minutely to compare two events which are separate in time. And this difficulty is due, in large part, to immediate-forgetting. It is worth mentioning that there are various procedures by which people attempt to overcome, or at least reduce, this difficulty. One of the most powerful of these is the kind of procedure known as measurement. For example, it may not be possible to compare two distances simultaneously by laying them side to side. But they can be compared closely if each distance in turn is compared simultaneously against a standard measuring tape. It is not misleading to say that immediate-forgetting is one of the circumstances which has prompted man to develop techniques of measurement.

4 Defects of Short-term Memory

There are various conditions in which people show defects of short-term memory. Some of these conditions are clearly abnormal, as in patients suffering from brain injury. Others must, at least up to the present day, be regarded as normal, e.g., the reduction in capacities which occurs as a function of ageing. The study of such defects is important for both practical and theoretical reasons. From a practical point of view, a defective person is best helped if the detailed nature and extent of his defects are known. This helps towards predicting what he will, and will not, be able to do. And it helps towards discovering ways of lessening his disabilities; either directly by reducing the extent of the defects themselves, or indirectly by training the person to use what capabilities he has in order to compensate for or circumvent his defects. From a theoretical point of view, the study of defects may well throw light on the nature of normal functioning. This section will outline three fairly well known defects of short-term memory, namely, 'memorizing-defect', momentary retrograde amnesia, and the reduction in short-term memory which comes about with ageing.

Memorizing-defect. The year 1887 was a notable one for the study of short-term memory. In that year, Jacobs reported his pioneer experiments on immediate memory span. In that same year, a Russian physician, S. S. Korsakoff, described an abnormal condition whose dominant symptom is failure to retain events for more than a few seconds or minutes. There is still no generally agreed name for this memory defect. Sometimes it is called 'short-term memory defect', sometimes 'fixation amnesia', sometimes 'memorizing-defect'. For convenience, this last term will be used here. The salient features of the defect can be outlined briefly under three headings. (*a*) The patient is unable to retain events which he experienced more than some seconds previously. Thus, he forgets the meal he has just eaten, the news he has just heard, the visit he has just been paid. (*b*) He shows little or no impairment in ability to remember events from before the start of his illness. Thus, he can recollect his life history up to the time of illness, he can use language, he can recognize objects and people who became familiar to him before his illness, and he can recite poems he used to know. (*c*) He shows little or no impairment in immediate retaining. Thus, he can perform immediate memory span tasks, he can retain the theme of what he is saying long enough to complete a short simple narrative, he can remember a short question long enough to answer it appropriately.

It is almost possible to predict the general behaviour of someone with the combination of abilities and disabilities so baldly outlined above. Nevertheless, some of these more general features of the patient's behaviour are worth describing. However, one cautionary point must be stressed. The same basic defect gives rise to behaviour patterns which, in detail, are different from one person to another. Even in the absence of other defects, the ways in which a person behaves after the onset of illness are dependent on the capabilities, attitudes, and behaviour patterns which are carried over from before the illness. They also depend on his present surroundings, the demands made on him, and the attitudes of other people to him. The main point is that in illness, as in health, no two people are identical. This means that we must beware general descriptions which oversimplify by leaving no room for individual differences. It does not, of course, mean that we are unable to make any general descriptions of a useful kind.

Defects of Short-term Memory

Because the patient forgets all, or nearly all, current events within some seconds, he is unable to solve problems which require the piecing together and the holding together of more than a few items of evidence. He cannot meet the demands of sustained conversation on a developing theme, nor carry out errands which require him to retain instructions received more than a few seconds before. He is constantly mislaying things and losing his way about the hospital and even his own room. He is disoriented in time as well as in space, since the present is not, for him, part of a continuous temporal context. He is unable to recollect that part of his life history which follows the onset of illness, and is not sure whether he entered hospital yesterday or some years before. He can give virtually no information about how long he has been ill or about the hospital and its staff. He is liable to misrecognize people and objects, and to meet the demands of recall by fabrication, i.e., in all sincerity he makes up a likely but untrue story about the past. The following quotation depicts some of the cumulative effects of memorizing-defect and some of the differences between one patient and another. It comes from an article by J. Barbizet, of Paris, which reviews current knowledge about memorizing-defect. (This rather technical review is entitled 'Defect of memorizing of hippocampal-mammillary origin: a review,' *Journal of Neurology, Neurosurgery and Psychiatry*, 1963, vol. 26, pp. 127–35.)

Such patients therefore who no longer fix the present live constantly in a past which preceded the onset of their illness. Their disengagement from the present is, however, far from complete. Some are conscious of the disorder of memory, like Émilienne, who said: 'When I watch closely I know, but I soon forget. My brain feels like a sieve, I forget everything. Even in my tiny room, I keep losing things. It all fades away.' Questioned on some events of the previous day, most often she will merely say: 'I don't remember.' However, if one insists and gives her some details of these events, this stirs up some old memories which, mixed with the information just received, lead to an erroneous answer, sometimes of simple paramnesia, and sometimes a more elaborate and fabricated story; she remains hesitant, however, and unsure of her answer. Confronted with a doctor she saw the day before, she says she does not recognize him, but when pushed she answers: 'I must have seen him last summer in Bréhat.' When asked whether she is sure of this, the answer is No. ... In other instances, the patient is not aware of his own inability to fix new facts, and consequently does not criticize his answers when these are drawn from past memories and are used to clothe today's environment and acquaintances. Thus, Germaine mistakes the head nurse for her relative and the medical student for her daughter. To Maurice, all doctors are citizens from Murat, a town in his native Cantal. Both patients are unable to memorize the present but can tell without mistakes the events of their childhood, and it seems that fabrication is with them an attempt to meet present situations using old memories in the absence of new ones, the acquirement of which has become impossible. (p. 128.)

Memorizing-defect was originally described by Korsakoff as the outcome of brain damage due to chronic alcoholism. The alcohol poisoning sets up a chain of physiological changes which culminate in damage to the brain. It is now known that, while alcoholism is the most frequent single cause of memorizing-defect, this defect can arise from a variety of other factors. Moreover, it is likely that these diverse factors all have their effect by leading to damage in the same particular part of the brain. In recent years, progress has been made in narrowing down the anatomical site of this damage, and it now seems probable that the basic cause of the defect is the destruction of nervous tissue in the brain structures known as the mammillary body, and the hippocampus. The anatomical and physiological aspects of memorizing-defect need not be discussed here (see Barbizet's article for a review). However, it should be mentioned that this defect lends further support to the functional differences between short-term and long-term retaining. The defect seems to involve an inability to establish any new patterns of long-term retaining. In-coming information can be remembered for as long as it is actively retained but it does not give rise to any lasting modifications. Already established patterns of long-term retaining can be utilized, but they are not capable of being extended and brought up to date in relation to recent events.

Momentary Retrograde Amnesia. This particular form of defect occurs in many, but not all, people who have recovered from concussion. These people are unable to recall events which took place immediately *before* the moment of concussion. The occurrence of this particular gap in recall is seldom of any practical concern. But it has important theoretical implications. The defect is best introduced by giving a brief account of concussion and its after-effects. (For a fuller account, see *Brain, Memory, Learning,* by W. R. Russell, especially Chapters 6 and 7, Oxford University Press, 1959.) In concussion, a person loses consciousness and becomes paralysed due to a sudden blow on the head. Unconsciousness may last for only a moment or for many days, depending on the severity of the impact; but the direct cause of unconsciousness is probably mechanical disturbance of nervous tissues in the brain. Now, when a person is recovering from concussion, he does not return to normal in the manner of someone awaking from sleep. Rather, he passes through a succession of stages which are marked by the return of progressively more complex modes of functioning. The total time required to progress through these stages is highly variable, but the sequences of the stages is fairly constant. First, there is return of simple reflex activities, then of restless purposeless movement involving the body as a whole. Then comes more purposeful movement and the ability to utter a few disconnected words and phrases. Then follows progressively more purposeful movements and coherent speech until, at length, there is full return to the complexity of normal functioning.

Short-term Memory

When, in the course of this recovery, the person reaches the stage of being able to converse with reasonable coherence, some curious defects begin to show. He fails to recognize some familiar objects and people, he misrecognizes others, and he rapidly forgets events as soon as they occur. That is, he shows symptoms of memorizing-defect. If questioned about the accident, he either can remember very little or he gives a fabricated description of what happened. In short, while he is normal in some respects, he is not yet in a state to comprehend current happenings fully nor to retain them for later recall. Nor is he yet in a state to be able to recall readily events which preceded the accident. This inability is called retrograde amnesia (that is, backwards loss of memory) and may cover events which preceded the accident by, in some cases, years. It is typical that, as recovery proceeds, the first events to be recalled are those which took place furthest back in time. As recovery continues, the person is able to recall events which occurred progressively nearer in time. These features are well illustrated by the following case, reported by Russell.

A green-keeper, aged 22, was thrown from his motor-cycle in August 1933. There was a bruise in the left frontal region and slight bleeding from the left ear, but no fracture was seen on X-ray examination. A week after the accident he was able to converse sensibly, and the nursing staff considered that he had fully recovered consciousness. When questioned, however, he said that the date was February 1922, and that he was a schoolboy. He had no recollection of five years spent in Australia, and two years in this country working on a golf course. Two weeks after the injury he remembered the five years spent in Australia, and remembered returning to this country; the past two years were, however, a complete blank as far as his memory was concerned. Three weeks after the injury he returned to the village where he had been working for two years. Everything looked strange, and he had no recollection of ever having been there before. He lost his way on more than one occasion. Still feeling a stranger to the

district he returned to work; he was able to do his work satis-
factorily, but had difficulty in remembering what he had actually
done during the day. About ten weeks after the accident, the
events of the past two years were gradually recollected and finally
he was able to remember everything up to within a few minutes of
the accident. (pp. 69–70.)

This report illustrates that the recollecting of a continuous
personal past is one of the last accomplishments to recover;
thus indicating that such recollecting is a more complex,
high-level achievement than its everyday commonness
would suggest. The report also illustrates that, during
recovery, it is the oldest, most distant events which are
recalled first, and then events which took place in the progressively more recent past. This points to the conclusion
that it is the recalling of more recently past events which is
most vulnerable to the effects of general brain dysfunction.
This conclusion is supported by conditions of progressive
worsening of brain dysfunction. In such deterioration, it is
the recent events which are forgotten first. Then it is the
progressively more distant events which cannot be recalled.
The general conclusion is, therefore, that the longer a person
has already retained the effects of some past event, the less
likely is it that his recalling of this event will be disrupted by
brain dysfunction. The final point made by the above
report, is that the period covered by retrograde amnesia
does not shrink up to the very moment of the blow. Even
after full return to normality, the man could not recall the
events which immediately preceded the blow on the head.
This permanent residual loss of recall is momentary retrograde amnesia.

Momentary retrograde amnesia is typical of most people
who have recovered from concussion. For example, the
motorist can recollect approaching the crossroads, but
nothing more; the workman can recollect the ladder
slipping away from him, but nothing more. Why this short
blank period? In every case, the person must have

experienced much more, often of a highly dramatic kind. So why is he now unable to recall these vivid experiences which took place just before the blow and while he was still conscious? The answer seems fairly certain to be that there is complete failure to retain the effects of these experiences. The information was taken in and gave rise to appropriate patterns of central nervous activities; but these activities were abruptly abolished by the blow; they did not persist long enough to effect any lasting modifications of the nervous system. The sudden paralysis of nervous activities prevented the establishment of those neural changes which underly long-term retaining.

This prevention of 'consolidation' also occurs in what is known as electro-convulsive therapy. Such therapy is found to benefit patients suffering from certain types of mental disorder. What happens is that a brief electric current is passed through the head so as to produce sudden paralysis of nervous activity. In some respects, the effects of this electric shock are similar to the effects of concussion. In particular, the recovered patient often has the same inability to recall experiences which immediately preceded the sudden paralysis of the nervous system. This effect of electrically paralysing the brain has been confirmed by experiments on animals. In these experiments, the animal, say a white rat, is given repeated opportunity to master some simple task. For example, he runs towards two doors, side by side; one door is black, the other white; if he pushes through the black door, he finds food; but if he pushes through the white door he finds himself in an unpleasant compartment without food. The rat is presented repeatedly with this choice between the two doors and, in time, the cumulative effects of his experiences lead him to choose the 'correct' door on every trial. Now, what happens if, following each trial, his brain is electrically paralysed? When the shock comes an hour after each trial, nothing happens to his progressive learning. But when he receives this shock some fifteen minutes or less after each trial, he shows impaired remembering; he takes more trials to master the task, implying some failure to retain the effects of past choices. The sooner shock is administered after each choice, the greater the impairment of retaining. With a delay of about twenty seconds, there is (under certain circumstances) complete and permanent forgetting. The rat fails to benefit by his repeated experience and does not master the task.

Incidentally, it might be suggested that momentary retrograde amnesia in concussion is due to repressing. That is, the experiences which precede the blow are retained, but they are so unpleasant that the recovered patient cannot bring himself to recall them. This suggestion does not seem at all feasible. For one thing, the recovered patient does not seem able to recall these experiences under any circumstances, even under hypnosis or hypnotic-type drugs. (The term 'truth drugs' is misleading. Such drugs have their effect by inducing a relaxed, suggestible state. The person in this state can be persuaded to answer questions cooperatively and to 'concentrate' on recalling events which, under normal circumstances, he does not care to recall, even to himself.) For another thing, this momentary retrograde amnesia is not typical of all unpleasant head injuries. It may often be absent in high velocity missile wounds, for example, when a bullet enters the brain, causing damage but not necessarily loss of consciousness. Also, it is typically absent in crush injuries, when gradually increasing pressure on the skull leads to brain injury but, again, not necessarily to unconsciousness. Experiences in these kinds of injury can be terrifyingly unpleasant, but they are far from being subsequently forgotten.

In conclusion then, a sudden paralysis of brain activity can be caused mechanically or electrically. And when it occurs, there is consequent failure to retain the effects of whatever experiences took place some seconds before the paralysis. This failure points, yet again, to a distinction between short-term and long-term retaining. The general implication is that incoming information does not, at once, effect modifications in long-term retaining. The neural activity patterns occasioned by recent experience seem to require time to 'make contact with' and 'join on to' already established patterns of long-term retaining, and so be assured some chance of longer survival.

Ageing and Short-term Memory. It is dangerous to make general statements about the long-term functional changes which take place as a person ages from the twenties onwards. So much depends on the individual, his circumstances and interests, the sorts of accomplishments he has acquired, whether he continues to use these accomplishments or not, whether they help or hinder him in acquiring new accomplishments. Some people become 'old before their time' while others continue to function at high levels of achievement into extreme old age. Provided these considerable individual differences are kept in view, it is possible to summarize some of the findings about ageing by simply referring to two broad trends. The first trend is the cumulative effects of past experience. These effects were mentioned in Chapter One and are acknowledged in everyday speech by phrases like 'the wisdom of age', 'the knowledge of a lifetime', and 'the maturity of experience'. Cumulative experience counts for much. It is no accident that in, for example, the professions of the historian, the politician, and the lawyer, the older man often outshines his younger colleague. The older man has a greater fund of cumulative experience on which to draw, and a practised skill in dealing with the issues likely to arise in his field of specialization. The broad trend of cumulative experience is, then, towards increasing efficacy of functioning (even if, in some circumstances, it has drawbacks). By contrast, the second broad trend is towards progressive impairment of functioning.

At basis, this trend seems to stem from a mild but cumulative form of brain injury. Brain cells, once lost, are not replaced and, as a person lives on, some brain cells die off or are destroyed by minute injuries of various kinds. The result is a progressive loss of vital brain tissue.

For some tasks, the moderate loss of brain tissue does not matter: the person has, so to speak, more than enough component parts to do the job. For other tasks, this loss does matter but is more than compensated for by the effects of cumulative experience: the gains outweigh the losses. For yet other tasks, this loss may lead to demonstrable impairment of functioning. The kinds of task showing such impairment are, notably, those which make heavy demands on short-term memory. Experimental studies find that, on average, older people are less able to 'hold in mind' a complexity of information. The older person does less well than the younger on tasks which require him to take in and retain a set of information while, at the same time, carrying through other activities: his short-term memory is more vulnerable to distractions. Older people are also less able to accomplish those feats of comprehending which are so important in solving complex problems, especially of novel kinds: part of the data keep 'slipping from mind'. In his book, *Ageing and Human Skill* (Oxford University Press, 1958), A. T. Welford has surveyed several of these experiments which indicate progressive impairment of short-term memory with ageing. He summarizes a chapter on learning and memory in the following words:

The evidence upon changes with age of ability to learn is still fragmentary and to some extent conflicting, but would seem in its present state to support two broad conclusions. (1) Much of the apparent difficulty of learning by older people is not due to any true incapacity of learning or recall as such but to inability to comprehend the material or to deal with the conditions under which it is presented. (2) Increased liability to interference with short-term retention by other activity would seem capable of accounting, directly or indirectly, for many if not all of the cases where true learning or retention deficiency can be shown, even those where other explanations seem at first sight more obvious. (p. 256.)

Many middle-aged to elderly people are aware of their own lessened ability to 'hold' a complex of information. Many are also aware that, to avoid failure in some situations, they must modify their previously established procedures, for these are no longer adequate. They find that, in various ways and with varying success, they must alter their problem-solving procedures so as to allow for reduction in short-term memory.

Before concluding this chapter, it should be mentioned that perhaps the most general point to emerge is the progressive selecting of what is retained. Not all the physical energies which reach a person from his environment are capable of exciting his sense organs. And not all physical energies which can excite his sense organs do so at any one time. In these two respects, there is heavy selection of information for intake. But once information is received, there are yet further stages of selection. Within a second or so, much received information is permanently lost and only some fragmentary characteristics of it are retained. Of these fragmentary characteristics, even less are selected for longer retention over a period of minutes. And as will be seen in the following chapters, this loss of the retained effects of past experience continues into the future. In short, the person's ongoing activities exert a continuing and progressive natural selection on what he retains from his past for use in the future. This very general point was expressed many years ago by William James (1842–1910), the great American psychologist whose book, *Principles of Psychology*, is probably the most rewarding single work ever written by a student of mental life. In speaking of the retained effects of a person's ongoing activities and experiences, James said this. 'Of some, no memory survives the instant of their passage. Of others, it is confined to a few moments, hours, or days. Others, again, leave vestiges which are indestructible, and by means of which they may be recalled as long as life endures.'

III Memorizing

An alternative title for this chapter might be 'Memory for Precise Detail'. The word memorizing will be used here to refer to the activities of learning, retaining, and remembering with detailed precision. When we undertake to memorize a poem or a quotation, our aim is to be able to recall it with word-by-word accuracy. Similarly, when we have successfully memorized a name, or a fact, or a number, then we are able to characterize the item of information closely; we are able to recall the exact name, the detailed fact, the precise number. In short, we will use the word memorizing to refer to learning and remembering which is relatively precise and specific: the material involved is either factual or verbatim in nature.

It is typically the case with memorizing that it requires a repeated going over of whatever is being memorized. It is true that we can often recall a strange name, a telephone number, or a particular phrase in a foreign language after only a single hearing or reading. But such learning is the exception rather than the rule and is certainly not typical of memorizing a poem or passage of prose. Material which is lengthy or unfamiliar has to be read or heard several times before it can be recalled with memorized exactness. And even then, it must usually be rehearsed from time to time if it is not to be forgotten. Memorizing, then, achieves detailed recall and typically does so through repetition. This makes memorizing, for all its complexities, relatively easy to study. Since exactness is its aim, it is easy to tell when a person has accomplished his task. Since repeated attempts must usually be made at mastering the material, it is relatively easy to tell how a person is progressing from one attempt to the next. And since learned material must usually be repeated from time to time if it is not to be forgotten, it is relatively easy to follow the course of forgetting over various lapses of time. All this has made memorizing a favoured topic for experimental study, not only in the laboratory but also in the school classroom.

1 Memorizing Activities

Despite its literal and repetitive features, memorizing is not a passive affair. It is part of a person's ongoing biographical change. It involves the person in relating new material to what he has already learned, and in relating the component parts of the new material to each other. Because of this, the experimental study of memorizing is dominated by two broad issues, namely, the role of meaning and the role of repetition. One point must be stressed straight away: each of these issues is complex in itself and the two issues are not independent the one from the other. This point is admirably brought out by William James in a passage which refers to commonplace, yet fundamental, aspects of everyday memorizing.

Most men have a good memory for facts connected with their own pursuits. The college athlete who remains a dunce at his books will astonish you by his knowledge of men's 'records' in various feats and games, and will be a walking dictionary of sporting statistics. The reason is that he is constantly going over these things in his mind, and comparing and making series of them. They form for him not so many odd facts, but a concept-system – so they stick. So the merchant remembers prices, the politician other politicians' speeches and votes, with a copiousness which amazes outsiders, but which the amount of thinking they bestow on these subjects easily explains. The great memory for facts which a Darwin and a Spencer reveal in their books is not incompatible with the possession on their part of a brain with only a middling degree of physiological retentiveness. Let a man early in life set himself the task of verifying such a theory as that of evolution, and facts will soon cluster and cling to him like grapes to their stem. Their relations to the theory will hold them fast; and the more of these the mind is able to discern, the greater the erudition will become. Meanwhile the theorist may have little, if any, desultory memory. Unutilizable facts may be unnoted by him and forgotten as soon as heard. An ignorance almost as encyclopaedic as his erudition may coexist with the latter, and hide, as it were, in the interstices of its web. Those who have had much to do with scholars and 'savants' will readily think of examples of the class of mind I mean.

In a system, every fact is connected with every other by some thought-relation. The consequence is that every fact is retained by the combined suggestive power of all the other facts in the system, and forgetfulness is well-nigh impossible. (*Principles of Psychology*, vol. 1, 1891, pp. 662-3.)

In this passage, James raises a number of aspects of memorizing. There is reference to the matter of interest or value. A person is likely to select out from current events those which interest him, which have relevance to his long-standing concerns and aims and aspirations, which are likely to be of future use to him. For example, the sports enthusiast is predisposed to seize upon events related to his interests, whereas another person may let the same events pass by almost unnoticed, and forget their details immediately. There is, too, reference to the ease with which material can be memorized when it can be related to material that is already familiar to the person. When the new fact fits into a system of interrelated facts, this facilitates its being memorized in the first place. Somewhat familiar material is more easily committed to memory than material which is unfamiliar, strange, and does not fit with what is known already. Again, there is reference to the role of repetition in preventing subsequent forgetting of the memorized fact. Since the person is interested in the material, he has frequent occasion to recall it, and thereby keep it alive. Once material has been memorized, its frequent use serves to maintain its retention. Lastly, there is reference to what might be called the issue of memorizing and understanding. This is an important issue which merits some discussion.

Memorizing and Understanding. 'Memorizing' is sometimes contrasted unfavourably with 'understanding'. At a superficial level, such a contrast is valid and worthy of emphasis. But on closer inspection, the antithesis between understanding and memorizing is found to break down into several more basic questions. The fundamental questions are these. How does the person deal with the material which is presented to him? What characteristics does he abstract from the material? How does he relate these characteristics to each other and to what he knows already? Out of these basic questions there arise subsidiary questions. What characteristics of the material can he subsequently remember? And under what circumstances does he remember them?

In Chapter One, it was mentioned that students proceed in diverse ways when asked to memorize the magic-square array of digits. At one extreme, there is little emphasis on interpreting the material; the student repeats a digit sequence over and over again until he can depend on being able to run through this sequence when required, and so reconstruct the array from memory. At another extreme, there is emphasis on interpreting the array and less on repetition: the student works on the material and selects out a few higher-order characteristics which economically serve to specify the whole: to reconstruct the array, he expands these remembered relationships so as to recreate the details of the original. At one extreme then, there is heavy emphasis on rote repetition. At the other extreme, there is emphasis on economical abstraction. And between these two extremes, there lies a wealth of compromise procedures. In this situation, the use of any of these procedures may suffice to ensure the same accomplishment, namely, the ability to reconstruct the array from memory. However, the 'understanders' are perhaps less likely to forget the array subsequently because their recall procedure involves the production of fewer independent characteristics. Let us cite one further example of divergent methods of dealing with material which is to be reconstructed from memory. This simple example is taken from a book by the American, G. Katona (*Organizing and Memorizing*, 1940). He presented adults with the array of digits shown in Figure 3. One group

$$2 \quad 9 \quad 3 \quad 3 \quad 3 \quad 6 \quad 4 \quad 0 \quad 4 \quad 3 \quad 4 \quad 7$$
$$5 \quad 8 \quad 1 \quad 2 \quad 1 \quad 5 \quad 1 \quad 9 \quad 2 \quad 2 \quad 2 \quad 6$$

Figure 3

of subjects was given three minutes to master the above array by repeating the digits in groups of three. Another group of subjects was given three minutes to discover some principle of construction in the array: and most of these adults discovered that the digits did, indeed, conform to a pattern which might be expressed as follows. Start at the bottom line with 5; then add 3 to get 8; then add 4 to get 12; then add 3 to get 15. Continue in this way, adding 3 and 4 alternately, until twenty-four digits are obtained in two rows of equal length. In short, the two groups were deliberately led into dealing with the material in different ways. Three weeks later, both groups of subjects were asked to write out the array. Of the principle-seekers, 23 per cent reproduced the digits accurately. But none of the 'repeaters' were able to do so. In order to reconstruct the material, the 'repeaters' had to be able to produce a larger number of unrelated characteristics; they had more to remember; and not surprisingly, their reconstructing was less successful than that of the 'understanders'. This simple experiment demonstrates that subsequent reproducing of the material is facilitated if the material can be characterized in terms of a few higher-level relationships, i.e., if the principles are understood. Now, there are innumerable real-life situations where this procedure of abstracting higher-level characteristics is a powerful economy. But notice that the gains are won at a cost. As in the experiment with binary digit span, there is the cost of translation work to be considered. In any particular situation, this cost of translation may or may not outweigh its gains.

It is often the case that when 'memorizing' is compared unfavourably with 'understanding', what is meant is that the person has abstracted and retained from the material details which are specific and not generalizable. For example, if a person is shown a table of experimental results, he is not usually expected to learn the exact figures off by heart. What he is expected to do is to abstract the general trends and significances of the data. The merit of such abstracting is that these higher-order characteristics can be used in other contexts. These principles enable him to note similarities between this particular set of data and other, superficially different, sets of data. They enable him to predict the likely outcome of new experiments and observations. By contrast, memorizing the exact data does not, in itself, guarantee such higher-order abstracting. His mastery of the data may enable him to do only one thing, namely, recall these details when they are specifically requested.

In the passage quoted from James there is an implied reference to the role of repetition in enriching understanding. If a memorized fact is frequently recalled in a variety of contexts, this enables the person to relate the fact to an increasing range of other facts. Such diversified repetition gives opportunity to relate the fact to others which have already been memorized, or are being encountered for the first time. The outcome of this is that the particular fact can be recalled more flexibly. The person is more able to recall it under a variety of relevant circumstances and not merely when prompted by some specific and narrow circumstance to which it is exclusively related. The utility of such increasing flexibility of recall is obvious. The value of any fact lies in its being available for use when required; and it may be required in a variety of contexts. For example, a common failure in problem-solving is inability to recall relevant information. The information has been acquired and can be recalled if specifically asked for; but the problem situation is not sufficient to prompt its recall, and does not serve to bring the relevant information to mind. Every teacher knows how worthwhile it is to present the same factual material in a variety of contexts. The aim of this is not merely to prevent forgetting of the fact. The aim is also to encourage the child to discover the relatedness of the fact to other facts, to work it into a more comprehensive system of interrelated facts, to make the fact available for use in an increasing variety of contexts. After all, what is important is not only what and how much a person can recall, but also the circumstances under which he can recall it: in short, the use he can make of his past experiences in meeting the demands of present circumstances. In brief, repetition of the fact in diversified contexts increases the range of circumstances which will prompt its recall. This makes the fact usable in a more flexible fashion: it can, so to speak, be asked for in various ways. This also makes it less likely that the person will fail to recall the fact when asked for it in any one particular way. For if one recall procedure does not suffice to produce the fact, then he has alternative recall procedures at his disposal.

These introductory considerations emphasize that memorizing may be looked at from many viewpoints. It involves a complex of issues and a diversity of activities. Several issues all operate at one and the same time although, of course, their relative importance differs from one situation to the next. Let us now consider some of these factors separately.

2 Repetition

There is no question about the importance of repetition in memorizing. In the previous chapter, it was seen that repetition seems to play a central role in short-term retaining. When information is received and must be retained for use a short time hence, the retaining appears to be accomplished by some sort of repetitive rehearsal of the information. Furthermore, it was seen that if, say, a digit sequence could be recalled immediately after being received, this was no guarantee that it could be retained for a matter of minutes: it must usually be repeated several more times. And even then, still longer retaining often requires that the information be repeated yet again from time to time if it is not to be forgotten. So, repetition plays a crucial part in acquiring mastery of the material and, subsequently, in maintaining this mastery. In this section, we shall consider some very general, perhaps obvious, aspects of repetition.

Active Repetition. Every teacher knows that there is little to be gained by going over a piece of information again and again if the pupils are not even listening. To be effective, repetition must be, in some degree, active. The learner must be doing something in relation to the information, using it in some way and making its use part of his activity repertoire. This truth may be borne in on the teacher who reads out a short poem several times to his class so that it can be memorized. The children do memorize it, and then the teacher is shocked to discover that he cannot recite it from memory himself. The children were intent on memorizing, relating the words together in sequence, and mastering the whole. But the teacher did not do this: he merely read the words out without doing anything to memorize them. Mere repeated encounter with material does not, of itself, enable the person to memorize it. This general point may be made more explicit by outlining a simple demonstration experiment.

In this demonstration, people are asked to memorize pairs of words. Unrelated words are read out to them slowly, e.g., OMELET, BURGLAR; FREEZE, DESIGN; KITCHEN, LIGHTNING; TIGER, MUSIC. There are several pairs of words, and people are asked to memorize them so that, if they are given the first word of any pair, they can recall the second. In one use of this demonstration, there were twenty such pairs of words, that is, forty words in all: there were sixteen adult subjects: and the list was read out three times. After the presentations were completed, the subjects were asked to show what they had memorized. They were given the first word in the list and then had five seconds in which to write down the second word. Then, contrary to expectation, they were given this second word and asked to write down the third, that is, the first word of the next pair. Perhaps this request seems unfair, and, in a sense, it is. But the forty words had, in fact, been read out at a completely uniform rate; so if mere repeated presentations were sufficient for memorizing, it should be as easy to recall the third word in response to the second as to recall the second in response to the first. When the subjects had attempted to recall the whole list, word by word in this way, what was the outcome? On average, the second word in each pair was recalled correctly in seventy-four per cent of cases. But the first word of each pair was recalled correctly in only seven per cent of cases. Why this great difference? It cannot be due to the way in which the words were read out. For

example, BURGLAR followed OMELET on three occasions
and, likewise, FREEZE followed BURGLAR on three occasions, with the same length of pause between each successive
item. The difference is due to how the subjects dealt with
what was presented. They complied with the original
instructions. They attempted to relate together the words
of each 'pair', whereas they neglected the sequence of the
'pairs' as being of no relevance. This simple demonstration
serves to underline the point that merely being presented
with two words in succession does not ensure their being
memorized as a pair. What does ensure such memorizing
is the person's actively relating the words together. In more
general terms, the important thing is not so much what
is presented as what the person does with the material
presented.

As a general practical rule, it may be said that repetition
must involve appropriate activity on the part of the memorizer if it is to be effective. In memorizing many kinds of
material, one such appropriate procedure involves active
anticipation. Consider, for example, the task of memorizing
the Morse code equivalents of English letters, or the foreign
language equivalents of English words. One way of proceeding is to read each English item and then its equivalent,
and do this repeatedly. A better procedure is to read the
English item and attempt to recall (anticipate) its equivalent. And then, and only then, look at this equivalent to
check whether the anticipation has been correct or not.
The procedure involves getting some initial familiarity with
the material and then attempting to anticipate the next
portion of the lesson before actually looking to see what it is.
The operation of this 'recitation' procedure is evident in the
following demonstration conducted by the writer with
university students acting as subjects.

Each student in the group was given a printed selection
from Mrs Browning's poem 'Aurora Leigh'. The selection
contained 112 words and 16 lines with each line numbered

in sequence. He was given exactly five minutes in which to attempt to memorize the selection and told that, afterwards, he would be asked for an accurate recall, i.e., he must write out the correct words in their proper sequence and in their appropriate lines. The time given was long enough to enable every student to master a fair proportion of the poem but not sufficiently long to enable any, except a very few, to master it completely. Half of the students were to use recitation and the other half were not. Those using non-recitation were instructed as follows. 'Begin at the first line and read through the material to the end. Then read the material through repeatedly from beginning to end. Keep your eyes on the printed material at all times and make no attempt to recite or anticipate what comes next. Work as quickly as possible.' The other half of the students were instructed in recitation. 'For the first minute, read the material through from beginning to end as in the non-recitation method. Then, when I give the signal, begin recitation. Read a line, then close your eyes and try to repeat it silently to yourself. If you cannot repeat it, read it again and, if necessary, again. Then read the next line, close your eyes, try to recall it, check if necessary, and go on to the next line again. Work as quickly as possible and don't waste time trying to recall lines which you obviously haven't yet mastered.' After these instructions were given, each student spent five minutes in memorizing and then spent a further five minutes trying to write out as much as he could recall. He then scored his recall by counting up the total number of words correctly reproduced. Over a number of different class sessions, 150 students acted as subjects in this experiment, half of them using recitation and the other half non-recitation. Those using recitation recalled, on the average, 46 words while those not using recitation had an average recall score of only 33 words. Thus, the best learning was obtained by those who devoted a large share of their time to recitation.

Other investigations show that, as expected, the superiority of the recitation group is still present when remembering is tested not immediately after memorizing but some considerable time later. It is also found that the superiority of recitation is greater with material which is relatively meaningless and difficult to master. (With highly meaningful material such as simple poetry, it is difficult for the memorizer not to engage in anticipation to some extent.)

In general, then, a large number of investigations have agreed in finding that reading-with-recitation makes for faster memorizing than does reading alone. Why should this be? In the first place, the need to anticipate successive portions of the lesson ensures that the memorizer is actively involved in his task and does not lapse into inattentive re-readings. Secondly, he must engage in recalling the material, that is, he begins to practise just that activity which it is his ultimate aim to accomplish. Being able to read something is not the same as being able to produce that something from memory. Such production requires a different kind of activity, and the use of recitation ensures that this recalling activity is practised directly. Thirdly, recitation provides the memorizer with immediate knowledge of results, it lets him know how and where he is progressing towards mastery, lets him know at once if he is recalling incorrectly, lets him know where he must concentrate his memorizing efforts. Lastly, recitation may encourage the memorizer by letting him know that he is making progress and, perhaps, by spurring him to improve his own record with each successive re-reading of the material.

It should be obvious that repetition may take many different forms. For example, a student who has just read and memorized some facts about physics can repeat these facts by re-reading them, by recalling them to himself, by bringing them into an essay or a report, by bringing them into conversation and talking about them. The oftener he uses these facts, in whatever way, the less likely he is to forget them. One of the reasons why the enthusiast about any topic has a ready mastery of many facts related to that topic is that he is frequently bringing these facts to mind. He thinks about them, talks about them, and in this way maintains his mastery of them.

Repetition and Maintenance. Once material has been memorized, it can be maintained by frequent use. This fact has just been referred to. The maintenance function of repetition is familiar enough – even if, to our cost, we ignore this fact surprisingly often in everyday life. This maintenance effect of repeated use may be exemplified explicitly by outlining an investigation reported in 1939 by the American psychologist, H. F. Spitzer. The subjects in this investigation were more than three thousand 11-year-old school children.

As part of Spitzer's investigation, every child was given eight minutes to study an article about bamboo plants. The article was some six-hundred words long and made points of a factual nature which were unfamiliar to the child. Each child's remembering of these points was assessed by giving him a multiple-choice test containing twenty-five questions such as the following. 'To which family of plants do bamboos belong? Trees, ferns, grasses, mosses, fungi.' The child had to recognize which alternative answer was correct. His answers were then scored in the usual fashion which makes a so-called 'correction for guessing'. In brief, every child read a factual article and subsequently took a multiple-choice recognition test on its contents.

However, not all children took this test immediately after reading the article. The children were divided into groups, and each group was treated differently. In some groups, the children took the test only once, but at different lengths of time after reading. That is, some children were given the test immediately after reading the article; some were not given the test until a day later; others not until seven days later; and so on. Conditions were arranged so that children who were given a delayed test did not, in fact, expect that they would be tested on the article. The scores which these children made on the test are shown, in percentages, on the top row of Table 3. It will be seen that children who took the test immediately scored an average of 53 per cent correct. Children who did not take the test until the following day scored less, namely, 38 per cent. Children who did not take the test until sixty-three days later scored 26 per cent. These results illustrate the general finding that forgetting is rapid shortly after learning, and then proceeds less and less rapidly as time goes on. For example, there is a big drop in recognition score between children who took the test immediately after reading and those who took it one day after: but there is no difference between those children who took the test twenty-one days after reading and those who took it sixty-three days after.

Table 3

Days Since Learning	0	1	7	14	21	63
Average Scores on Single Tests	% 53	% 38	% 32	% 28	% 26	% 26
Average Scores on Successive Tests						
Group I	53	53	—	—	49	—
Group II	53	—	48	—	—	43
Group III	—	—	32	—	32	—

Other groups of children took the same test more than once. For example, children in Group I took the test immediately after reading, then again the following day, and then again twenty-one days after the original reading. The scores made by these children are shown above, and the effect of the successive tests is evident. After twenty-one days, these children scored an average of 49 per cent correct: but children who took the test for the first time after twenty-one days scored only 26 per cent. Clearly, Group I had benefited from taking the test before. The repetition involved had helped to maintain what they had learned. In taking the test, they had used the information acquired, and this had provided a further opportunity to learn and maintain that information. The same general conclusion emerges from other groups of children who took the test more than once. The results for some of these groups are also shown in Table 3.

The main outcome of this investigation is that repeated use of what has been memorized favours later remembering. And by and large, the sooner the repetition follows original learning, the better. In these children, the repetition was occasioned by their taking a multiple-choice exam. But repetition could have been occasioned in other ways. For example, the teacher might have talked about the material in class, or the children might have been given opportunity to bring the material into essays or discussions, or they might have been given incentive to talk about the material among themselves or at home. Many circumstances could serve to keep the material alive for them by inducing its repetition. With regard to the especial value of repetition which closely follows original learning, it is worth mentioning that many university students have discovered for themselves the worth of reviewing material shortly after learning it or receiving it. Many students report the saving of effort which results from making habitual use of the following rule. Never finish a reading session without reviewing in outline the main points of what has just been read. This practical rule is found by many to be about the most important single step they can take to prevent subsequent forgetting of the material. By giving an additional active review to what has been read, the student not only discovers how much he has learned or failed to learn, but also learns the material further before he has had much opportunity to forget it. Subsequently, this saves efforts to re-learn material which has been forgotten shortly after original learning. Likewise in dealing with lecture notes. These are best gone over and their details filled out while the original lecture is still fresh in mind, that is, before too much forgetting can take place.

Some Effects of Massed Repetition. Before concluding our general survey of repetition, brief mention may be made of some curious effects which arise when repetitions are carried out in close succession. If we pronounce a word over and over again, rapidly and without pause, then the word is felt to lose meaning. Take any word, say, CHIMNEY. Say it repeatedly and in rapid succession. Within some seconds, the word loses meaning. This loss is referred to as 'semantic satiation'. What seems to happen is that the word forms a kind of closed loop with itself. One utterance leads into a second utterance of the same word, this leads into a third, and so on. Now this is a highly unusual sequence of events. Normally, when a word is used it has meaning in the sense that it is a momentary component of some developing theme. The word normally arises in the course of a train of activity and leads on, through some of its attributes, to further related attributes and a continuation of the theme. But after repeated pronunciation, this meaningful continuation of the word is blocked since, now, the word leads only to its own recurrence. It is found, for example, that if a digit, say 'seven', is repeatedly pronounced, this impedes its use in a calculation which is attempted immediately afterwards. That is, the person finds, for some short time, difficulty in using the number in meaningful relationships with other numbers. It is noteworthy that in such rapidly repeated speech, some words may even become difficult to pronounce. This effect is sometimes comparable to the familiar confusion which arises in so-called tongue-twisters: the difficulty is to switch rapidly between two closely similar but different patterns of vocal articulation.

Another effect of massed repetition is akin to semantic satiation. But this time, the person simply listens to the speech of someone else. A phrase is recorded on tape, e.g., 'drop salt into milk'. And the tape is formed into a loop so that the same phrase is played over and over again, rather like a gramophone when the needle is stuck in a groove. Now if we listen to this repeated utterance, it seems to change. We hear other words, we hear nonsense sounds, it is difficult to believe that we are merely listening to the same phrase over and over. This so-called 'verbal transformation effect' is all the stronger if we are not told beforehand about the closed-loop nature of the material being presented, but are told to expect changes in what is being heard.

The above effects of closely massed repetition of verbal material are paralleled in a variety of situations where the same material is rapidly repeated. For example, prolonged inspection of some visual figures may give rise to peculiar alterations in the appearance of the material. Such effects are perhaps of limited practical concern, but they are of interest in discovering the functional principles which govern the organization of human activities.

3 Meaning

The word 'meaning' is, like the word 'memory', both abstract and used to refer to a variety of different issues. Here, we shall be concerned with four issues. Firstly, the familiarity of the material to the memorizer. Secondly, the advantage of memorizing material which is part of a larger meaningful context: the issues of whole versus part memorizing. Thirdly, individual differences concerning what is, and what is not, familiar. And fourthly, the individual's interest in memorizing the material, that is, the extent to which he feels its acquisition to be worthwhile.

Familiarity of the Material. Familiar material is easier to memorize than unfamiliar material. This obvious fact would need no discussion if it did not have so many practical and theoretical implications for memory in general. Let us begin with two simple illustrations of this fact.

Consider the following three lists of material. (1) TAS – YAL – DOP – SIW – MEL – YOS – HIW – LON – MAF – GIW – NAL – WOH. (2) WAS – TIN – LAY – WHY – OLD – WOE – NIL – LOW – HAM – FIG – MOP – ASS. (3) WE – ALL – SAW – A – TINY – GOLDFISH – WHO – SWAM – IN – MY – POOL. No experimental investigation is required to tell us that these lists would not be equally easy to learn. We would have to read through the first list several times before we could recall it. The second list would be recalled after a smaller number of readings. And the third list would be reproduced after no more than two readings. Now each list is made up from exactly the same letters. So why should they not be equally easy to memorize? The answer is obvious. The second list is easier than the first because it contains familiar, though unrelated, words. The third list is easier still because it contains familiar words which, in addition, occur in a familiar kind of sequence, that is, a sequence which makes sense. The three lists, then, differ in the extent to which they can be characterized in terms which are already familiar to us by virtue of the cumulative effects of our past experience. To someone who had never learned to read English, each of these three lists would be equally unfamiliar. They would appear as so many meaningless marks on paper, just as a text of Chinese characters would to those of us who know no Chinese. But granted past experience of English, the three lists are not equally familiar, and so not equally easy to memorize.

Consider now the two patterns, A and B, shown in

Memorizing

Figure 4. Each pattern contains the same lines, but in a different spatial arrangement.

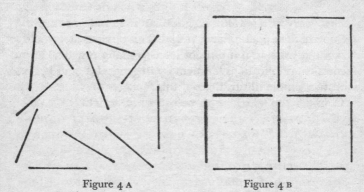

Figure 4 A   Figure 4 B

Which is easier to memorize, A or B? The answer is clear. In B the lines are embodied in a simple, overall pattern. The whole can be characterized in terms which are both familiar and few. This makes the figure easy to memorize. It also makes the figure easy to recall, that is, to characterize in its absence; and easy to recognize if encountered among several other patterns. None of this is the case with A. Suppose someone seriously tried to commit A to memory. How would he do it? He would certainly have to work on the figure, devise what might be called its rules of construction. These rules might be visual or verbal or numerical; but the fewer and more coherent he could make them, the less difficulty he would have in memorizing the figure.

What has just been said may be rephrased in more general terms as follows. When a person approaches any memorizing task, he brings to it those long-term patterns of retaining which he has cumulatively built up through past experience. It is in terms of these patterns that he recognizes and interprets the material. And it is by modifications to these patterns that he succeeds in retaining the characteristics of this material for use in the future. In so far as the material can be characterized in ways which are already part of these long-term patterns, then no modifications are required for their retaining. These characteristics are already in the person's repertoire of activities and do not need to be acquired afresh. All that need be memorized are the novel characteristics of the material: the unfamiliar parts, or the unfamiliar relationships between parts which, in themselves, are already familiar. Only the novel characteristics of the material need give rise to new patterns of retaining. And the fewer these novel characteristics are, the less modification is needed to secure the retaining of the material as a whole.

This fundamental effect of familiarity is alluded to in the passages quoted earlier from James and from Bain. The effect can be seen whenever a person attempts to memorize material which is relatively strange to him. He attempts to translate the material into familiar terms. He makes effort after meaning. He masters the unfamiliar by extending the familiar so as to incorporate it. For example, suppose he is memorizing the longest word in the English language. This word is (the writer believes) FLOCCIPAUCINIHILIPILI-FICATION. What does he do? In one way or another, he breaks up the letter sequence into some five or six groups which have some kind of familiarity for him, and then he fixes the sequence of these groups, possibly by repeatedly saying them over to himself. In school work, teachers know the advantage of introducing a topic in terms which are already familiar to the pupils and only gradually extending the familiar to embrace the unfamiliar. The devices used to this end may include analogy, metaphor, homely illustrations, models, charts. And again, the efficacy of mnemonic systems and devices is largely due to their providing the person with procedures for relating the unfamiliar to the already familiar. Let us cite only one instance of this pervasive attempt to characterize new material in familiar ways. This instance serves to illustrate effort-after-meaning, and also to introduce the issue of whole-part memorizing. It comes from an experiment reported in 1961 by the British psychologist, Dr Mary Allan.

In this experiment, the subjects were young naval ratings, and their task was to memorize a random sequence of letters of the alphabet. Each letter was printed on a separate card, like a playing card, and the twenty-six cards made up a pack in which the letters occurred in a jumbled, non-alphabetical order. This pack was handed to a rating who had to turn over each successive card, name it aloud, and try to note the sequence in which the letters followed each other. He had to do this at a steady rate of about one card every second. As soon as he had gone through the pack in this way, he was asked to recall the letters in as nearly the correct sequence as he could. Then he went through the whole procedure again with the cards still in the same order. Again he attempted recall. And these trials were repeated until he could recite the letter sequence correctly. How did the naval ratings deal with this task? At first, they expected that they could never manage it. But when they were encouraged to make serious efforts, they began, of their own accord, to group the letters into short sequences which had some meaning for them. The particular groupings used varied from one man to another, and even when two men used the same grouping they often made it meaningful in quite different ways. As they proceeded with this flexible type of group-labelling procedure, they also attempted to assign each group to a fixed position in the sequence. The final effort was to build bridging relationships between these groups which did not seem to follow easily out of each other. In short, the men dealt with the material by grouping letters together, translating these groups into units which had meaningful familiarity, and establishing the sequence of these groups by elaborating yet further meaningful connexions. They organized their progressive mastery of the list around reference points which, in some way, stood out for them and seemed useful for later recall. In all this, there were clear differences in the detailed procedures of the individual men; as always happens when people are left free to memorize in their own way, there are common general procedures which vary from person to person in the details of their execution. From a quantitative point of view, the task turned out to be less difficult than the men had imagined it would be. No man took more than six trials to achieve a completely correct recall.

Notice that these men were forced to treat the letter sequence as a whole and that, at least to start with, this seemed a formidable undertaking. Might it not be easier to pursue a part-method of memorizing? Why not break the sequence into several shorter sequences and memorize each before going on to memorize the next? Allan tried this. She divided the total pack into five portions, four sub-series of five letters each and one sub-series of six letters. The subject went through the first sub-pack, then recalled the letter sequence in it. And he repeated this eight times. He then dealt with the second sub-pack in the same way. Then the third. And so on to the fifth and last sub-pack. In other words, each sub-pack was gone through and recalled eight times before the next sub-pack was dealt with. Finally, the men were asked to recall the entire sequence of twenty-six letters by recalling each sub-sequence in correct order. Curiously enough, not a single subject could do this. They were not able to recall every sub-series correctly in itself much less recall the order in which the sub-series came. Now notice that eight trials, by the whole-method, was more than enough to master the entire sequence; yet eight trials on each of five sub-sequences was not sufficient for mastering the whole. The part-method, albeit less of a strain, was less efficient in terms of the number of trials and the time spent on the memorizing task. Given eight trials in all, it was clearly more efficient to use these trials in a whole-method rather than a part-method. Why should there be this difference between the two methods? In the part-method, it is relatively undemanding to turn over a sequence of five cards and recall this sequence immediately afterwards: the series falls within the immediate memory span. There is little need to work over the sequence and translate it into familiar terms. But by the time the man has gone through all five sub-packs, each making little demand in itself, he finds he has forgotten parts of the earlier sequences. He finds also that he has established no means of specifying the order in which the sub-sequences follow one another. In brief, he has failed to memorize the sequence as a whole. By contrast, the whole-method forces the subject into dealing with the entire sequence. It forces him to work over the material as a whole, read meaning into it, note the ways in which one part relates to another, note focal reference points around which to hinge the sequence. The demands of the task force him to work more actively at organizing the whole sequence, and this leads to faster memorizing.

Whole-part Memorizing. In the above experiment, a whole-method of approach led to faster memorizing than a part-method. By the whole-method, the person had to make more effort to organize the material, relate its components to each other and to what was already familiar. But this greater memorizing effort payed off in terms of the time taken to master the entire sequence. Now, there are many situations where we have a choice between whole- and part-methods of memorizing. For example, a poem or speech may be read through repeatedly from beginning to end until it is mastered. Alternatively, the material may be divided into sections and each section memorized separately before a recital of the whole is attempted. Which method is better? The whole-method or the part-method? It should be said at once that there is no straight answer to this question. The merits and demerits of each method depend on the material and, of course, on the individual person who is doing the memorizing. Furthermore, this question does not always arise in clear-cut form. The whole-method and the part-method are two extreme procedures between which there are various compromise procedures. In each specific situation, the most effective procedure depends on a balance of considerations. Some of these considerations will now be discussed.

Consider an actor faced with the formidable task of memorizing a role in a play. How does he proceed? To start with, he familiarizes himself with the play as a whole. He reads the script through to extract its general characteristics. As he reads, he retains successive words only long enough to build up a cumulative abstract of the play, a general impression of its plot, sub-plots, the personalities involved, the essential conflicts and their final resolution. He gets a synoptic overview of the whole and of his own role in relation to this whole. He then proceeds to concentrate on smaller themes. The development of his role in each act of the play, the nature of his relationships with various other characters, the mood to be conveyed. And only then does he get down to the details of particular sequences of action, lines, moves, gestures. In summary, his memorizing procedure is to work from the general to the particular: he familiarizes himself with the whole and then with progressively smaller parts of this whole. He does not, if he can avoid it, proceed to memorize his first speech, then his second, and so on. What is the merit of this whole-to-part procedure? There are several merits, but the chief one is this: familiarity with the outline of the whole serves to specify the component parts. The parts fall into their proper sequence in reference to the whole which they subserve. At each moment, the actor is helped to recall what follows because it is already characterized in outline by the developing theme of the play. For him, the whole context specifies the broad features of each part-theme and leaves him then to fill out the outlines by recalling detail.

Memorizing

His action at each moment is supported by the context in which it occurs: familiarity with the whole gives significance to the component parts.

This example, of the actor mastering his role, gives point to the chief merit of the whole-method of memorizing. Familiarity with the outline of the whole provides a context of meaning for each part and, at each moment, serves to prompt recall of what comes next. This influence of whole-context is especially evident when the material involves a developing theme, e.g., a narrative poem or a speech. It is also of assistance even when the material is relatively meaningless, e.g., as in Allan's experiment with random letter sequences. There are, then, many situations where familiarity with the whole facilitates detailed mastery of the parts.

The chief de-merit of the whole-method, especially in its strict form, is that it takes the memorizer a long time before he has anything to show for his efforts. Suppose, for example, an adult is attempting to memorize a prose passage of five-hundred words. In one investigation, the passage was gone over again and again from start to finish; and it took, in all, sixty-five minutes to achieve verbatim mastery. However, under comparable conditions, a hundred-word portion of this passage took only nine minutes to master. With the smaller portion, the adult has something to show after nine minutes. Whereas the same nine minutes devoted to the whole passage yields very little achievement of an obvious kind: he may not be able to recall even a single sentence correctly. Now this apparent lack of progress may discourage some people. They may feel that they are getting nowhere, that the task is altogether too much for them, that they had best stop even trying. In objective fact, this attitude may not be justified. When this attitude is absent, it can be shown that the nine minutes spent on the whole passage is leading towards mastery. It can also be shown that the nine minutes spent on the portion is taking the memorizer less far than it seems. He has four more portions still to memorize, and he is likely to forget some of each while he is memorizing another; furthermore he still has the task of joining the portions into a whole sequence. Nevertheless, these facts may not necessarily prevent the person from being discouraged by apparent lack of progress with the whole-method. And if this attitude arises, then it impedes further progress in memorizing. The effects of this attitude are well expressed by a passage from the book, *The Nature and Conditions of Learning*, 1946, by H. L. Kingsley.

Children often prefer the part method, and unpractised adults are often sceptical of the advantages of the whole method. With the whole method much more time and work is required before any results of learning are manifest. One may read a long poem through a dozen times without being able to recite a single line, while with the same amount of work by the part method the learner would probably be able to recite several stanzas. For this reason a learner gets the feeling of success sooner with the part method. The recitation of parts become sub-goals, which provide a series of steps toward the main goal, the ability to recite the whole. These intermediate goals and the satisfactions derived from reaching them no doubt favour the part method, particularly with children and with adults unaccustomed to rote memory work. The whole method is likely to be discouraging because the learner has to work so long before he can see any returns for his effort. He may feel that he is not making any progress or that he is wasting his time with this 'new-fangled method'. This attitude operates against the success of the method. The experienced and informed learner knows that the readings in the whole method are not a waste of time. He knows, as Ebbinghaus demonstrated, that every reading yields an increment of learning, which is spread over the whole, and that if he continues, he will eventually find the whole selection rising above the threshold of recall. He knows that while he must work longer before results are manifest, the final returns fully justify his patience and endurance.

This attitude is probably responsible for the general finding that the advantages of the whole-method tend only to emerge after the memorizer has acquired experience of and confidence in this procedure.

In very general terms, it may be said that the whole-method is best with experienced and accomplished memorizers and comparatively short lengths of material. With large amounts of material and inexperienced or poor memorizers, say children, the part-method is best, the size of the part being the largest the person can grasp as an overall, meaningful unit. With a moderate length of material, the best plan seems to be the flexible one of starting by getting an overview of the whole, pursuing the whole-method as far as possible, but keeping a watch for any difficult parts requiring special attention and extra memorizing effort.

Individual Differences. Material which is familiarly meaningful to one person may not be so to another. This fact is so obvious that it needs no elaboration. What is perhaps not so obvious is that this fact gives rise to a variety of individual differences in memorizing performance which are sometimes attributed to other causes. A few of these differences can be cited by referring merely to the memorizing of word lists. In memorizing lists of random words, the effect of familiarity is evident in several ways. The words which are memorized soonest are, other things equal, the words which are common in everyday usage, i.e. the words which are most familiar to the average memorizer. It is these words (along with others which are especially striking or significant for the person) that tend to be made the focal reference points in the mastery of the list as a whole. Again, if people are given a random list of, say, twenty commonly used words to memorize, they master this list more quickly than an equally long list of words which are relatively uncommon in everyday usage. The greater familiarity of the common words enables them to be related together more rapidly. And again, if the words are presented, not in random order but in a sequence which approximates some sort of sense, this makes mastery easier. The closer the list comes to familiar words in a familiar kind of sequence, the easier it is to memorize. All these effects apply to the average person since they embody degrees of familiarity which are inherent in common everyday experience with language. However, word lists can be made up which are more familiar to some people than to others, for example, a list of anatomical names is likely to be memorized more quickly by medical students than by students of, say, modern poetry. Also, some word lists are, on average, more easily memorized by women than by men. Words which refer to 'feminine pursuits' such as dressmaking and cosmetics are, by and large, more familiar to women than to men. And such lists are memorized more quickly by women. In contrast, word lists which comprise items drawn from 'masculine pursuits' such as carpentry and mechanics are, by and large, memorized more quickly by men rather than women. It is noteworthy that, as the material is made less and less meaningful, any sex differences in memory abilities become progressively less evident. There are memorizing tasks on which women do better on average than men. There are memorizing tasks in which the reverse is the case. But it seems that if the task is robbed of these features which make it more familiar or appealing to one sex rather than another, then there is no basic sex-difference in memory abilities.

Material which is immediately and unthinkingly familiar to one person may be strange and incomprehensible to another. This raises important practical problems in the fields of instruction and of communication generally. Suppose we try to 'get across' to someone by presenting material in a way which is familiar to him. We must first discover what is and what is not familiar as far as he is concerned. We must assess the relevant cumulative effects of his background experiences. All teachers know how difficult a problem this can be in practice. They also know how easy it is to make the error of assuming that what is familiar, indeed obvious, to them is also familiar to their pupils. One great problem in all communication is to discover the nature and extent not only of another person's knowledge but also of his ignorance.

Interest in Learning. In everyday life, we all encounter material which we could memorize if we wished. But much of this material is, we feel, not worth memorizing. It does not mean anything to us in the sense that its acquisition seems unlikely to serve any future use. There is also factual material of a kind which is relevant to our interests but which we still do not memorize. This is because we are satisfied merely to know where to find the material should it be needed. We feel that the gain of being able to reconstruct the material from memory does not justify our labour in committing it to memory. Now, it is the common experience of most people that they have difficulty in bringing themselves to memorize material which they feel will be of no value to them. In more general terms, if they regard an accomplishment as useless, then they are reluctant to expend the effort necessary for its acquisition. This familiar phenomenon is referred to in various terms. We say, for example, that we lack motive, or interest, or will, or concentration, or incentive, or intention to learn. And we know from our experience how greatly this lack obstructs learning. The student will recollect that on those occasions when he 'could not work up any enthusiasm' for study, it was hardly worth his while to continue. Teachers too are aware of the difference it makes if their pupils are interested in a lesson or can be made to want to learn about it. People who claim to be 'just no good' with, say, mathematics or car repairing or essay writing often mean, in fact, that they have never been sufficiently interested in these activities to learn the necessary skills and knowledge. And there seems to be no truth whatever in the claim that people who are deeply asleep can memorize words played over to them through earphones.

Little of a brief and general nature can be said about this important matter of interest in learning. It can only be mentioned that slight progress is made if the learning activities do not, in some way, fit into the patterns of a person's ongoing activities. And furthermore, that these patterns are of many different kinds and arise in many different ways. Some samples of different 'interests' will suffice to illustrate their variety. The 'interest' of the baby in repeating vocal sounds he has just heard seems to derive from instinctive disposition. The 'interest' of the young child in memorizing jingles and rhymes does not derive from his intending to master these activities for use in the distant future: it derives from the immediate pleasure of joining in a repetitive social game involving exercise of his developing vocal accomplishments. The 'interest' of a schoolboy in memorizing a poem may have little to do with any concern for the poem itself: it may derive from the contrived system of rewards and punishments which the teacher has made contingent on his memorizing: take these away, and the boy may have no other 'interest' in learning the poem. By contrast, the 'interest' of the dedicated scholar in learning about his subject derives from his concern for the subject itself, his genuine curiosity about the issues involved, his need to resolve perplexities: so strong is his interest in the subject that he memorizes a great deal in an 'incidental' way, that is, without explicitly intending to memorize; his actively working with and thinking about the material is sufficient for its memorizing without his having to set himself the task of learning it.

4 The Ebbinghaus Experiments

Hermann Ebbinghaus (1850–1909) made several contributions to psychology, but is best known for his work on memorizing. This work, involving six years of arduous research, was published in 1885 in a book, *Über das Gedächtnis*, which is now a landmark in the history of inquiry into mental life. It was the first systematic study of memory activities, and most of our present day knowledge about memorizing stems more or less directly from this pioneer investigation. Ebbinghaus approached the problems of memory in the spirit of an experimental physical scientist. His aim was to introduce into the study of human functioning the methods of strict experimental control and quantitative treatment of results. These methods had recently reaped rich rewards in physics and physiology, so he deployed them in psychology. He was, of course, well aware of the complexity of his subject matter. For example, he knew that memorizing is powerfully influenced by the meaning which the material has for the memorizer. And so, he had to simplify the questions he asked. He had to ask, in effect: How does memorizing proceed when, as far as possible, the influence of meaning is eliminated? In other words, he deliberately asked questions about meaningless rote memorizing. Ebbinghaus has sometimes been criticized for making this policy decision. But in the event, his policy was a wise one. It led to conclusions which have stood the test of repeated examination. Furthermore, these conclusions have been found, within limits, relevant to learning performances of a more meaningful kind than those he studied.

The Ebbinghaus Experiments

Throughout his lengthy series of experiments, Ebbinghaus used himself as subject. That is, he assumed the dual role of experimenter and memorizer. He also took every precaution to keep conditions as standard and as constant as he could. He required particularly to standardize three things: the material to be memorized; the procedure used in memorizing; and the methods of measuring the results of memorizing. He needed large amounts of material which would be equally easy or difficult to memorize. Poetry, prose, even random lists of words would not meet this requirement. So he invented the nonsense syllable. Each syllable was formed by placing a vowel between two consonants to give letter triplets like the following: TAJ, ZIN, VEC, YOX, DAK, JOF, HUQ. Now, these syllables are not altogether meaningless, e.g. HUQ might be interpreted to resemble the word 'hook'. Nor do lists of these syllables fail to vary from each other in meaning. But the extent of variation in memorizing difficulty from one list to the next is relatively slight, especially if certain precautions are followed in constructing the lists. This, then, was his material: lists of nonsense syllables.

He also needed to standardize the procedure used in memorizing, so he devised the 'anticipation method'. On the first trial, he would take the list of syllables and read through it from start to finish, spelling out each item aloud at a steady rate. On the next trial, he would start by attempting to anticipate the first item, then look at it to see whether his anticipation was correct or not: then he would attempt to anticipate the second item. He would continue in this way, and at his steady rate of working, until the end of the list was reached. Then he would go over the list again, and again, until he came to a trial where every item was anticipated correctly. Notice that in this method, the reading of each item serves a dual function. It serves to confirm or to correct the anticipation just made; and it serves to prompt anticipatory recall of the item which is next on the list. Throughout these repeated readings-with-recitation, he schooled himself to make no effort after meaning. This is, in fact, not an easy thing to do. Anyone who makes his first attempt at memorizing nonsense syllables automatically reads meaning into the list. And this effort after meaning plays an important part in determining the course of his mastery. But Ebbinghaus deliberately trained himself not to read meaning into the material (in the same way as a proof-reader must train himself to ignore the sense of the print he is reading for errors).

The above discussion should have made clear that, in considering the outcome of these experiments, two things must be borne in mind. First, the material is standard and meaningless. Secondly, the memorizing procedure is itself standard in a special rote fashion. This rigid standardization lends artificiality to the entire enterprise but, on the other hand, it makes it possible to draw highly precise conclusions which are unaffected by the many ambiguities that beset the study of memorizing under more 'real life' conditions. The drastic simplification of these experiments served to raise and answer a number of questions. It served to clarify notions about memorizing. And this clarification led to better informed inquiries into more complex forms of memorizing and learning.

The method of treating the results and the sort of conclusions arrived at are best illustrated by outlining one of the experiments conducted by Ebbinghaus.

An Illustrative Experiment. The question was this. When material has been memorized, how rapidly is it forgotten? To answer this question, Ebbinghaus memorized lists of nonsense syllables: then he put them aside for some specified period of time: at the end of this time, he re-learned the same lists and noted the extent to which re-learning required fewer trials than original learning. During the course of this experiment, he submitted himself to this procedure no fewer

The Ebbinghaus Experiments

than 163 times. Each time, he learned eight thirteen-syllable lists by his anticipation method. He took the first list, read it aloud at a steady rate of one syllable every 0·4 seconds, and continued the readings until he was able to give two errorless anticipations of the entire list. After a pause of fifteen seconds, during which the number of readings was recorded, the second list was memorized in the same way to the same criterion of two errorless recitals. Then the third list was tackled, and so on, until all eight lists had been mastered. The total number of readings required to memorize these eight lists gave the 'learning-time'. (Since each reading is done at exactly the same rate, it is a simple matter to work out the total learning-time.) After a lapse of from twenty minutes to one month, the same set of lists was re-learned exactly as before. The total time required for this second learning was the 're-learning-time'. By comparing the re-learning-time with the original learning-time, he derived a measure of the retained effects of the original memorizing. For example, if 1,000 seconds were required for original learning, and if re-learning took 600 seconds, then the saving of effort was 400 seconds, or 40 per cent of the original time. This 40 per cent exemplifies a 'saving score'. It reflects the amount of learning-time or effort saved in consequence of previous learning. If this material had not been learned before, he would require 1,000 seconds for its mastery. But because it has been learned once before, he saves himself 40 per cent of this time.

In this experiment, there were seven different intervals between original learning and re-learning. These intervals are shown in Table 4. The average saving score at each

Table 4

Time Since Learning	min. 20	hr 1	hrs 9	hrs 24	days 2	days 6	days 31
Average Saving Score	58%	44%	36%	34%	28%	25%	21%

interval is also shown. These results illustrate that forgetting was rapid at first and then became progressively slower as the interval between original learning and re-learning increased. One hour after learning, more than half of the original work had to be done again before the material could be brought back to its former level of mastery. Nine hours after learning, about two-thirds of the original work had to be done again. After six-days, three-quarters of the original work had to be put in; and after a month, some four-fifths.

Two points must be mentioned in relation to this experiment. First, these results derive from the method of single testing. Each set of material is learned twice only: once at the beginning and once again at the time interval stated. Each time interval is the time which elapses between the original learning and the re-learning of the same material. The results would be quite different if they derived from successive re-learnings of the same material, e.g. if the material were re-learned twenty minutes after original learning, and then re-learned the next day, and then again a week later, and so on. The different results obtained by the methods of single and successive tests have already been illustrated in the data of Spitzer's experiment. The second point concerns the use of the re-learning method itself. This method measures not only remembering but learning ability as well. So if, for whatever reason, the person's learning ability changes between the times of learning and re-learning, this will influence the amount of saving. (It is by no means impossible for a person to need longer to re-learn a set of material than he originally took to learn it.) For example, Ebbinghaus discovered that it always took him 12 per cent longer to learn material around 7 p.m. than it did around 10 a.m. This means that if the original learning took place at 10 a.m. it occurred at a favourable time of day. And if the re-learning took place at 7 p.m. it occurred at an unfavourable time of day, and for this reason would indicate a spuriously high rate of forgetting. Accordingly, a deduction of 12 per cent of the re-learning time would be made before calculating the saving score.

By means of such painstaking experiments, Ebbinghaus arrived at a number of conclusions about memorizing and the factors which influence it. Some of these conclusions will now be summarized.

Rate of Forgetting. This is the issue with which the above experiment was concerned. The answer of this experiment is unambiguous (see Table 4). If these results are plotted on a graph, we get a smooth curve which falls rapidly at first and then more and more slowly. (Such a curve is referred to as a negatively accelerated decay curve.) Since 1885, other investigators have asked this question about rate of forgetting. They have used a variety of material, e.g. passages of prose, lists of factual material, geometrical figures, poetry. They have also measured remembering by means of recall scores and recognition scores as well as saving scores. And they have almost always found that forgetting follows this progressively diminishing trend. So general has been this finding that the classical curve of Ebbinghaus has sometimes been called *the* curve of forgetting. However, this is an overstatement. His curve holds over a wide variety of conditions but there are exceptions to this rule that forgetting is rapid immediately after learning and then takes place more and more slowly. The exact extent and rate of forgetting depends on various circumstances. For example, if a person is given a factual prose passage to study, we may ask him to remember either the exact words (literal remembering), or the general sense of the points as expressed in his own words (content remembering). Now, the amount and rate of forgetting is different in these two cases. Literal remembering typically falls off much more rapidly than content remembering. Again, there is the phenomenon known as the 'reminiscence effect'. Suppose a person is

Memorizing

given a poem to memorize but is not given long enough for complete mastery. We now ask him to recall the poem and we note which lines he gives correctly. Suppose, say two days later, we ask this person to recall the poem again. We find that he fails to recall some lines which he recalled before. But we also find that he may recall lines which he did not recall on the first occasion. This subsequent recall of material not recalled before is known as 'reminiscence'. It may even lead to a reversal of the forgetting curve. That is, the total number of lines correctly recalled immediately after learning may actually be less than the total number of lines recalled a day or two later. This 'negative forgetting' is, however, both small in amount and transitory. As a general rule, it might be said that the Ebbinghaus curve of forgetting is the 'ideal' curve which holds over most conditions but, in practice, is very often obscured by a complexity of circumstances.

Number of Learning Trials. What happens if the number of learning trials given to a particular list is either less than or more than the number required to reach the criterion of two errorless recitals? If, for a particular list, twelve trials are needed to reach the criterion, what would happen if he took twenty-four trials? Or if he took only six? To answer this question, Ebbinghaus conducted tests in each of which material was read a given number of times that varied, from test to test, between eight and sixty-four. Then a day later, he applied his usual re-learning method to determine the amount of saving. He found that surplus repetitions were not wasted. Even though the immediate effect (a smooth errorless recital) was not affected, overlearning made it easier to re-learn the material on a subsequent occasion. The more trials he gave to original learning, the fewer trials he needed for re-learning. Even original practice which was insufficient to accomplish an errorless recital was not without effect: a few readings made the material

130

easier to master on a subsequent occasion than no readings at all. Ebbinghaus described these findings by saying that it was as though each repetition engraved the material more and more deeply on the nervous system. Later investigators have confirmed these findings and extended them by show- ing that each learning trial does not result in a constant amount of saving. The increase in remembering which results from an increasing number of trials shows diminish- ing returns. To illustrate this point, we may cite some of the results obtained in 1929 by W. Krueger, working in Chicago.

Krueger had three groups of adult subjects learn a list of twelve unrelated nouns. The first group was given repeated learning trials and stopped after their first errorless recital. The second group also learned up to this point, but then continued overlearning for half as many trials again. The third group was taken to the point of one perfect recital, and then given as many overlearning trials again. Thus, if a subject required ten trials to reach the criterion, he would be given ten trials in Group I, fifteen trials in Group II, and twenty trials in Group III. After an interval of time which varied from one to twenty-eight days, each subject re-learned the list under conditions which yielded both a recall score and a saving score. Examples of these scores are shown in Table 5. These data show that the amount remembered

Table 5

	Group I	Group II	Group III
Saving after 1 day	21·7%	36·2%	47·1%
Saving after 28 days	1·5%	20·5%	25·1%
Words recalled after 1 day	3·1	4·6	5·8
Words recalled after 28 days	0·0	0·3	0·4

increases with an increase in the number of learning trials. But increasing this number from ten to fifteen results in greater improvement than increasing the number from fifteen to twenty. Incidentally, these data also show that the re-learning method provides a more sensitive measure of remembering than does a simple recall score.

In summary, there is a uniformly positive relation between amount of practice devoted to original learning and the amount remembered. But there are diminishing returns at the higher degrees of practice. Thus, a student who wants to be sure of remembering a lesson would not stop studying at the moment when he had just mastered it. He would overlearn by continuing his study longer. However, he would be unwise to continue overlearning for too long because, after a time, the additional effort involved would not justify the progressively smaller gains in later remembering.

Amount of Material to be Memorized. If it requires so many readings to memorize a list of twelve nonsense syllables, how many readings will be required to memorize a list of twenty-four? It might be expected that, if the amount to be memorized is doubled, then the time to memorize would also be doubled. In fact, this expectation is not borne out. It takes more than twice as long. In one study, different lengths of syllable lists were presented to adult subjects. These lists contained, respectively, 12, 24, 48, 100, 200 and 300 syllables. The total time required to memorize these lists to a criterion of one errorless recital was, respectively, 1·5 minutes, 5 minutes, 14, 37, 93, and 195 minutes. These results are typical. They show that, as the amount of the material increases, learning time not only increases but does so at a disproportionate rate. It takes more than twice as long to memorize 24 items as to memorize 12. Again, it takes more than twice as long to memorize 200 as to memorize 100 items. Where lists of nonsense syllables are concerned, a fairly general finding is that the learning-time-per-syllable increases in proportion to the square root of the number of syllables in the lists. Lists which are shorter than the immediate memory span are, of course, exceptions to this general rule.

Broadly speaking, the above rule applies to the memorizing of any kind of material. For example, it also applies to meaningful material such as prose or poetry. To be sure, there are exceptions. It can happen that, depending on the difficulty of the material, a longish passage is mastered in as few readings as a shorter one. But on the whole, the time taken to learn increases disproportionately with increasing length of passage. For example, in one typical experiment, prose passages were memorized. These passages were comparable to each other in content and difficulty, but they differed in length. A passage of 100 words required a total learning-time of 9 minutes: one of 200 words required 24 minutes; one of 500 words required 65 minutes; and a passage of 1,000 words required 165 minutes. In conclusion, then, it is generally true to say that the more there is of any material for memorizing, the more time will memorizing take; and if the amount is doubled or trebled, it will take more than twice or three times as long for memorizing.

The Spacing of Trials. Does it make any difference whether successive trials occur close together in time or are spaced apart? Ever since the issue of distributed practice was raised by Ebbinghaus, experiments have agreed that, in general, it is better to have several short learning sessions spaced out at intervals than to have one long unbroken period of work. The sort of investigation which gives rise to this agreement is that published in 1940 by an American psychologist, A. P. Bumstead. Bumstead, like Ebbinghaus, used only himself as subject, although most experimenters have employed groups of subjects, either school-children or students. In one session, he would read a fifty-line excerpt from Milton's *Paradise Lost*, beginning at the first line and reading through to the end at his normal reading speed. In each successive session, he would repeat this process, trying to anticipate what came next and prompting himself from the text whenever his recall faltered. These sessions continued until he could recite the whole passage without referring to the text. Altogether, he memorized nine such fifty-line selections with each session spaced at intervals which varied from one hour to eight days. The results showed that increasing the interval between memorizing sessions progressively reduced the time actually devoted to memorizing. When sessions were spaced at one-hour intervals (in the daytime only), forty-three readings were required involving a study time of 140 minutes. When sessions were spaced at one-day intervals, the number of readings required was only nineteen with an actual study time of 60 minutes. With eight-day spacing, the readings dropped to thirteen and the study time to 46 minutes. Now, these rather typical results reveal that the greater the spacing, the smaller is the amount of time spent in actual study, while, of course, the total time required increases. This means that spacing can only be profitably used where there is a lengthy time available for study, and the problem is how best to distribute this time among a number of learning activities. Spacing would be of little use to a student 'cramming' for an exam.

Apart from giving the opportunity for additional and perhaps surreptitious practice, moderate spacing appears to owe its general superiority to a number of different factors which are not quite fully understood as yet. Broadly speaking, these factors are of the inhibitory and interfering kind from which the learner can only recover by giving up his specific learning task and doing something else.

In deciding how to distribute practice in any practical learning situation, we are faced with the double problem of discovering the optimal length of the practice period and the optimal length of the interval in terms of the total amount of time available for study. As regards the practice period, it would seem that it should be short but not so short that the learner has no time to warm-up, to 'get into the swing' of the task. With more difficult tasks, with younger and more inexperienced learners, and in the earlier stages of learning, the practice period should be shorter than with easy tasks, mature learners, and tasks which are in an advanced stage of practice. The reason for this is simple. The more difficult the task, the more fatiguing it is; and the same task is more difficult for young children, for people unaccustomed to concentrated learning, and for people to whom the specific task is unfamiliar. As regards the length of the interval between sessions, little of a general nature can be said since the optimum depends on the nature of the task, the characteristics of the learner, the stage of mastery of the task, and also the nature of the activities engaged in during the interval. All that can be said is that if the task is relatively easy or short, then no distribution of practice will be necessary at all. If the task is difficult or long, then practice should be spaced in such a way that the learner will not have time to lose interest in the work or forget too much of what he has already learned.

Serial-position Effects. As the person proceeds from one memorizing trial to the next, certain items in the list are learned more rapidly than others. The items which are memorized soonest are those which occur at the beginning of the list, and the items which are memorized slowest are those in the middle. In other words, the readiness with which any item is memorized depends not only on the item itself but also on the position it occupies in the list as a whole: whether it comes near the start of the list, or the middle, or the end. This is known as the 'serial-position effect'. When a sequence of items is being memorized in sequence, this effect takes a typical form: it is the first items in the sequence which are mastered soonest; next soonest are the very last items in the sequence; and the slowest items to be got correct are those in the middle. Notice that if the sequence is repeated to the point of mastery, then the items at the beginning and end of the list will be over-learned relative to the items in the middle. This means that the items which are forgotten soonest are these middle ones, and the items forgotten most slowly are the ones which start the sequence. In brief, the usual and classical form taken by the serial-position effect is early–late–middle.

There are, of course, circumstances in which the serial-position effect does not take this classical form. One such circumstance occurs in what is known as 'free recall'. Suppose we read out a random list of twenty unrelated words to a person and ask him to listen to these words so that, immediately afterwards, he can recall as many of them as possible irrespective of their order. It typically happens that the best recalled words are those which came at the end of the presented list. What happens is that the person recalls those last few words while they are still fresh in mind; he 'gets them out' before he has much chance to forget them. In this kind of situation, then, it is the last items which are best recalled, the beginning items next best, and the middle items most poorly. Incidentally, this result does not apply if the person is asked to try to recall the items in the order in which they were presented. When he tries this, he finds that, by the time he comes to recall the last items, he has forgotten them. The same is true if the words which are presented form a somewhat meaningful sequence. This disposes the person to start by recalling the items at the beginning of the list, and so the serial-position effect once more takes the form of early–late–middle.

Another circumstance which competes with and may out-weigh the serial-position effect is the 'strikingness' of par-ticular items. If the items of a list are, for the memorizer, not all of the same kind then some items may 'stand out' more than others. For example, a nonsense syllable in a list of words; a long word in a list of short words; a familiar word among unfamiliar words; an unfamiliar word among familiar ones. Anything which makes an item 'stand out' from the others is memorized soonest and becomes a distinctive reference point around which the remainder of the memorizing task is organized.

Bearing the above exceptions in mind, the serial-position effect usually takes the classical early-late-middle form. This is true for syllable lists, word lists, poetry and prose. In everyday life, we can often recall the first few lines and the last few lines of a poem, or the beginning and end of a novel, or a sermon, or a lecture; but still not be able to recall what came in the middle. It might be said that the progressive mastering of most sequences builds up from the beginning and from the end inwards to the middle. And in practice, it is the middle parts of most lessons which require additional care and effort.

Rapid versus Slow Memorizers. Does the person who memorizes rapidly also forget rapidly? Is his memorizing a matter of quickly come and quickly go? Or, by contrast, does the slow memorizer remember better? Slow, but sure? These are not questions which Ebbinghaus studied directly because, of course, he used only himself as subject. But they are questions which can be answered within the limits of his experimental procedures. It should be said at once that, like most obvious questions about psychological issues, these questions turn out to be more complex than they seem: there is no simple answer to them. The critical issue is not the speed with which learning is accomplished but, rather, what the person learns and the degree to which he learns it. In detail, these issues, concerning what and how thoroughly a person learns, rapidly become technical. And these technicalities cannot be gone into here. (They are well presented in a difficult article by B. J. Underwood published in *The Psychological Bulletin*, 1954.)

When several people are given lists of nonsense syllables

to memorize by the 'anticipation method' it is found that some people consistently achieve mastery in fewer trials than other people. At one extreme, there are rapid memorizers. At the other extreme, there are slow memorizers. What happens when these people are tested some time later on the same material? Do the rapid memorizers remember more, or less, than the slow memorizers? When all people are given the same number of learning trials, that is, the same amount of time for memorizing, the answer is quite clear. Given the same amount of time for learning, the rapid memorizer achieves a higher degree of mastery; and later on, he still shows this higher degree of mastery, that is, he remembers more of the material than does the slow memorizer. This finding reflects the maxim that the higher the degree of initial mastery then the higher the degree of mastery even after a lapse of time.

Suppose now that the learning conditions are changed. Each memorizer has as many trials as he needs to reach, say, one completely correct recital of the list. The slow learners will, of course, take more trials than the rapid learners. But what is their relative standing some time later? The answer to this question varies according to circumstances but, on the whole, the fast memorizer still shows the greater degree of mastery. However, on detailed analyses of the memorizing performances, it is found that the rapid memorizer has actually memorized the list to a higher degree of mastery: despite the fact that all learners are stopped when they reach their first all-correct recital. It is at this point in our inquiries that matters begin to get rather technical. So it must suffice merely to state the main conclusion. When rapid and slow memorizers are carefully equated for degree of mastery of the material (a complex procedure which can only be done mathematically using the detailed records of learning progress), then there is no difference whatever in their later remembering performances. This is, of course, a mere restatement of the maxim that the amount remembered depends directly on the degree of original mastery.

It is of interest to note that, if people are repeatedly required to memorize lists for immediate reproduction, they gradually adjust to this situation by altering their memory procedures. The person is given a list to memorize until he can recite it. Then he moves on to another list until he can recite that. Then he takes another list, and so on. This continues, list after list, a few lists each day for several days. Now, as the person continues day after day to memorize different lists, he masters successive lists more and more rapidly; but he also forgets each list more rapidly. In other words, the person adjusts to the requirements of the situation by developing techniques for rapid but temporary mastery of the material. He learns how to master the material rapidly, and also how to 'let it go' and so leave himself free to deal with new lists, which are now to be mastered for immediate reproduction.

It can be seen that the issue of rapid versus slow memorizers is a complex one. When this issue is studied under the controlled experimental conditions of the laboratory, it turns out to hinge on a more basic issue, namely, what the person is learning and the degree to which he is learning it. In the schoolroom situation, this is really the important issue. The child who, on average, is a slow learner is handicapped in nearly all kinds of memory activities. But people with the same memory abilities may make very different uses of these abilities. Thus, one person may take longer to master a lesson than another because he is learning it in a different way. One pupil may deal rapidly with material so as to be able to recite its details and answer specific questions about it. By contrast, another person may spend longer over the material so as to be able to abstract higher-order characteristics and relate them to other material which he already knows. In brief, one person may work for rapid superficial mastery and specific details, and another for slower but more comprehensive understanding of generalizable relationships. It is one of the great problems in any instructional situation to discover the relative merits and demerits of these two extreme approaches, and to encourage or discourage them accordingly. It is also important to remember that 'memory abilities' is an ambiguous term which refers to a wide diversity of different activities. Given the same degree of 'memory ability' for the same kind of subject-matter, one person may, through persistent application and appropriate guidance, make better use of this ability. He may achieve more in the long run and, through this achievement, become better able to learn still more new material. Initial 'talent' is only one of the ingredients which make for eventual intellectual mastery.

5 Rules for Directing Memorizing

Our brief survey of the Ebbinghaus experiments shows how the very artificiality of his approach served to raise clear issues which are of relevance to the problems of memory in general. His work established a number of 'laws' which have been confirmed over and over again whenever his procedures have been followed. Furthermore, these 'laws' have been found, with certain modifications, to apply to memorizing activities which do not conform to his experimental strictures. The follow-up of the Ebbinghaus work has given rise to a tradition of experimental inquiry which, at the present day, represents the most rigorous and detailed body of knowledge in the whole vast field of psychology. Much of this detailed knowledge has, as yet, found no practical applications, although recent technological developments in what is called 'programmed instruction' are drawing heavily on the fruits of the Ebbinghaus tradition.

Rules for Directing Memorizing

Here, it may suffice to attempt an outline of general rules for the guidance of memorizing, especially by the teacher in the schoolroom situation.

It must be stressed that these rules are not to be applied slavishly. They must be applied only after due consideration for the particulars of the memorizing situation. It may often be found that the use of one rule is incompatible with the use of another and that the final form of guidance must be based on a balance of considerations. There are many basic preliminary questions to be answered before we can get down to the detailed design of any memorizing situation. Some of these basic questions are as follows. What is to be accomplished, and who by? What is it we want the person to be able to do which he cannot do now? What can he accomplish already, and how can his present accomplishments be best utilized in building up this new achievement? How can the task, and the material, be made most meaningful to him? Once he has mastered the task, how can it best be maintained? To what other accomplishments should this new accomplishment be related so that he can use it most effectively? All of these are fundamental questions which should, as nearly as possible, be answered before the detailed guidance of learning is considered. Finally, it should be remembered that the only person who can accomplish the learning is the learner himself. No one else can learn the material for him. All an instructor can hope to do is arrange conditions which will facilitate the person's learning in the best possible ways.

(1) *Motivation.* Secure and maintain interest in learning by providing appropriate incentives. Utilize existing interest by integrating the task into activities which are already interesting.

(2) *Material.* Present the material in ways which emphasize whatever characteristics are to be memorized and do so in a form which is as familiar as possible to the learner.

Memorizing

As far as possible, enable the learner to gain an overview of the whole before proceeding to the parts. Items to be remembered together and in sequence should be presented together and in that sequence.

(3) *Repetition.* Encourage active use of the material. Introduce anticipatory recall early, but not so early as to encourage guessing errors. Ensure accurate first impressions, avoiding errors if possible, and correcting them immediately on their first appearance. Use the whole-method for short, easy lessons; and a combination of whole- and part-methods for longer, more difficult lessons, giving special attention to difficult parts. Distribute practice, making memory drills short and stopping at the first signs of fatigue.

(4) *Maintenance.* After learning, ensure adequate over-learning: directly by reviewing frequently at first and, later, at progressively longer intervals; indirectly, by integrating what has been learned into further activities. Encourage understanding of what has been learned by securing its use in relation to other relevant learning.

IV Memory for Stories

Memory for stories and for story-like material plays a large part in daily affairs. And in social situations, the recall of such material usually takes the form of narrative, that is, description in words. We retell stories and anecdotes. We recount items of news and gossip. We report conversations in which we have taken part. We tell about social gatherings we have attended. We give accounts of plays we have seen and books we have read. There are innumerable occasions on which we characterize in words some past experience of a thematic, story-like kind. Now, what happens when someone reads or listens to a story and subsequently retells it? The first person to attempt a systematic exploration of this question was Professor (now Sir) Frederic Bartlett of Cambridge University. He published his findings in a book (*Remembering*, 1932) which has now become one of the classical works in psychology because of its conclusions regarding memory. In this chapter, we will start by considering these experiments of Bartlett, and then go on to mention some of their implications. It is helpful to bear in mind that the word 'story' will be used in three different senses. First, to refer to the original story as it took place in objective fact, as actually given to the person; second, the story as perceived and interpreted by the person at the time, the story as he 'sees it'; third, the story as subsequently recalled by the person, as he remembers it. As we shall see, these three versions of the story may be very different from one another.

1 The Bartlett Experiments

Bartlett's procedure was to present an adult with a story, or an argumentative prose passage, or a picture, and have him recall it some days, weeks, or even years afterwards. In his Method of Repeated Reproduction, he asked the same individual to recall the same event again and again at intervals. If the reproductions were given frequently and at short intervals, he found that they rapidly became fixed in form while, if long intervals elapsed between successive reproductions, the process of gradual transformation continued almost indefinitely. In his Method of Serial Reproduction, he adopted a procedure which duplicated, to some extent, the conditions under which rumours spread from one person to another and legends are handed down from one generation to the next. He had one person reproduce the original; he then handed this reproduction to a second person; this second person's reproduction was presented to a third, and so on. Both of these methods – of repeated and serial reproduction – yielded results which are of interest not only to the study of memory but also to the study of rumour and folk-lore. Subsequent investigations, conducted mainly in Cambridge, have extended and refined Bartlett's conclusions. But Bartlett's book still remains the most comprehensive account of this type of psychological research. Results cannot be given in detail here, but what can be done is to take one of the pieces of material used by Bartlett and give some indication of the qualitative changes which occur when people try to reproduce it. The material is a story adapted by Bartlett from the translation of a North

American folk-tale and is entitled 'The War of the Ghosts'. The story is of interest since, coming from another culture, it presents difficulties to British people because of the strange conventions and beliefs which it reflects, its apparently disconnected narrative, and the purely decorative detail which it contains. First, some results will be presented which were obtained by the writer. A discussion will then be given of the characteristic changes which occur with regard to this particular story.

The writer explained to a group of students that a story would be heard and that it was to be repeated as accurately as possible by one of them. It was also explained that the first retelling of the story would be heard by a second student who had not heard the original. This second student would then reproduce the story for a third student who would be hearing it for the first time. The third student would retell the story to a fourth, and so on. Seven students were then asked to volunteer as subjects and six of them left the room. The remaining student listened carefully to the story and the second student was called in to hear the first student recount the story as accurately as he could. This procedure was repeated with the remaining five subjects, the last simply telling the story to the group. The original story and each retelling of it was recorded on a tape machine so that the entire series of reproductions could be played back to the assembled class. A specimen series of reproductions, written down verbatim from the recording, is given below. It should be pointed out that this specimen is not selected because of being unusually dramatic. The writer has used this experiment repeatedly as a classroom demonstration and the example to be given is typical of his collection of records.

Original Story: The title of this story is 'The War of the Ghosts'. One night two young men from Egulac went down to the river to hunt seals, and while they were there it became foggy and calm. Then they heard war-cries, and they thought: 'Maybe this is a war-party.' They escaped to the shore, and hid behind a log. Now canoes came up, and they heard the noise of paddles, and saw one canoe coming up to them. There were five men in the canoe, and they said: 'What do you think? We wish to take you along. We are going up the river to make war on the people.' One of the young men said: 'I have no arrows.' 'Arrows are in the canoe', they said. 'I will not go along. I might be killed. My relatives do not know where I have gone. But you', he said, turning to the other, 'may go with them.' So one of the young men went, but the other returned home. And the warriors went on up the river to a town on the other side of Kalama. The people came down to the water, and they began to fight, and many were killed. But presently the young man heard one of the warriors say: 'Quick, let us go home: that Indian has been hit.' Now he thought: 'Oh, they are ghosts.' He did not feel sick, but they said he had been shot. So the canoes went back to Egulac, and the young man went ashore to his house, and made a fire. And he told everybody and said: 'Behold I accompanied the ghosts, and we went to fight. Many of our fellows were killed, and many of those who attacked us were killed. They said I was hit, and I did not feel sick.' He told it all, and then he became quiet. When the sun rose he fell down. Something black came out of his mouth. His face became contorted. The people jumped up and cried. He was dead.

First Reproduction: The title of this story is 'The War of the Ghosts'. Two young men went out to hunt seals. It was foggy. They heard war-cries and hid behind a log. Then they heard the splash of paddles and a canoe came up in which there were five young men. 'Come with us' they said 'we are going to make war on the people up the river.' One of the young men went with them (long pause) and took part in the battle which followed. He saw one of the Indians being killed and someone shouted: 'He is killed, let us go home now.' He felt sick and someone told him that he had been hit. They left and returned to the village. (Long pause.) He did not feel well the next morning. Something black came out of his mouth and he was dead.

Second Reproduction: The title of this story is 'The War of the Ghosts'. The interest of the story takes place in a foggy situation with a group of people in a small boat. The idea of the story is a seal hunt. There are five men who prepare to go upon this seal hunt and they select one of their number to accompany them to a battle. This battle occurs between some Indians and, in the course of the battle, evidently someone is killed and evidently it is this one individual who has been selected to accompany this group. Then someone shouts: 'Let's go home. He's been hit – or something's been done to him.' So they find themselves back in the original situation – back where they were. And this selected individual finds himself rather ill. And in the course of a day or so, this illness seems to become worse. And eventually something black comes out of his mouth and he's dead.

Third Reproduction: On a foggy day, five men go out on a seal hunt. They select one of the men – no – while they're out in the seal boat, a battle breaks out somewhere or other and they select one of the five to fight in this battle. So he is hit in the battle and he dies after a day or so, after the illness has worsened. And the others decide to – er – er – go back to the seal hunt. One of them has been hit for a second time in the battle and something black comes out of his mouth and he dies.

Fourth Reproduction: On a foggy day, five men go out in a boat on a seal hunt. While they're there, a battle breaks out and one of the men is sent to fight. He gets wounded and later dies. The other four men decide to continue on the seal hunt. One of these has been wounded and becomes sick. He too, later, dies, something black coming out of his mouth.

Fifth Reproduction: Five men set out in a boat on a seal hunt. While they were there, a battle breaks out. One of the men is killed in the battle. The other four continue on the hunt but one of them has been wounded and he becomes worse and dies with something black coming out of his mouth.

Sixth Reproduction: Well, five men were out on a seal hunt. One dies. That leaves four. The four go on their way. They start scrapping with each other and soon one of them is killed and something black comes out of his mouth.

Seventh Reproduction: Five men go on a seal hunt. One of them dies. That leaves four of them. One of them goes away. The other three start scrapping. One of *them* dies and something black comes out of his mouth.

Two points strike us at once regarding the above series. First, the story is much shortened. This is really no more than is to be expected since few adults could, at a single hearing, memorize the original word for word. Much is necessarily omitted. Notice that, as the tale becomes shorter, each successive version omits progressively less. Had the series been continued, we would have found it settling down to a relatively fixed form – a form which is sufficiently terse and conventional to be grasped and reproduced with literal accuracy. Second, despite omissions, the story becomes more coherent. There is no question of isolated and unrelated recall of bits of the original. The story, no matter how distorted it becomes, remains a story to the end. This is because the subjects interpret the story as a whole, both in listening to it and in retelling it.

With the Method of Serial Reproduction, changes take place which are more dramatic than those ·found in the Method of Repeated Reproduction where having experienced the original acts as a certain restraint to improvisation. This is especially the case under the conditions of the present experiment where the subject is reproducing the story orally in front of an audience and so under a degree of mild stress. If he were writing out the story with time at his disposal, he would check and re-check his statements, correct his ambiguous expressions, and produce a narrative which is as explicit and orderly as he can make it. Here, he cannot do this. He may know what he wants to say but, because of nervousness or inarticulateness, he may not express himself as clearly as he would like. And some imperfection in the wording, some alteration in the order of events, some omission which, at the time, seems trivial may be misinterpreted by his hearer and so prepare the way for a succession of further and more dramatic changes. Now, it might be argued that all this additional opportunity for misunderstanding would rob the above demonstration of its value. There are, however, two good reasons why this is not so. First, it often happens in everyday life that gossip, rumours, and so on are passed round by word of mouth under conditions where fluster and distraction are present. Just consider the news which is exchanged over coffee cups! Second, even where conditions are most favourable to quiet and reflective recall, the same kinds of distortion appear as are reported above – especially if we try to recall any event which happened a long time ago. It is found that long-distance recall involves both the presence of one or two isolated details and also the presence of the general setting, expressed mainly through the subject's emotional attitude to the original event. Sometimes, only the details are present: a name, a phrase, a perfume, a sound – and nothing else. Sometimes, only the general atmosphere is present: we may recall only the unpleasantness, the eeriness, or the exhilaration of the situation. But detail and 'tone' may both be present. And it is when this happens that recall is most conspicuously inferential and constructive in character. What the above demonstration does is to elicit, over a short time interval and in an exaggerated way, exactly those changes which have been found by Bartlett and others to occur, over a longer time interval, in real life.

Further examples of distortion can be seen in the five additional records given at the end of this section. These were obtained from five different groups of students by a procedure identical with that outlined above and each record is the seventh version of an independent reproduction series. The reader should compare these versions with the original. In this way, he will probably learn more about the qualitative changes involved in remembering complex events than he could by reading any brief description of them. It may, however, be helpful to consider, in very general terms, the conclusions pointed to by these experiments with 'The War of the Ghosts'.

The main conclusion is that interpreting plays a large, and usually unrecognized, role in the remembering of stories and events. The event, as perceived and as recalled, has to be connected, certainly as a whole and, if possible, as regards its details also, with something which is already familiar. A story which is foreign to the subject's mode of thinking is not recalled accurately either in general theme or in detail. Events drop out of the account unless they can be fitted into a familiar framework either naturally or in that specially incongruous way which provides an unexpected dramatic or comic turn of events. All this is evident in 'The War of the Ghosts'. At one reading or hearing, British subjects fail to grasp the true nature of the theme. The wound becomes an affair of the flesh rather than of the spirit; the initial appearance of the warriors remains unexplained; and the ghosts either drop out of the story altogether, or remain in a rather detached context, or are brought in at the end as a comic or dramatic climax. The interpretation which any one person puts on the story may be unusual and its rationale not immediately apparent. Such individualistic interpretations often mark distinct turning-points in a series of reproductions but, as we would expect, they rarely survive in their original form. In being passed on from subject to subject, the story becomes, in a word, conventional. It retains only those characteristics which can be readily assimilated to that background of past experience which all the members of the chain share in common. The story is shorn of its individualizing features, the descriptive passages lose most of what peculiarities of style and content they possess, and the original phrasing is replaced by current, commonplace *clichés*. When descriptive and argumentative passages are used as material, conventionalization and a bias towards the concrete are also found. Illustrative examples survive the general moral which they point; every argument or piece of reasoning is quickly dropped and replaced by a bald expression of fact or of conventional opinion.

An instructive illustration is reported by Bartlett of the way in which the person's cultural background determines which elements of an experience will be dominant. He used 'The War of the Ghosts' in experiments which were conducted both during and after the 1914–18 war. During the war, the first excuse given by the young men for not joining the war-party ('we have no arrows') was rarely retained by his men subjects, whereas the second excuse (referring to relatives) persisted in almost all cases. At this time, these men had either seen war service or were likely to do so soon. Thus, it seems probable that this part of the story reminded them of their own situation. Indeed, some subjects admitted that it did. The reference to relatives was personally relevant. In experiments conducted after the war, it was found that this second excuse, like the first one, tended to drop out since it played a small part in the central theme of the story. Once social conditions had removed the anxious preoccupation with the possible effects of war service on relatives, there was a reduced tendency for the second excuse to be outstanding.

An element of the story which is conspicuously difficult for British subjects to assimilate is the 'sympathetic weather'. In the original, the coming of the warriors is heralded by fog and calm just as, in many plays and novels, a storm blows up at the moment of tragedy or peaceful skies accompany a happy ending. This sympathetic weather is often reacted to as establishing an eerie mood, yet it is rarely reproduced as such. The title of the story, too, is commonly omitted although it is clearly enough stated in the original presentation. It seems as though both the title and the sympathetic weather belong to a class of features which are effective in setting up a vague expectation of what is to follow but which are not, in themselves, outstanding details. Like the unusual literary style of the original, the impression they make is general rather than specific. They contribute to the subject's interpretation of the story without being remembered in detail.

The last of the common omissions are definite numbers and proper names. These usually disappear altogether and, if they do not, they are transformed or transposed.

Memory for Stories

For example, 'Kalama' may be transformed into 'Colombo' and – as in the above record – the number five may persist but be transposed from its original context to another part of the story. Omission goes, of course, hand in hand with an emphasizing of what is retained. And, in certain instances, this emphasis is pointed up by elaboration. The elaboration usually involves the adding of detail as where the young man's reference to his relatives is expanded and made more concrete in the statement that 'he had a wife and family to look after'. Elaboration may, however, involve the invention of whole new episodes when the story is of the cumulative, repetitive, house-that-Jack-built variety. A tendency towards this cumulative elaboration seems to be showing itself in the later versions of the series recorded above.

This section may now be concluded by quoting a number of versions of 'The War of the Ghosts' which occurred, in different groups of adult British subjects, at the end of a reproduction series.

Seventh Reproduction of Group A: Well, this is a story about a battle between some ghosts. Five chaps went to hunt for seals. They arrived on a rocky coast and discovered another five chaps hiding behind a rock. They asked them if they would join in the hunt and one of them refused because he had no arrows. The other four went off to fight in a battle. It was a great battle and everyone was killed. Well, when the chaps came back, the one they had left behind was dead also.

Seventh Reproduction of Group B: This is a story about warriors and ghosts. The warriors went down to a lake where they met some men in a boat. One of the warriors got an arrow in his back. He felt no pain but his face was distorted. So he went back to bed where he felt better.

Seventh Reproduction of Group C: This is the story of two men who went fishing for seals. The story took place in Canada or India or some place like that. When they were out fishing, they saw five men in the distance. They wanted to fight with them and so they had a battle. During the battle, two of the men were killed. And they went back and told their parents.

Seventh Reproduction of Group D: There were two men in a canoe. They paddled along and came to a village. They both got out. They went to the village. They went back to the canoe and got into it. Then something black came out of the mouth of one of them and he fell dead. And then the other one fell dead too.

Seventh Reproduction of Group E: This story concerns three young men in a place called Igula. And they decided to have a trip up country and they went in a canoe taking bows and arrows with them. They went up so far, up to a part of the country called Colombo. But they found nothing at all and so they came back again. After a few days, one of the men became ill and yet none of them had been hurt in any way during the trip.

2 Interpreting and Reconstructing

As compared with the Ebbinghaus experiments, those of Bartlett place fewer restrictions on how the person should deal with the task in hand. And this greater freedom of action is both an advantage and a disadvantage. The advantage is that it enables us to observe a person acting in ways which obviously resemble his activities in a host of everyday circumstances. But this greater richness of observation is bought at a price, for it is difficult to treat the results in rigorous fashion. We must, as yet, be satisfied to draw conclusions which are largely qualitative rather than quantitative, relatively vague rather than relatively precise. In this section, we shall consider some of these general conclusions with emphasis on two basic features. First, in listening to the story, the person interprets it in his own way by abstracting those characteristics which seem important to him at the time. Secondly, in recalling, the person uses what he believes to be the characteristics of the original in an attempt to reconstruct the original.

Verbatim Memory. His main difficulty is that the presented sequence of words far exceeds his immediate memory span. Few people could be expected to listen to even a short story only once, retain it, and then repeat it with verbatim accuracy. The person cannot behave like a tape recorder. So what does he do? He interprets the material as he receives it. He retains the moment-by-moment details only long enough to build up a cumulative abstract of the story's characteristics, e.g. its main theme, its sub-themes, its style, its salient features. He engages in a complex kind of group-labelling procedure whereby sequences of words are grouped, translated into meaningful units or ideas; then the exact words are forgotten and their gist retained. This does not mean that the person never retains any of the original wording, for it may well happen that some words are themselves salient characteristics of the story. What it does mean is that the person deals with the story in terms of its content rather than its wording. He prepares a cumulative digest of the story and retains a complex of abstracted characteristics rather than a verbatim record. When he comes to recall, the best he can do is to produce this complex of abstracted characteristics and attempt to translate it into a word-by-word narrative. Even at best, then, his narrative will depart from the wording of the original; for it is a feature of language that the same theme or idea can be expressed in different words. In short, the very best we would expect of the retelling is that it should give the main characteristics of the story in words which are largely the person's own rather than those of the original.

So verbatim recall is hardly to be expected after only one presentation. To achieve such recall it would be necessary for the person to study the original repeatedly, just as an actor must study a speech before he can recall it in its original words. It may be mentioned that people seem to differ greatly in the extent to which they use abstracted characteristics which are, themselves, verbal in nature. Some people digest the story largely by constructing their own verbal précis of it. Others translate the story in predominantly non-verbal terms, e.g. they may see the action of the story in their mind's eye. Some experimental work has been done on such differences between individuals. This work shows that there are great divergences between one person and another regarding the extent to which they digest a story into verbal characteristics or otherwise; and these differences are reflected in recalling. More will be said about such individual differences when we discuss imaging activities. But with regard to the role of verbal and non-verbal modes of digesting stories there is, as yet, little to be reported of a firm and general kind.

Interpreting. While a person is listening to the story, he is digesting it, abstracting what seems to him to be, from one moment to the next, its important characteristics. Now, the person does not carry through these abstracting activities in, so to speak, a vacuum. He carries them through in terms of his interest in the task, in terms of what he believes the whole situation demands from him. In these experiments, the person's general approach to the task is relatively standard: the demand is that he deal with the story in such a way as to be able to retell it as exactly as possible. There are, however, everyday situations where a person's approach to story-like material is less dispassionate and more selective than this, e.g. the politician listening to a speech intent on hearing views or arguments which he can contradict. Yet even in the relatively dispassionate and 'disinterested' conditions of the experiments, it is clear that the characteristics which are abstracted from the story may be very different from one person to another. Each person delineates the story in a way which seems important to him, which fits in with that unique background of cumulative past experience and those momentary attitudes which he inevitably brings to bear on his abstracting. In short, each person interprets the story in his own way. The same drama is played out before two spectators; but each, as is popularly and so rightly said, puts his own construction on it.

Interpreting can be seen even more directly in situations where people are given a prose passage to paraphrase at their leisure. Here, they have time to study the passage, and all they need do is write out an abbreviated account of its essential points: the person is free both to read the material and to revise his précis as often as he wishes. Yet, as every teacher knows, the final précis of one person may be very different from that of another, not merely with regard to the detailed points selected as important but also with regard to the overall interpretation of the passage. One précis may seem to come from an original utterly different from that on which another précis seems to be based. Now, if there are effects of interpreting under these favourable conditions, it is not unexpected that the effects should be stronger still when the person is given only one hearing of a story. And it is not unexpected that these effects should be yet stronger again in everyday conditions where the person is emotionally involved in certain aspects of what he hears.

So each person puts his own construction on the material as he listens to it. He interprets the incoming story in his own way, often unaware that he is so doing, that he is emphasizing some features, ignoring others, perhaps reading into it what is not there. Each person abstracts a complex of characteristics which may differ from that abstracted by another person. This means that what different people retain will be different; and so too will be their subsequent retelling of the story.

Reconstructing. In retelling the story, the person does not behave like a tape-recording machine playing back a recorded sequence of signals. It would perhaps be nearer the truth to say that he behaves like a zoologist who, in the light of his accumulated experiences about biology, assembles a few fossilized remains so as to construct the likely appearance of some long extinct animal. In everyday life, people who are asked to recall an episode often say that they must take time to 'collect their ideas' and to 'set them in order'. We may, for the sake of convenience, over-simplify the narrator's activities by saying that he engages in three related phases of activity. If the following brief account of these three phases seems either complex or artificial, it should be borne in mind that recalling *is* complex, and that good experimental evidence exists for every feature mentioned.

First, the recaller produces, out of the cumulative effects of his past experiences, those characteristics which he believes to specify the story. Such production may be difficult, especially if recall is attempted a long time after hearing the original. The characteristics so produced may involve particular words or phrases, or general themes of a more or less synoptic kind, or the overall atmosphere or flavour of the story, or the setting in which the story was heard. Whatever their nature, the person is unlikely to recall any relevant characteristic which he did not originally abstract from the story: his reconstruction is hardly likely to be more faithful than his initial interpretation. However, his reconstruction may well be different from his original interpretation. Some abstracted characteristics may have been forgotten in the meantime or, if not forgotten, at least not brought to mind just when required. Some characteristics may have been thought about in the interval and, thereby, be retained through selective repetition and be given undue emphasis in present recall. Furthermore, some characteristics may be imported from other experiences. The cumulative, ongoing organization of long-term memory may make it difficult to distinguish between features which derived from this particular story and features which were taken in at other times and places. There may be confluence among the retained effects of different past experiences. In short, then, the characteristics produced by the person are those which, at the moment, he can recall from his original interpreting; and sometimes also characteristics which derive from other experiences and are now attributed to the story.

The second phase is to organize these characteristics together into an arrangement which seems plausible. In doing this, the person is governed by his general notions regarding what is likely and what is unlikely. If two characteristics seem incompatible with each other, he tends to resolve this by linking the characteristics together in a way that seems sensible to him. He seems to aim throughout at arranging his recalled characteristics into a story which is as coherent and reasonable as he can make it, even if this means discarding some features, exaggerating the importance of others, and rearranging their sequence. The third and final phase is to produce a word-by-word narrative which seems adequate to this arrangement, contains whatever exact words he can remember from the original, and conforms as nearly as he can make it to the general verbal style of the original. This phase is carried through under the influence of his knowledge about language, of what word sequences are likely to be so and what are unlikely. And it may be strongly influenced by attitudes and conditions operating from the immediate situation in which he finds himself.

Overview. This section may be summarized as follows. The story, as recalled by the person, is influenced by a wide diversity of circumstances and activities – some operating at the time of interpreting the story, some operating in the interval between receiving and recalling, some operating at the time of reconstructing. There is the influence of his original interpretation: the effects which his cumulative past experiences and his present attitudes have on what characteristics he abstracts from the ongoing story, and the relative priorities he gives to these characteristics. There is the influence of subsequent activities: the frequency and extent to which this or that feature of the story is used in relation to other experiences. Finally, there is the influence of conditions at the time of recalling: what he produces, at the moment, as the salient features of the story, and how he relates these together and translates them into a coherent narrative.

When memory for stories is viewed in terms of these complex 'compressions' and 'expansions', it is not surprising that the recalled story should deviate from the story originally presented. What is surprising is that the recalled story should resemble the original at all. Yet it often does, sometimes with astonishing fidelity. The writer has in his possession a recalled version of 'The War of the Ghosts' produced by a man after a lapse of twenty-nine years. Admittedly, this particular man is a genius, in any meaningful sense of that ambiguous word, and has among many talents the most remarkable long-term memory abilities. In 1932, he was given a modified version of the story to read for immediate recall. In 1961, he recalled what he could for the present writer. Subsequently, the writer was able to obtain the original version which had been used. And the two versions, the original and the recalled, tallied in every important respect, even to the details of place-names, numbers mentioned, literary style, and some of the wording. Bearing in mind the complex dynamics of memory activities, it is their successes which are very much more to be marvelled at than their failures.

3 Memory for Story-like Material

The memory dynamics just discussed enter into many every-day activities. Some of these will be discussed in subsequent sections but, here, four situations may be mentioned which illustrate the pervasive effects of interpreting and re-constructing.

The Episodes of a Meeting. What happens when people attend a meeting of some kind and later recount what took place? Does their narrative characterize the original happenings fully or only partly? Is it faithful to the original as far as it goes? These questions are sometimes of prac-tical importance, and they are not independent of each other. Thus, the narrative may faithfully characterize some aspects of the meeting, yet omit so much that it conveys a distorted impression. Again, an account may be detailed and full, yet inaccurate. On occasion, the narrator may not be aware of the inaccuracies and distortions but genuinely accept their veracity. On other occasions, the narrator may be aware that he is recounting inaccuracies. For example, he may include many allegedly direct quotations. 'He said to me . . . and I said to him . . .' and so on. Yet he may not believe these direct quotes to be exact reproductions of the words originally used: social convention may allow their inclusion merely to represent the general flavour of the remarks made and to give the narrative a more lively and personal appeal.

What is likely to happen in reporting a meeting is illus-trated in the results of an experiment reported by two

Cambridge psychologists, J. Blackburn and E. J. Lindgren. Without the knowledge of the people present, they made a recording of the discussion which followed a meeting of the Cambridge Psychological Society. Two weeks later, they wrote to all those who had attended and asked them to write down all they could recall about this discussion. When the reports were received, they were checked against the recorded version and it was found that the average number of specific points recalled by any individual was only 8·4 per cent of the total recorded. However, the really remarkable thing about these recalled points was that, on the average, no less than 42 per cent of them were substantially incorrect. A large variety of errors and confusions appeared. Happenings were reported which had never taken place at all or which had taken place on some other occasion and were wrongly recalled as having occurred at this particular discussion. Thus, a person might report a colleague as making a remark which he knew this colleague habitually made but which he did not happen to make on this particular occasion, e.g. the formal thanking of the speaker by the chairman of the meeting. There were also elaborations, as when some casual remark was expanded into a fairly lengthy contribution to the discussion, or when a point was reported as having been made explicitly whereas it had only been hinted at. In short, what was recalled was not only fragmentary but also distorted, and much was recalled which, in fact, had never happened. It is to minimize these omissions, importations, and distortions that committees have a secretary whose duty is to take notes during the meeting, prepare minutes of the proceedings soon after, and submit these minutes for collective approval.

Picture Material. As an example of the overall effect which interpretation has on recall, we may cite an experiment which was conducted in 1932 by the American psychologist Leonard Carmichael along with two other colleagues. The material used was a list of twelve more or less ambiguous line drawings. Four of these drawings are shown in Fig. 5. Adult subjects were told that they would be shown these drawings and that, immediately afterwards, they would be asked to draw the figures as accurately as possible but in any order. The figures were then shown one at a time.

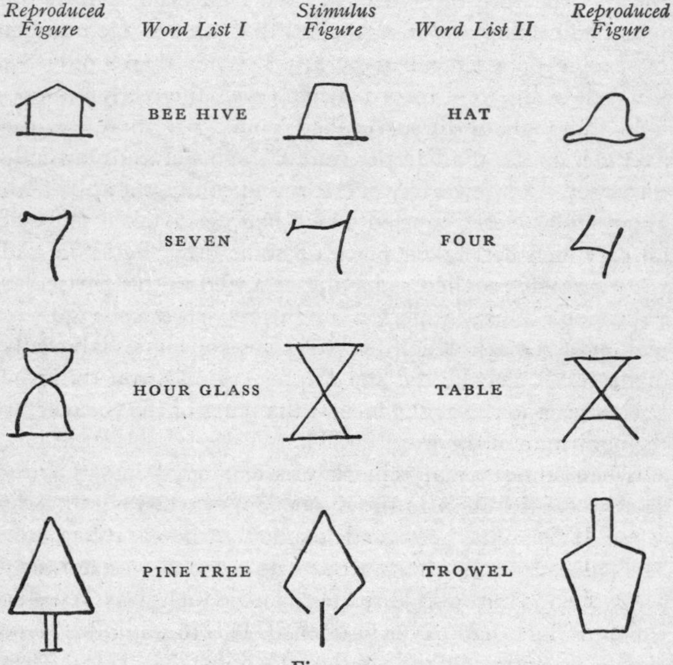

Reproduced Figure	*Word List I*	*Stimulus Figure*	*Word List II*	*Reproduced Figure*
	BEE HIVE		HAT	
	SEVEN		FOUR	
	HOUR GLASS		TABLE	
	PINE TREE		TROWEL	

Figure 5

However, before each, the experimenter said: 'The next figure resembles . . .' and gave a name to the figure. The purpose in doing this was to direct, through suggestion, the subject's interpretation of each figure. The ingenious turn in the experiment was that, while all subjects saw the same figures, half of the subjects were given one set of verbal labels and the other half a completely different set. Thus, the first drawing in Fig. 5 was labelled a 'beehive' for one group of subjects and a 'hat' for another. In the great majority of cases (an average of 87 per cent for the four drawings shown here), it was found that, when the subjects came to reproduce any figure, their drawings were clearly distorted in the direction of the particular verbal label which had been supplied. The nature of these distortions is apparent from the specimen reproductions shown in Fig. 5. The verbal label acted, in the first place, by predisposing the subject to perceive, say, the first drawing as resembling a hat. In the second place, it moulded his recall. He would recall the rough outline of the figure and perhaps some of its detail. He would also recall that it crudely represented a hat and his final drawing would be biased accordingly.

Lecture Material. Lectures provide university students with much of the information they have to study, understand, and retain for later use. This poses very real problems for the student. How should he deal with the ongoing lecture? What notes should he write? What should he do with these notes subsequently? These questions cannot be given straight answers because the optimal way of dealing with any lecture depends on a balance of many considerations. There is the lecture itself, its purpose, content, style and clarity. Not all lectures are the same. At one extreme, it may be discursive, concerned to present already familiar material in a new light. At the other extreme, it may be packed with new and detailed information. There is also the student himself, his previous knowledge, his working habits, the uses he will later make of the lecture material. Not all students attend the same lecture with the same background knowledge and the same purpose. Some students may be more interested in the lecturer than in the lecture, in the style and elegance of the delivery rather than in what is said. Others may want to take away every detailed fact mentioned. There are, then, many circumstances to be considered. We may now outline some of the problems they raise and assume, throughout, that the lecture is of the kind which presents material for subsequent private study and use.

It is helpful for the listener to bear in mind the following ideal. Try to understand the lecture while it is in progress, and do so in such a way as to be able to produce a précis of the lecture afterwards. A student will hear the lecture only once, so if he does not understand its main purpose and argument at the time, he is unlikely to do so later. Also, if he reminds himself that he should be able to précis the lecture after it is over, this will alert him to listen for the main points made, the sequence in which they are made, references cited, and outstanding details given. Now, if the student concentrates on this kind of ideal, he will find it necessary to take notes. This raises further problems and, here, perhaps the general rule is as follows. Make those brief jottings which will least distract from understanding the lecture in progress and best serve to prompt later recall of the essentials of the lecture. Note-making can distract from listening to the lecture. If the student attempts to write very full notes he cannot, at the same moment, be working at understanding what is currently being said. And there are inappropriate moments for note-making. For example, if a lecturer is making three points in rapid succession, the last two may be missed if the student starts elaborately writing out the first as soon as it is given. One objective, then, is to avoid losing the thread of the lecture through being preoccupied by writing notes: this means keeping notes to a minimum. The other objective is to ensure that the notes are sufficient to prompt later recall of what, otherwise, might not be recalled. The minimum notes sufficient for this purpose will differ widely according to the nature of the lecture and of the student. For most lectures, an occasional jotting in the student's own words will suffice for the reconstruction of the lecture's essentials. For some

lectures and some students, however, the notes may have
to be very full. For example, if a mathematics lecturer is
presenting the detailed step by step arguments of a new
proof, it may be necessary to copy down everything written
on the blackboard, plus explanatory comments about why
particular steps are taken: during such a lecture, it may be
impossible for the student to achieve understanding of the
proof, and so it is essential to take full notes whose subsequent study will lead to understanding.

Details heard during the lecture are liable to be forgotten
rapidly, and notes made during the lecture are not likely
to 'make sense' for long. So it is helpful to go over the notes
as soon as possible and, while the lecture is still fresh in
mind, prepare the précis. The sort of précis prepared
depends, again, on a balance of considerations and the
future utility of the material. Sometimes, it may suffice
merely to prepare a précis 'in the head', mentally review
the main points of the lecture. Sometimes, it may be necessary to write out a précis from the notes and from what can
still be recalled of the lecture: this written précis may have
to be used for revision purposes perhaps months or even
years hence: so it had best be well organized and legible
for a long time to come. Sometimes, it may be necessary to
do even more, that is, not merely write out a précis of the
lecture but also incorporate into it the fruits of private
reading and thinking. After all, the purpose of most university lectures is to provide the student with a starting
point and a direction for his private study. The aim is not
that the student should construct a word-by-word duplicate
of the lecture to be learnt off by heart. The aim is that he
should follow up the points made in the lecture, read more
about them, think about them, relate them to other
material which is already known and which is now being
studied, and so build up an increasing understanding of
some realm of knowledge. This aim can, of course, only be
accomplished by the student himself. Not only must he

ensure that he takes away from the lecture its main points, but he must also ensure that these points are worked on before they can be forgotten, that they are reviewed from time to time to ensure their being retained, and that they are related to diverse other points so as to become an intrinsic part of a growing intellectual mastery in which there is a ready and flexible use of relevant information and mental skills.

Introspective Reporting. 'Introspecting' literally means 'looking inwards'. And introspective reporting involves a person in describing, among other things, his private thinking procedures. The whole issue of thinking and its study is both fascinating and complex: but it cannot be pursued here. Our main concern will be to indicate briefly that introspective reporting is a form of recalling which is influenced by the effects of interpreting and reconstructing. Suppose we present someone with the following problem to solve.

A businessman works in the city and lives in the country. Every day, he leaves the city by the same train, and gets off at a station where his chauffeur meets him with the car and drives him to his home. One day, the businessman finishes his work early and takes a train which leaves the city one hour earlier than usual. When he gets off the train, there is, of course, no chauffeur to meet him. So he starts walking home. After walking for a while, he meets the car which has set out for the station at the usual time. So the last part of the way home, he goes by car. He arrives home ten minutes earlier than on the other days. How long did the businessman spend walking? Assume that his speed of walking is constant, that the speed of the car is constant, and that no time is lost either in waiting or changing.

As the person thinks out this problem, there may be very little for us to observe since most of his activity is mental. There are powerful economies inherent in the human development of these internalized thinking activities. For example, they enable the person to represent a line of action to himself and explore the likely consequences of this line without having to expend the time and effort necessary to carry out the action in actuality: they also enable him to bring together at the same time events which, in actuality, must occur objectively at widely separated times and in widely separated places. However, the great biological merits of internalized thinking make them especially difficult to study. They cannot be observed by another person nor, very often, by the thinker himself. But in so far as the thinker is aware of his own thinking activities, we may ask him to describe them for us. This request is, in fact, less simple than it seems.

Consider the person in process of solving the above problem. If we ask him to give a running commentary on his thinking, he finds that the activities of thinking and the activities of describing his thinking interfere with and disrupt each other. Strictly concurrent introspective reporting is probably an impossibility. So what we may do is to let him finish with the problem and then describe how he proceeded, that is, recall for us in words what he did in the course of thinking out the solution. Here we find a number of difficulties. For one thing, many detailed experiences cannot now be remembered. Anyone who thinks through even such simple problems as anagrams is frequently aware of some intriguing turn of experience, and knows that either he must drop the problem and write down this experience, or he must continue with the problem and later be unable to recall the experience. For another thing, there is real difficulty in translating what can be recalled into words. Anyone who works with the activities of introspecting rapidly discovers how impoverished a vehicle the English language is for communicating the rich nuances of subjective experience: much can only be hinted at by resort to inadequate and misleading metaphor. Then again, what the person reports is typically more coherent and rational than was his actual thinking.

This last point can easily be demonstrated as follows. Present a predominantly verbal problem, such as the above might be for some people, to a person whose solving of the problem is likely to be carried through by predominantly verbal activities. And ask the person to 'think aloud' while he works the problem, that is, utter his 'verbal thoughts' aloud as he goes along. Notice that such 'thinking aloud' is different from introspective reporting: the person focuses on the problem, rather than on his own activities, but in so far as verbal activities enter into his working, he expresses these aloud instead of keeping them sub-vocal. Such 'thinking aloud' cannot be done by all people with all problems and, even when it is done, it does not fully describe the person's every moment-by-moment activity. But it does give us some impression of the tortuous course of problem-solving, the many digressions, irrelevances, and false trails which typify most thinking activities. Now, after he has solved the problem and we have recorded what he has said, we ask him to report the course of his thinking in as much detail as he can. We want him to recall and describe everything which 'passed through his mind' during the working of the problem. When he has done this to the best of his ability, we compare his introspective report with the record of his 'thinking aloud'. This comparison typically shows that the former is more ordered and logical than the latter: it tends to omit those phases of his thinking which, by hindsight, seem irrelevant, stupid, and off the track. In brief, his introspective report, for all its value, describes his thinking as having been more directly to the point than it was. Out of what he can recall of his own experiences, he has reconstructed a story which accords more closely to a logical proof of his conclusion than it does to a description of all the prolix complexities through which he meandered prior to arriving at the solution. (Incidentally, the solution of the above problem may be arrived at as follows. Consider, not the businessman, but the car. The car saves ten minutes, that is, the last five minutes of the journey to the station and the first five minutes of the journey away from the station. Therefore, it meets the businessman one hour, less five minutes, after the time he arrived at the station. So the businessman must have spent fifty-five minutes in walking.)

It is noteworthy that many people are unaccustomed to observing their own thinking activities. For them, these experiences have only momentary value: the activities serve to carry forward some directed theme of thinking and are forgotten as soon as their purpose is served. When people do begin to observe their own thinking, they are commonly surprised at the wealth and complexity of experience which hitherto has gone unnoticed by them. This surprise was well expressed by Sir Francis Galton who, in 1883, wrote about his attempts at introspective reporting as follows.

They gave me an interesting and unexpected view of the number of the operations of the mind, and of the obscure depths in which they took place, of which I had been little conscious before. The general impression they have left upon me is like that which many of us have experienced when the basement of our house happens to be under thorough sanitary repairs, and we realise for the first time the complex system of drains and gas and water pipes, flues, bell-wires, and so forth, upon which our comfort depends, but which are usually hidden out of sight, and with whose existence, as long as they acted well, we had never troubled ourselves.

4 Giving Testimony

In practical life, we may be called upon to give an account to others of some incident which we have witnessed. We are present at the scene of a crime and, some time later, we are asked in a law court to give a description of what happened and answer questions about it. Even outside the field of jurisprudence, we often require, in the give and take of social life, to recount our experiences to our friends and satisfy their curiosities about them. The question arises, especially in the light of what was said above: How adequate is our account? Alfred Binet (1857–1911), the famous French psychologist, tackled this question experimentally as long ago as 1900 and, in the early years of the century, many others followed his lead in conducting investigations into testimony. In outline, the method of investigation is simple. The subject is, say, shown a picture, the picture is then removed and, after a lapse of time, he is asked to describe it. His description can be elicited by merely asking him to tell or to write down as much as he can recall. He can simply be asked for a 'report', that is, a free account. On the other hand, he can be asked questions about the details of the picture. This interrogation can be restricted to such aspects as have not been mentioned by the witness in his report: or it can be conducted by preparing a list of questions which cover exhaustively all the contents of the original and are posed to all witnesses in the same order and in the same manner. The answers to these questions must be considered separately from statements which are made spontaneously and, in contrast to the report, they are said to constitute a 'deposition'.

In interrogating a witness, much has been found to depend on the form of the questions asked, particularly if they are of the type known as 'leading' or 'suggestive'. Since most of us are not ordinarily aware of the many subtly different forms which the 'same' question can take, it will probably be instructive to characterize briefly six of the main forms which can be distinguished. A 'determinative' question is the least suggestive of all and is simply introduced by a pronoun or interrogative adverb, e.g. 'What colour was the dog?' A 'completely disjunctive' question forces the witness to choose between two specified alternatives, e.g. 'Was there a dog in the picture?' can only be answered by a 'yes' or a 'no'. An 'incompletely disjunctive' question offers a choice between two alternatives but does not completely preclude a third possibility, e.g. 'Was the dog white or black?' For many witnesses, and especially for children, this form of question is, in practice, completely disjunctive, since a certain independence is required in the choice of the third possibility, for example, that the dog was neither white nor black but was brown. An 'expectative' question is one which arouses a moderately strong suggestion of the answer by framing the question negatively, e.g. 'Was there not a dog in the picture?' An 'implicative' question is one which implies the presence of something which was not actually present in the original, e.g. 'What colour was the cat?' in reference to a picture which did not contain a cat. Lastly, a 'consecutive' question is any form of question used to augment a suggestion which has been developed by a previous question. In addition to these six forms of question, it is found that a question is more suggestive if it asks whether certain things happened or were present rather than whether the witness saw or heard them. Furthermore, any leading question increases in suggestiveness if it comes from the lips of someone who, to the witness, appears authoritative and (as we say with a revealing double use of the word) imposing.

Once the report or deposition has been obtained, it can be analysed under three main heads. First, there is the range, that is, the number of items mentioned. Second, there is the accuracy of each item as compared with the original. Third, there is the degree of assurance with which an item is given: this varies all the way from the total uncertainty reflected in 'I don't know', to the certainty which is so complete that the witness is willing to take an oath that his statement is correct.

Many experiments of the above sort have been performed. As regards the original experience, the favourite has been the showing of a picture. This is usually detailed and depicts, say, a harvest or a fishing scene in which there are a number of people and a variety of objects and activities. But random collections of objects have also been used, and so too have more real-life events. Carefully rehearsed little 'dramas' have been performed in a natural context and in an apparently spontaneous way. Or again, as in the experiment of Blackburn and Lindgren, the event may be one which, although recorded, is genuinely unrehearsed. It might be expected that these testimony experiments would yield rich observations on many facets of memory. And such indeed is the case. A few of the major findings may now be highlighted. Incidentally, it is to be emphasized that these findings are obtained from people who are performing to the best of their ability. We can never be absolutely certain that deliberate falsification is absent from any account, but the experiments are conducted in such a way that there is little reason to mistrust the subjects' sincerity. Lying is, of course, an interesting social phenomenon but it is not one which is relevant in the context of a book on memory.

The completely accurate testimony is rare. The errorless account is an exception even when given by competent people under favourable conditions. Thus, one German investigator collected a total of 240 testimonies and found only five errorless reports and one errorless deposition. These errorless accounts are commonly given by witnesses who are extremely cautious and make only those few statements of which they are absolutely certain. It is also found that a detail may be in error even although it is given by the majority of witnesses. The testimony of the majority may be as inaccurate as that of the minority. Especially is this so with short time intervals between events: these are usually overestimated. It also tends to happen with the sequence of events, with the exact time of day at which they took place, with the relative spatial positions of people or objects in a scene, and with definite numbers of objects. These details are particularly liable to errors of interpretation and tend to be recalled in accordance with what would normally be expected rather than in accordance with what was, in fact, the case. A good example of this distorting effect of interpretation is given by the German psychologist, William Stern. During a lecture, a strange man walked into the room, asked permission to look at a book on one of the shelves there, spent a short time reading in the room, and then went away taking the book with him. The incident had, of course, been carefully rehearsed and one important feature of it was the taking away of the book, since the removal of any book from that room was strictly against the regulations. During the incident, the lecture continued and the students paid no particular attention to the stranger or to what he was doing. A week later, these students were asked to report on the incident and then answer a comprehensive list of questions concerning it. They might reasonably have declined to commit themselves on the grounds that they had paid very little attention at the time. However, they avoided this cautious procedure and made numerous statements about the man's appearance and actions. Many of these were, of course, incorrect. In the interrogation, the crucial question was: 'What happened to the book he was reading?' A few students answered this correctly and a few abstained from answering, but the majority declared unhesitatingly and in all sincerity that the man returned the book to its shelf.

The effect of the interrogation is to elicit more statements than appear in the report but also to reduce the overall accuracy of testimony. In quite a number of investigations, for example, it is found that the proportion of inaccurate items (contained in all the items given in testimony) is something like a tenth for report and a quarter for deposition. It is understandable why this should be so. In giving a report, the witness is free to describe only those circumstances which he can recall vividly and with a certain assurance. But as soon as he is interrogated, he may have to deal with features of the original which he can recall but vaguely, if at all. To be sure, it is always possible for him to say: 'I don't know.' But, in not a few cases, the witness is unprepared to confess his ignorance. It is as though the very fact of being questioned constrains him to feel that he must give an answer – and that he is capable of giving it. So, what he can recollect but dimly and inaccurately is constructed into a definite reply to the question posed. It may be that this reply is not formulated with full conviction but, rather, is given to satisfy the demands of an insistent interrogator. But once the reply has actually been given, there is a tendency for the witness to leave doubts behind and accept it as the outcome of genuine recall, especially if the interrogator seems to be satisfied with the answer and proceeds to ask further 'consecutive' questions. Now, if merely being questioned is likely to lead to false testimony, how much more must this be so when the questions are put in suggestive form. This is especially true when the witness is a child. It is found that children are inferior to adults in both the range and accuracy of their testimony, that is, they give fewer items and what they do give is more likely to be inaccurate. In part, this is due to their poorer ability to observe, to understand, and to use language – all natural consequences of their more limited past experience. But, in part, it is due to their greater suggestibility. They are particularly likely to answer leading questions in accordance with the suggestion they carry. Thus, William Stern has estimated that 7-year-old children are misled by some 50 per cent of leading questions as contrasted with 18-year-olds who are misled by only some 20 per cent of such questions.

The assurance with which testimony is given is found to be no absolute guarantee of accuracy. Less error is found in sworn testimony than in unsworn, but inaccuracies still remain, especially if there has been a considerable lapse of time since the original experience. This is illustrated by figures which the writer has recalculated from data published by Karl Dallenbach, an American psychologist, in 1913. These figures are given below. Dallenbach allowed fifteen men students to scrutinize a picture and then asked them a set of sixty questions which were prearranged to cover all the details. The students knew the object of the experiment and were told not to attempt to answer any question about which they felt uncertain. After giving each answer, they indicated whether they would be prepared to take an oath as to its accuracy or whether they were only moderately certain about it. They were given the same interrogation on four different occasions: immediately after seeing the picture, five days after, fifteen days after, and forty-five days after. The main results were as follows:

Number of days since experience	0	5	15	45
Average number of questions answered	59	57	57	57
Average number of wrong answers	8	10	12	13
Average number of questions answered and sworn to	42	39	38	35
Average number of wrong sworn answers	3	4	6	7

The number of wrong answers is, it is true, small but, in a court of law, it might be just those answers which would tip the balance of a final judgement.

In summary of this section, it may be said that errors of testimony are almost unavoidable and that, while interrogation is an excellent means of filling out the gaps in spontaneous report, it has its dangers. It leads witnesses, especially children and unsophisticated adults, into false deposition. Falsification can be reduced, but not completely eliminated, by: asking for sworn testimony; obtaining the testimony as soon after the event as possible; and confining the testimony to that given in a spontaneous report and in answer to questions which are framed as non-suggestively as possible.

5 Rumours and Folk-tales

In an earlier section, it was indicated that the results obtained by the Method of Serial Reproduction are of interest in two main respects. They illustrate the distortions which occur in long-term remembering; and they represent an analogy to the way in which rumours and folk-tales grow and change in the growing. A rumour may be broadly defined as information, purporting to be about some real event, which is passed on from person to person, usually by word of mouth, without secure standards of evidence being present. We are all familiar with rumours, both complimentary and scandalous. Typically, they have a fairly well identified central figure such as Professor X or the Government; they specify fairly clearly the character of the action, the destructiveness, the meanness, the beneficence which gives the tone to the story; and their source is vague, whether it be an insubstantial 'they' or an equally elusive 'good authority'. Rumours are, despite their social importance, short-lived. They rise, circulate for a few days or weeks or months, then disappear when they are no longer topical. Folk-tales, on the other hand, possess remarkable longevity. Whether they deal with the mundane or the super-natural, whether they preserve in oral tradition the deeds of long ago or explain why this house is uninhabited or how the bear lost his tail, they appeal to long-term interests. They are rumours which have persisted to become part of the verbal heritage of a people.

It is obvious that both rumours and folk-tales merit mention in any book devoted to memory. And for this reason, the present section is devoted to these social pheno-mena. But an exhaustive discussion would be out of place – it would lead us too far into the fields of social psychology and anthropology. The main outlines can be found in *The Psychology of Rumor*, a readable little book published in America by Gordon W. Allport and Leo Postman in 1947. Here, we shall discuss only those aspects of rumours and folk-tales which are of direct relevance to the psychology of memory.

We have seen that, as 'The War of The Ghosts' passed from mouth to mouth, there was such a change of emphasis, such a cumulation of omissions, transpositions, and inven-tions that the original became barely recognizable. We have also seen that the transformations in this laboratory-created rumour were the result of interpretation, of the unwitting effort of each member of the chain to make sense of the story. Now, exactly the same sorts of changes seem to occur in rumour. However, it should be realized that, despite their superficial similarity, there are three main points of difference between rumour as it is produced in the laboratory and as it occurs in real life. The first difference relates to the individual's concern with accuracy. Subjects participating in a serial reproduction experiment are instructed beforehand to recount the story as accurately as possible. These instructions produce a restraint. They diminish the exaggeration which stems from a person's attempts to impress his audience either with the drama of the tale, or with the extent to which he is 'in the know' regarding information not accessible to his hearers. They also check the more or less deliberate addition of gratuitous interpretations of the kind prefaced by phrases such as 'But if you ask me what really happened ...' In the social setting which is the medium for rumour, such restraint is absent. The second difference between the laboratory and the real-life rumour concerns the time which elapses between the individual's hearing of the story and his retelling it. In the laboratory, the time interval is usually negligible. In real life, this time lapse is variable and may be sufficiently long to enable the additional forgetting of details and the further introduction of distortions to take place. The third, and by far the most important, difference between the two situations is the motivation of the individuals concerned. The laboratory situation is relatively impersonal. The story has no intimate bearing on the lives of the subjects, and is repeated by them, not because of its interest but merely to comply with the experimenter's instructions. The motivation involved in listening to and passing on the story is the most distinctive characteristic of rumours and folk-tales. And something must now be said about it.

For a rumour to thrive, its theme must be of some importance to both speaker and listener, and also, the true facts must be shrouded in some sort of ambiguity. Neither importance nor ambiguity is, by itself, sufficient. If the government announces an increase in income tax and this increase is reliably reported to us through the newspapers and over the radio, rumours do not spring up regarding the increase, or at least regarding the increase as such: the event is important to most of us but it is not ambiguous. If changes occur in the market price of camels in Afghanistan, we are not likely to hear rumours about it: the event is ambiguous but is, as far as we are concerned, unimportant.

The fact that rumours depend on the ambiguity of important events means that they will be more prevalent in some situations than in others. They will not occur in intimate, settled groups of people who know one another so well that, despite gossip and endless discussion, a bizarre story concerning one of them will not be accepted and passed on. They will occur in situations where no one knows exactly what is happening, and where the human need to know makes any aspect of that situation good conversation. This is apparent during wars, strikes, and times of social crisis generally. It is also seen in large factories, schools, offices, and hospitals where little is known about the private lives and doings of those important people who wield administrative power. It follows that at least one method of arresting the growth of rumour is to remove ambiguity by supplying adequate information. If this information comes from a trusted source and is accepted by a group of people, then the rumour is scotched for this group.

The fact that rumours depend on the importance of ambiguous events means that a rumour which circulates widely through one section of society may not appear in others. Teachers, lawyers, bankers, tea clubs, and bridge parties all have their own set of rumours concerning these events which, for the particular group, are important enough to compete in the rivalry of general conversation. When we say that rumours circulate only where the story has importance for the members of the rumour-chain, we are drawing attention to the motivational factor. Any human motive, or more usually combination of motives, may be at work. Sex interest operates through much of gossip and most of scandal: anxiety is at work behind the macabre and threatening tales of disaster or impending disaster: hopes and desires underlie pipe-dream rumours: hate and jealousy sustain accusing tales. Rumour often gives verbal outlet and relief to our emotional tensions, enabling us to express our antipathies, fears, and desires. And, at the same time, it serves to justify us in feeling the way we do. It is often a subtle and metaphorical way of saying: 'Why shouldn't I dislike so-and-so? He got the job I wanted by unfair means', or 'Why shouldn't I feel superior? I don't behave in the outrageous way that he does', or 'Why shouldn't I feel optimistic? Other people like me have had lucky breaks'. Thus, they often protect and justify those attitudes which, if faced directly, might be distasteful to us. Apart from this emotional aspect, rumour also serves our need to understand events, to know just what is happening, and to find a reasonable explanation for it. We need to know the why, how, and wherefore of the surrounding world, and especially those features of it which are likely to affect us personally. And, as a substitute for reliable but unavailable news, curiosity rumours result. A stranger who has just come to live in our neighbourhood will soon become the subject of rumours which would explain who he is and why he has come. In short, nothing could be further from the truth than to describe rumours as idle. They are motivated in a complex way which is seldom, if ever, clearly understood by the rumour spreader and is difficult enough for even the psychologist to understand. This much, however, is certain. Any rumour serves one or more of at least four distinct functions. It may serve a social purpose in giving the story-teller the attention of the group, a moment of conversational leadership. It may relieve our emotional tension. It may justify us in holding the attitudes we do. And it may render the surrounding world intelligible.

As compared with rumour, the folk-tale has the additional distinction of treating issues which are of more than transitory importance. Like the rumour, it undergoes transformation until it assumes a relatively stereotyped form couched in simple and concrete terms. It is not expressed in abstract language but recounts specific happenings of a familiar or, at least, readily intelligible kind. The tale does not, however, owe its persistence so much to the specific circumstances it recounts as to its considerable metaphorical significance. Both teller and hearer may be aware that it contains no literal truth. But this is not important if it is metaphorically true. The Christmas rose, despite snow and ice, is said to burst into blossom at midnight on Christmas Eve: it may not do so in fact, but it might well as an expression of the gladness of that season. The folk-tale, like the great work of literary fiction, expresses through specific characters and concrete happenings the fears and wishes and problems which are common to every member of a particular society. For example, the mighty Icelandic sagas supply a sense of stability and comradeship, and a pride of ancestry. The deeds of their heroes and villains embody the universal and recurring features of human personality. Their account of the world's creation, of the seasons, and of the caprices of the gods furnish a plausible explanation of these cosmic riddles which are the most important and yet the most eternally ambiguous faced by man in his brief and confusing existence.

The differences between the rumour, the folk-tale, and the serial reproduction experiment have now been indicated. What of their similarities? It is difficult to obtain the detailed history of a rumour. It is more difficult still to trace the progress of a folk-tale. But what evidence there is suggests that all three phenomena follow the same basic pattern. Each undergoes progressive transformation in being passed on from individual to individual. Each takes on a form which is more intelligible and meaningful to the members of the group among which it passes. And each assumes this form through the interpretations and reconstructions which each person has built up over his lifetime. These reflect his individual needs, preoccupations, fears, and doubts along with the attitudes and interests which he has acquired from the social group in which he lives. We may conclude this discussion of rumours and folk-tales by giving two examples of transformation.

Our first example illustrates the progressive distortion of 'history' by a succession of writers who rely on each other's interpretations rather than on the original evidence. This example is taken from a booklet published in 1956 by The Historical Association. The event is the signing of the National Covenant in Edinburgh in the year 1638 – an event which has aroused heated partisanship even up to the present day. The popular account of the signing is that, on 28 February, the people of Edinburgh thronged into

Greyfriars Church and overflowed into the churchyard to append their names, even in blood from their veins, to copies of the Covenant spread out on flat tombstones. This account is a simplified and dramatized version of the more complex and sober historical reality. What actually happened was that, on the day mentioned, there was only one copy of the Covenant which was subscribed in the church between 4 and 8 p.m. by some 150 to 200 nobles and gentlemen. On the following day, more copies were available in another part of Edinburgh for signing by nobles, clergy, and commissioners of burghs. The 'people of Edinburgh' did not sign till later and, when they did, it was neither in Greyfriars church nor in the churchyard. The stone traditionally associated with the event is, in fact, of a much later date than 1638. The popular account then continues to add that the first person to sign was the aged and sickly Earl of Sutherland, and we are given a picture of a life crowded with wisdom and nobility and crowned by one last defiant gesture. 'Accounts of the event illustrate the growth of a legend, because James Gordon in his *History of Scots Affairs* narrates that the first to subscribe was John Gordon, Earl of Sutherland: Robert Chambers, in *History of the Rebellions in Scotland*, added these words: "a nobleman venerable for his excellent domestic character"; Rev. John Aiton, in *Life and Times of Alexander Henderson* (1836), refers to him as "the venerable Earl of Sutherland"; Hetherington, in his *History of the Church of Scotland*, speaks of "an aged nobleman, the venerable Earl of Sutherland", stepping "slowly and reverentially forward" and subscribing "with throbbing heart and trembling hand". The object of all this veneration was under 29 years of age!'

Our second example illustrates how a folk-tale may be radically changed in passing from one cultural context to another. In Northern Europe, the bear is one of the few animals which does not possess a tail, and we find a folk-story to explain how it was lost. One winter night, it is said, the fox persuaded the bear to dip his tail into the water in order to catch fish: the water froze and, in pulling himself free, the bear left his tail behind and so lost it for ever. This story spread into southern countries and, in being assimilated by members of a different region, underwent transformation. In these countries there are no bears, and the story is told as one of several concerning the cunning of the fox. In place of the unknown bear, the familiar wolf is substituted. And, although the wolf does have a tail, this is a minor detail which does not affect the central theme which has now become concerned with the characteristic cunning of the fox.

In summary of this whole chapter, it may be said that the recall of stories and events is rarely accurate. There are omissions, transpositions, and additions resulting from interpretation, from the individual's making the account conform to his standards of intelligibility. Thus, recall is often less a matter of literal reproduction than of the imaginative construction of fragmentary recall into a coherent whole. Normally the individual is unaware of this constructive characteristic of his remembering. But on occasion, especially in the retelling of rumours and folk-tales, he may interpret deliberately in order to heighten the drama of the story and capture the attention of his audience.

V Imaging

Imaging refers to sensory-like experiencing which occurs in the absence of appropriate sensory stimulation. And this chapter is concerned with imaging activities and their role in memory. The 'mind's eye' is a phrase whose meaning is readily understood by most people except the congenitally blind. It is in the mind's eye that we see the face of an absent friend or, like Wordsworth, the poet, a host of dancing daffodils. We say we have an image of the friend or of the flowers. But although the word 'imaging' obviously derives from the realm of seeing, it is used also in regard to hearing, tasting, smelling, touching, experiences of temperature, of bodily conditions, of muscular movements and strains. In short, it is used to refer to all instances when we experience sensory qualities in the absence of appropriate sensory stimulation. Now, much of our remembering takes the form of imaging. In the quiet of our room, we may, as it were, re-live some past complex experience in vivid sensory terms. We may see again the high green hills, the blue sky, the light-flecked waves breaking against the rocks. We may hear again the cries of the sea-birds and the sound of the ship's hooter. We may smell again the odour of the wrack on the shore and the perfume of the rose in our lapel. We may taste again the chocolate we ate on that day, feel again the relaxing warmth of the sunshine, our movements in walking along the heaving deck of the ship, and the sinking feeling of oncoming sea-sickness. Throughout, we are recalling the past by reconstructing its sensory characteristics. Memory-imaging, more than any other kind of recalling, gives us the illusion that we are actually going back in time and reliving moments of our past.

There are three general points to be stressed about imaging. The first is that imaging is an activity. In the interests of easy expression, we may talk of 'an image' as though it were a static thing which occurs to us rather than an activity which we carry out. But it should be borne in mind that, strictly speaking, imaging is a form of activity; in the same general sense as 'a memory' of whatever sort is also a form of activity. The second point is that we cannot directly observe anyone's imaging except our own. We must infer the nature and extent of a person's imaging from what he does, and especially from what he tells us about his private experiencing. This raises difficulties in the study of imaging since introspective reports, even when given in good faith, cannot always be accepted at their face value. But it does not, of course, mean that we cannot discover a great deal about imaging. The third general point is that the nature and extent of imaging differs widely from one person to another, and that most people are unaware of this. Each person accepts his own modes of imaging uncritically and tends to assume that everyone else experiences in the same ways as he does himself. This egocentric assumption may make it difficult for him to comprehend the descriptions which other people give of their imaging.

1 After-imaging

It may be useful to start our discussions of imaging by referring to some short-term after-effects of sensory stimulation. One such after-effect is called 'positive after-imaging'. This refers to the fact, mentioned in Chapter Two, that the

Imaging

effects of sensory stimulation outlast stimulation itself by a very short period, e.g. if a visual array of digits is exposed for a fraction of a second, it is possible for the person still to see and read off some of the digits after the exposure has actually ended. Much more commonly experienced is negative after-imaging. The reader who has not experienced a negative after-image for himself might care to try the following little experiment. Take as the stimulus a scrap of brightly coloured paper about, say, the size of a penny, and make a tiny pencil mark or pin-prick near its centre. Lay this on a sheet of white paper and look fixedly at the mark in its centre for perhaps twenty seconds. Remove the coloured stimulus and fixate with the eyes some tiny mark on the large white sheet. After a few seconds during which nothing may happen, a patch of colour will be seen. If we continue fixating, this patch will vanish, then return only to vanish once more; it may alternately appear and disappear as many as twenty or thirty times, growing fainter with each successive reappearance until a time is reached after a minute or so when it disappears altogether. Now, there are two surprising things about this image. The first is its colour. If the stimulus is red, the image is green; if the stimulus is blue, the image is yellow; if the stimulus is black, the image is white. The image has, in short, that colour which is described as being complementary to the colour of the stimulus, and it is for this reason that the after-image is called 'negative'. If, after fixating the stimulus, we fixate not the white sheet but some coloured surface, the image changes colour accordingly. Suppose the stimulus had been green. On a white or grey surface, the image is red; on a yellow surface, the image is orange; on a blue surface, the image is purple; on a green surface (the same colour as the stimulus), the image is grey and colourless; and on a red surface, the image is a highly saturated red of great brilliance. The second surprising thing about the negative after-image is its size. Suppose a 1-inch square stimulus is fixated at a distance of 1 foot from the eye. If the after-image is then obtained by fixating a surface which is also 1 foot away, the image will cover exactly 1 square inch of this surface. But if this surface is 2, 5, 10, or 15 feet distant from the eye, the image will be 2, 5, 10, or 15 inches in diameter. Thus, the size of the image varies with the distance between the observer and the surface on which he projects the image. In fact, the size of the image is directly proportional to the distance of the projection surface from the eye. This generalization is known as Emmert's Law, and we will have occasion to refer back to it later in the chapter.

The reader can fairly readily obtain all the above-mentioned effects for himself, although a little trial and error may be necessary to establish the most favourable conditions. The clearness and duration of the negative after-image depend on such factors as the colour and brilliance of the stimulus, the background on which it lies, the conditions of illumination, and the length and accuracy of fixation. The image is clearer the simpler the stimulus; complicated stimuli, such as a detailed picture, give either a very poor image or none at all. These effects are all readily understandable in terms of the psycho-physical properties of light but, in this book, there is neither the space nor the necessity to give an account of these properties. Here, it suffices merely to say that the effects are due to the adaptation or 'fatigue' of the colour- and light-sensitive tissue (the retina) which lies at the back of the eyeball. In fixating the red stimulus patch, we continuously stimulate the same area of the retina until it becomes no longer sensitive to the red of the patch. (As we fixate the stimulus, we may notice that it seems to lose its colour except round the edges.) Then when we fixate some other surface, this adapted retinal area is insensitive to whatever red component the surface possesses, and the negative after-image results. As we continue to fixate, the retina adapts to the colour of the new surface and the image wanes. The important point is that the image is the after-effect of continuously stimulating, and so 'fatiguing', a specific area of the retina.

The positive after-image is essentially in the nature of perseveration. Some stimulus is present for a moment and then vanishes, but we continue to experience the effects of the stimulus as though it still persisted. The positive after-image is less easy to demonstrate than is the negative, but we have probably all experienced it at some time or other. We glance at a brightly lit object, then turn our eyes to a dark wall and see 'inwardly' the object still before us and in its original colour. The majority of us have experienced the positive after-image which follows our looking at the sun or a dazzling light. In the realm of hearing, we have had the embarrassing experience of not 'catching' a question, asking for it to be repeated, and then hearing the words 'in the mind's ear' and answering them before our questioner can say the words again. It is also well known that the strokes of a clock which have not been attended to during the striking may sometimes be counted immediately afterwards and the whole succession of strokes may be repeated in awareness with a vividness almost comparable to an actual perceiving of the sounds at the time. Usually such perseveration is extremely short-lived, but there are circumstances under which it may persist for a considerable time. For example, many people are troubled by experiencing continued movement after a journey by sea or train; and people who are exceptionally sensitive to light often report that a long day's fishing in bright light is followed by positive after-images of the pools and foliage which are so vivid as to interfere with relaxation and reading.

Both the negative and positive after-image resemble the memory image proper in that they exist in the absence of a present, appropriate, external stimulus. But they can be distinguished from the memory image, in relative if not in absolute terms, by the conditions of their appearance. They occur very shortly after the withdrawal of the stimulus, whereas the memory image typically occurs much later and is subject to a distinctly voluntary control not shared by the after-images as such.

2 Memory-imaging

In 1883, Sir Francis Galton published a book entitled *Inquiries into Human Faculty and its Development*. In this work, he reported the outcome of several ingenious investigations into the activities of human beings, and made not a few observations which presaged much of later psychological investigation. It is written with the modest and lively simplicity of true greatness and, although some of its conclusions have had to be revised, it remains into the present day a book which well repays reading. Our present interest in Galton's book lies in the account given of the answers to a questionnaire which he sent out to a hundred men, at least half of whom were distinguished in science or some other field of intellectual endeavour. In this questionnaire, he asked his respondents to recall their breakfast table as they sat down to it that morning, to consider carefully the pictures which arise in their 'mind's eye', and to answer a list of searching questions about these pictures. They were also asked about the vividness and detail with which they could image experiences to do with hearing, smelling, tasting, touching, and such bodily experiences as cold, hunger, drowsiness, and fever. They were further asked to contribute supplementary information and general remarks as they felt inclined.

When Galton had received the answers and tabulated them, the most outstanding result was the enormous range of differences between one individual and the next. At one extreme, there were individuals who reported imagery as bright and clear as the actually perceived scene. Their images were never blotchy or indistinct, but brilliant and as rich in their particulars as though the breakfast table were, at this moment, in front of them. At the other extreme, there were individuals who could report no imagery at all. They could recollect the table in verbal terms, even as regards colour, but there were no images of it. One artist reported that he could draw a likeness of both people and places some days or weeks after seeing them, but this was the result of having studied the appearances while present, and of trial and error sketching at the time of reproduction: no visual imagery was involved. Several individuals reported that their only experience of imagery had occurred in that drowsy state which lies between waking and sleeping. But some individuals had, presumably, not experienced imagery even during this state and could not even understand what was meant by Galton's questions. So deficient were they in imaging that they regarded other people's accounts of their imaging as mere romancing. Such an individual is in the same position regarding images as is a colour-blind man regarding colour – it falls completely outside his range of awareness.

Since Galton's time, other psychologists have supplemented his findings by asking people questions about their imaging. In order to facilitate comparisons between individuals, the subjects are usually asked to rate each image in terms of a prearranged set of categories such as the following. (i) Perfectly clear and as vivid as the actual experience: (ii) Very clear and comparable in vividness to the actual experience: (iii) Moderately clear and vivid: (iv) Not clear or vivid but recognizable: (v) Vague and dim: (vi) So vague and dim as to be hardly noticeable: (vii) No image present at all. Once these categories have been explained, subjects are asked to apply them while trying to image a variety of different experiences. They may be asked, for example, to attempt the following. Try to get a visual image of a glove, house, fire burning, sunset: try to get an auditory image of the bark of a dog, beat of rain on a window, click of a teaspoon in a saucer, swish of a silk dress, honk of a motor car: try to get a kinaesthetic image of marching, lifting a heavy weight, running upstairs, saying 'God save the King', nodding your head in assent: try to get a tactile image of velvet, emery-paper, heat of a warm fire, wet soap, cold rain on your face: try to get a gustatory image of salt, orange juice, chocolate, cheese, coffee: try to get an olfactory image of cigar smoke, tar, onions, camphor, roses: try to get an organic image of a headache, fatigue, a sore throat, nausea, repletion after a full meal.

The answers given by people to such questions as the above serve mainly to emphasize the wide range of individual differences noted by Galton. As indicated, imaging may occur in any one of at least seven sensory modes: it may be visual, tactile, and so on. One person may report imaging which is as vivid in any mode as in any other. Another may report poor ability to image in any mode. Yet another may report vivid imaging in one mode or some combination of modes and little or none in the remainder. Differences even occur within a single mode, as, for example, in the ability to obtain coloured imaging. In short, the possible variations both between and within modes are so tremendous that it is impossible to make any simple generalizations about them. Early psychologists hoped that it might be possible to classify people into groups or types according to the characteristics of their imaging. The terms 'visile', 'audile', and 'motile' were coined for those whose imaging was predominantly visual, auditory, and kinaesthetic respectively. However, although often suggestive, people's reports fail to furnish definite evidence that clear-cut categories can be established.

Despite these enormous, and as yet unclassifiable, differences between individuals, it is possible to draw four conclusions concerning general tendencies. First, visual imaging is the most common and, for most people, is also the most vivid. Auditory imaging is next most frequent, followed by tactile imagery. Kinaesthetic, gustatory, and organic imagery occur next with about the same frequency, while olfactory imaging is the least common and vivid mode of all. Second, people who report being particularly good in one mode of imaging also tend to report being above average in other modes as well. This would seem to indicate that the majority of us are versatile rather than restricted in our modes of imaging. While there are notable individual exceptions, it therefore appears that what imaging ability we have tends to be all-round rather than limited to one or a few sensory modes. Third, imaging occurs with especial frequency and vividness in the hypnagogic state, that is, the state between waking and sleeping. For many people, this state is particularly rich in imagery. Vivid, life-like scenes pass before the 'inner eye' and voices are distinctly heard. Usually such hypnagogic imaging requires no voluntary effort and may even occur despite our attempts to suppress it, the images sometimes appearing to be so real as to approach or attain the character of hallucinations.

The fourth and last – and in some ways the most interesting – general finding has two related aspects. One aspect is that the imaging of the self-same person varies according to what he is trying to recall. If it is a concrete, unique object such as a face or a voice, imaging tends to occur more frequently than if it is an abstract argument, a decision, or a logical deduction. Even although these latter items were originally experienced in concrete terms, such as a seen or heard communication, their recalling is accomplished with a lesser accompaniment of imaging. The second aspect of this fourth conclusion is that people who deal chiefly with abstract lines of thinking report a less than average ability to 'summon up' images. This fact was first noted by Galton who found his hundred men of intellectual distinction lower in imaging ability than children and adults selected from non-professional walks of life. Confirmation came in 1909 from an American psychologist, G. H. Betts, when he asked both college students and professors about their imaging. The students most frequently reported their imaging as slightly better than 'moderately clear and vivid' while the professors most frequently reported it as slightly better than 'vague and dim'. The relation between skill in abstract thinking and lack of imaging ability seems well established, although it is to be emphasized that it holds only in average terms and that there are, as always, individuals who constitute striking exceptions to the rule. We shall return to this relation again at the end of the chapter but, here, it may be said that the reason for it seems to be that the more efficient and successful the thinking, at least of a logical nature, the less it is accompanied for most people by imaging. It would appear that images are too concrete and specific to be of great service in reaching solutions by high-level thinking. And as the individual's skill in abstract thinking develops, it increasingly interferes with and weakens his somewhat outmoded skill in imaging, until he may not be able to image even when specifically asked to do so.

Image-association. Before leaving this section, one last and curious finding may be mentioned, namely, that of 'image-association'. There are people whose recalling of certain items is consistently accompanied by imaging which has no apparent relation to the items concerned. Thus, individuals manifest what is known as a 'number-form'. This involves imaging a spatial arrangement of numbers and, whenever a number is thought of, it is imaged in this way. The number-form may be a sloping curve with irregularities at the points of important numbers, or it may be a three-dimensional lattice of some sort. The form varies much

Imaging

from individual to individual and is usually complex. But despite its complexity, there is nothing vague about the form, and its possessor is confident of being able to construct, say, a wire model of it. These forms are also persistent, remaining largely unchanged throughout the years. (For descriptions and drawings of various number-forms, the reader is referred to Galton's book.) Incredible though such forms may seem to those of us who do not experience them ourselves, it is probable that most of us have the undeveloped foundations of one in our own awareness. Thus, one investigator questioned 250 people who claimed to have no number-forms and found that no fewer than 210 reported a feeling that numbers somehow receded from them: some reported that numbers had a vague upward movement and others that they seemed to recede in a straight line or at an angle.

The number-form is not the only example of image-association. Numbers, months of the year, and days of the week are also quite commonly recalled in terms of visual imaging involving either spatial relations or colours or objects. One case reported to the writer involves the vivid visual imaging of objects whenever the days of the week are thought of. This imaging has, to the writer's knowledge, remained substantially unchanged for the past ten years and his informant (whom we may call X) claims to have had just these particular image-associations since as far back as he can recollect. In very brief, the associations are as follows. Monday – a window of a factory where X's father worked when X was a child (and to which he returned on Mondays): Tuesday – a small white handkerchief with 'A Merry Christmas' embroidered in red across one corner: Wednesday – a man's black striped trousers (such as X's father wore to attend a committee which met every Wednesday during X's childhood): Thursday – a light-brown earthenware jar: Friday – an earthenware jar similar to the former but much darker in colour: Saturday

– a saucer with a pattern of brown and gold squares round the edge (this was part of the 'good china' which was used on Saturdays because X's father was at home for tea on that day): Sunday – a metal cream pitcher (used only on Sundays when X's family had cream instead of milk for lunch and tea). It seems clear from this sketchy report that at least four of these associations derive from those recurrent events which, for the young child, differentiated one day of the week from another. Unfortunately, the sources of most image-associations are not so evident and are often completely obscure. Why these associations should persist over the years and whether they serve any function are questions which have not yet been answered.

3 Photographic Memory

From time to time we hear people refer to 'photographic memory' and say wistfully how useful the gift must be. By this term is meant, presumably, the ability to image an absent scene with all the vividness, distinctness, and detail of a photographic print. Since many people suppose such an ability to exist, this section is devoted to an examination of the evidence for such a supposition. What approximates most closely to the popular notion of 'photographic memory' is a remarkable form of visual imaging which has been estimated to occur in something like 1 to 10 per cent of the adult population and 50 to 60 per cent of children under the age of 12 years. This form of imaging was first investigated by the German psychologist, E. R. Jaensch, and found to have so many unique characteristics that it was given the name 'eidetic' (virtually, identical or duplicative).

The observations of Jaensch and others on eidetic imaging have been summarized by G. W. Allport in an

Imaging

article published in 1924 in the *British Journal of Psychology*.
Allport himself worked in Cambridge with some sixty
11-year-old children, and his procedure may be mentioned
because it is typical. At a normal reading distance from the
child, he propped up a 2-foot square dark grey mat on which
he placed, one at a time, pictures cut from an ordinary
picture book. The pictures were rich in detail and action,
the principal features being in silhouette and the background
objects coloured in delicate tints. A picture was left on the
mat for thirty-five seconds, during which time the child
scrutinized it carefully. It was then removed and the child
was simply asked to look at the grey mat and report what
he saw. Thirty of the children then behaved in a most
striking manner. It was as though they were still actually
seeing the picture. Their imaging was unusually vivid and
contained details of the absent picture with an almost
photographic fidelity. This is eidetic imaging, and it differs
from the more usual forms of imaging in a number of respects, the chief of which concern its localization, its intensity,
and its richness of detail.

As regards localization, the eidetic image is seen as
situated in outer space. It is never localized 'within the
head', as the usual memory image so often is, but 'out there',
attached to the mat or a wall or some other surface. It is as
though the child were looking at a picture on this surface
and, indeed, if the surface is folded or bent then the 'picture'
too is likewise folded or bent. However, despite this 'outer'
character of the image, the subject always recognizes that
it is a purely subjective phenomenon, that it is an effect
which he is voluntarily producing, and that it has no outer,
objective existence. As regards vividness, the image is so
clear and strong that it tends to obscure the background
against which it is projected. In this respect again, it is as
though there were a filmy but almost opaque picture on
the projection surface. In always appearing as projected on
a surface in outer space, the eidetic image closely resembles

the negative after-image. However, the two phenomena are by no means identical. For one thing, the negative after-image occurs only after the prolonged fixation of a relatively simple object, whereas the eidetic image occurs after the very different activity of letting the eyes rove hither and thither over an object rich in complex detail. For another thing, the eidetic image differs from both the positive and negative after-image in being more persistent: not only does it last longer, but it can be voluntarily revived some hours, weeks, or even months later. A further difference is that the eidetic image does not, like the negative after-image, vary its size with the distance between the subject and the projection surface: it does not obey Emmert's Law, for, while undergoing some slight change in size with distance, it is roughly constant for positions of the projection surface, at least between 25 and 100 cm. A final difference between the eidetic and the after-image is that, as we shall shortly see, the former is subject to qualitative distortions of a kind which never occur in the latter.

The most striking characteristic of the eidetic image is the wealth of detail it contains. Details are reported from the image such as the number of buttons on the jacket of a passer-by, the length and direction of the lines of shading in a stretch of roadway, and the number of whiskers on a cat's lip. The individual appears to be able to focus upon any detail and make it become gradually clearer so that the rest of the 'picture' becomes obscure. It is this richness of detail which sets the eidetic image apart from the usual memory image, and this difference between the two can be demonstrated directly. When, after the picture is removed, the children are not asked to look at the grey mat but are asked merely to describe the picture, they do this without recourse to eidetic imaging. If they are then asked to turn their eyes to the grey mat, they supplement their account with what they 'see' there. Allport found that, with scarcely a single exception, the eidetic imaging supplied detail lacking in conventional recalling, and it sometimes happened that a child, on the evidence of his eidetic image, would spontaneously correct a misstatement which he had made in his previous account 'from memory'. We may give just one example of the amazing details which may be 'read off' the image. One of the pictures used by Allport depicted a street scene and contained, among other details, the German word *Gartenwirthschaft* written above the door of an inn in the background. This word was quite meaningless for the English children and was not usually reported at first, the subjects starting with descriptions of the more outstanding and dramatic features of the image. But on being pressed to observe more closely, each of the thirty children whose eidetic imaging was strong saw, often to his surprise, the small letters above the door. Three of these children spelled out the word without error, seven got no more than two of the letters wrong, and only five failed to give at least five letters correctly. In all cases, the letters were given with equal accuracy whether 'read off' from left to right or in the reverse order. There was, of course, no question of the word having been memorized. The exposure of thirty-five seconds was insufficient for this, especially since the picture itself was filled with incident and details of lively interest which the child was likewise able to describe from his imaging.

From what has been said, it might well be supposed that eidetic imaging is photographic in its accuracy. Such, however, is not the case. The child cannot see each and every detail of the original, as witness the fact that the majority of Allport's 'eidetic children' were unable to 'read off' every letter in the long German word. Thus, the imaging, although truly remarkable in its detail, is not to be compared with a photographic reproducing of the original. Those parts of the picture which proved most interesting are likely to be seen in the image, while the less interesting parts tend to be either faint or absent altogether. For example, one investigator found that, of a group of children who gave a vivid eidetic image of a picture depicting a monkey, half failed to image an uninteresting picture of an ordinary house. In addition to the tendency to omit uninteresting details, there are also qualitative distortions. The child may change the position or character of some of the details or even add an item entirely lacking in the original. These distortions and added details are also vividly seen in the image and there is nothing to distinguish them as innovations. Such changes are especially frequent when the picture is imaged after a considerable lapse of time. But this is not all. Many pictures portraying action result in an image where the action is carried to completion. On occasion, this movement in the image is voluntarily produced: a carriage is made to drive away, turn a corner in the road, and so disappear altogether from the image; people are made to enter and leave the 'scene' and perform various normal actions. Sometimes this movement may also be produced at the suggestion of the experimenter. In an investigation reported in 1926 by the American psychologist H. Kluver, both voluntary and spontaneous movements appeared in the eidetic images of animal pictures. In imaging a picture containing a donkey standing some distance from a manger, the donkey crossed over to the manger, moved his ears, bent his neck, and began to eat. Suggestions from Kluver to the effect that the donkey was hungry sometimes served to set in motion a series of changes which surprised the imaging subjects themselves. It was as if they were not now looking at a static picture but at a living scene, for, as soon as the suggestion was given, the donkey would 'spontaneously' race over to the manger. It is noteworthy that all these distortions, additions, and movements which occur in eidetic imaging are, like the qualitative changes which occur in recalling generally, in full accordance with the subject's framework of expectations. They are always consistent with the child's normal experiences and he is definitely unable to introduce into his imaging features which are ridiculous or unnatural.

Thus, for all its rich detail, eidetic imaging is neither literally reproductive nor static, and the longer the interval between the original seeing and the imaging, the greater the likelihood of distortion and change. Even in the eidetic image – the nearest approximation which psychology has found to 'photographic memory' – there are additions, omissions, and distortions and, as in recalling generally, the role of selective interests and accumulated past experiences is evident. The same is true of eidetic imaging in adults. Some remarkable examples of this have been recorded but, wherever these have been adequately investigated, it has been found that the imaging is far from being photographic. We may here cite only one investigation, that reported by W. A. Bousfield and H. Barry in the *American Journal of Psychology* in 1933. The subject of their study was Mr Salo Finkelstein, a Polish calculating genius who must be placed among the world's foremost calculators. He was hired by an American broadcasting company to tally returns of the 1932 Presidential election because, it was stated, he was faster than any calculating machine. Shortly after the election, he allowed himself to be experimented upon in various ways by Bousfield and Barry, and the results of these experiments revealed the truly amazing quality of his genius which concerned, first, his extraordinary speed in the mental manipulation of figures and, second, his vivid visual imaging. It is this second characteristic which is of interest here, and we could do no better than quote what Bousfield and Barry have to say concerning it.

In respect to the question of visual imagery, it is evident that the imaginal process is virtually integrated into the processes of memorization and calculation, and without it the involved manipulations of figures would undoubtedly be impossible. The imagery may be said to serve a reference function, since numbers resulting

Photographic Memory

from various calculations and numbers which have acquired significance through associations are chalked down, so to speak, and held in readiness for subsequent reference. The imagery, accordingly, leaves the attention free for subsequent calculations, and there is no necessity for continuous review of the figures in order that retention may take place. Certain of the more prominent features of this imagery for numbers are as follows: (a) The numbers appear as if written with chalk on a freshly washed blackboard. (b) The numbers are in Mr Finkelstein's own handwriting regardless of the form of presentation. (c) Ordinarily the numbers appear to be from 5 to 7 cm. in height. (d) The images normally appear to be at a distance of 35 to 40 cm. from the eyes. (e) The span of imagery includes about six figures with a definite preference for their horizontal arrangement. If, for example, a list of 200 numbers has been memorized, at any one moment any group of about six figures may be made to stand out clearly. (f) When the figures are visualized on a ground at a distance of about $1\frac{1}{2}$ m., they are about 30 per cent smaller and less distinct. Emmert's law of the proportionate variation of the size of the after-image with the distance of the projection ground from the eye seems to be reversed.

Notice that the imaging is, again, not photographic. The numbers always appear in Mr Finkelstein's own handwriting. Furthermore, his ability to image depends on his interest in the material as shown by his imaging letters of the alphabet as being both smaller in size and less distinct than his images of numbers. (His inability to image the colour of numbers originally presented in colour was found to be partly, but not entirely, due to an actual defect in his colour vision.) There are also instances of errors in his imaging. He can voluntarily and accurately image a square of digits, composed of five rows of five digits each, shown to him two hours before. But his imaging is not always accurate, for there are definite indications of retroactive interference, errors occasionally being introduced in the imaging as a result of having memorized a subsequent list. Thus, in all these respects, his imaging departs markedly from a photograph of the original. Nor is his memorizing at the time of original presentation accomplished through the passive ease of clicking any mental camera shutter. It is a process which requires deliberate and fully conscious handling of the figures, and the active relating of them to number sequences and combinations already made familiar by past experiences.

Does there, then, exist anything to correspond with the popular notion of 'photographic memory'? From what has been said, the answer is clearly in the negative. Remarkable though eidetic imaging may be, it in no wise suggests the static, duplicative characteristics of a photograph. It resembles any other instance of recalling in being a constructive process and it manifests the same forms of distortion which have already been seen to be typical of such constructing. Exactly how this re-constructing of the past is achieved is the chief mystery of memory. It is a mystery which psychology has failed to dispel. Perhaps it is a mystery which will never yield up its secrets to the methods of empirical scientific investigation. But the fact that it is a re-constructing rather than a literal reproducing points up a principle which seems to have universal application (a principle which is eloquently elaborated by Sir Frederic Bartlett in his book *Remembering*). Nowhere, in either human or animal activity, do we ever find the individual doing or experiencing exactly the same thing twice. He often does the same sort of thing, but he never literally duplicates any single activity, whether it be a performance or a conscious experience. The steps of a dance, the recital of a poem, the stroke of a tennis match – if these are closely observed there is little difficulty in detecting differences between the 'same' performance as executed today and at some other time. The same is true of recalling it: it never literally reinstates a past experience or activity. And indeed there seems to be no biologically sound reason why it should. The constantly changing world around us demands that we interact with it in an ever-changing way, and to react to the events of today strictly in terms of the performances and experiences of yesterday would be inappropriate. The utility of memory for living lies not in facilitating the operation of the past as it operated before, but rather in facilitating the operation of the past in relation to the somewhat changed conditions of the present. Memory seems to have been evolved to deal only incidentally with those rare situations where we are required to give a flawlessly accurate account of the past. Its primary function is not to conserve the past but to make possible adjustment to the requirements of the present.

Before leaving eidetic imaging, one last characteristic of it deserves mention, namely, its decline with age. It is found that the proportion of people showing eidetic imaging decreases sharply after the age of about eleven years – an age, incidentally, which marks a critical turning-point in the intellectual life of the individual, for it is at this age, on the average, that what we call 'logical' thinking finally emerges. The reason for this decline is not clearly understood, but a large contributing factor seems to be that, with the development of logical thinking, the eidetic image ceases to serve any very useful function for the majority of people. The function of eidetic imaging for the young child has been well expressed by Allport in his 1924 article as follows.

The eidetic image seems to serve essentially the same purpose in the mental development of the child as does the repetition of a stimulus situation. It permits the concrete 'sensory' aspects of the surrounding world to penetrate thoroughly into his mind. The young child delights in conjuring up his images: a parade of soldiers, a circus, a train journey, or even a trivial domestic scene may haunt him for days or weeks, furnishing him material of great interest for his play activities. It is sometimes only with difficulty that he is persuaded to distrust the reality of these vivid images. He reacts to them with the same degree of seriousness as to a genuine stimulus situation: he is terrified by his image of a wild animal; he is contented for hours with the companionship of his imaginary playmate; and he insists dogmatically upon the reality of his most fanciful visions. Such pseudo-sensory experience enables him to 'study out' in his own way and in his own time the various possibilities for response contained within the stimulus situation. His reaction when the situation is first presented is often incomplete, the presence of adults, or the lack of time, preventing him from becoming thoroughly acquainted with its properties. A period of reflection is necessary, during which he may experiment in various ways with his image, varying his behaviour to conform sometimes to one and sometimes to another aspect of the situation, gradually gaining a comprehension of the full meaning of the whole, and building up the attitude which is to determine his future response to the same or to analagous situations.

When he has reached adolescence, the individual's adjustments to the concrete aspects of his environment are reasonably well established, and he now turns from the conquest of the tangible world to the conquest of abstract thinking and personal emotional experiences. In this conquest and in the changing behaviour organization which emerges from it, there is little need for imaging of the eidetic sort. Individuals for whom imaging continues to be especially useful appear to be those who pursue literary or artistic vocations or who are required to manipulate, on a practical level, complex spatial relationships as in architecture or in surgery. But even in these individuals, eidetic imaging would be clearly anomalous. Its function is performed only in the earlier years of mental development, and eidetic imaging must now be kept strictly in check if it is not to become a serious liability.

4 Synaesthesia

'Synaesthesia' literally means 'experiencing together', and it is an activity which is much more familiar to some people than to others. The word is used to refer to imaging which follows closely and automatically on sensory stimulation, and is typically very different in nature from the sensory stimulation. For example, some people react to sounds by visual imaging or by tactile or kinaesthetic imaging; for them, music may be a vivid visual or tactile experience. The forms taken by such synaesthetic imaging are highly characteristic for the individual person but vary from one person to the next. A readable survey of synaesthesia and other issues about imaging is given by the book, *Imagination and Thinking* by Dr Peter McKellar (Cohen and West, 1957). Here, we shall consider the synaesthetic imaging of only one highly exceptional man who happens also to be an astonishingly able memorizer. These considerations will illustrate the general nature of synaesthesia and the role which imaging plays in the functioning of one individual. The man in question, S. V. Shereshevskii, was studied over a period of years by A. R. Luria, the distinguished Soviet psychologist, who reported the case in 1960. (An English translation of this report is an article 'Memory and the structure of mental processes' by A. R. Luria, in *Problems of Psychology*, No. 1, Pergamon Press, 1960. It is from this article that the quotations given below are taken.)

In 1926, Shereshevskii was a reporter for a Moscow newspaper. One day his editor gave him several verbal messages to deliver to other people and noticed that, although nothing was written down, the reporter repeated word for word all the messages he was given. Shereshevskii himself saw nothing unusual about this memorizing feat. So the editor sent him to see Luria who, he knew, would be interested in such unusual capabilities. Luria and his colleagues gave Shereshevskii a variety of material to memorize, and there seemed no limit to the amount he could commit to memory. He memorized lists of a hundred and more digits, lists of words, nonsense syllables, words in an unknown language, lists of geometrical figures, lengthy formulae, musical motifs. If given an item chosen at random from a memorized list, he could readily say which other item came before it and after it in the sequence. He could repeat a sequence of items either in the given order or in reverse. Furthermore, he could still recall these lists years later. Luria reports as follows:

Having carried out a great number of experiments with Shereshevskii and recorded them, I suggested to him after 10, 15, and 20 years that he should try to recall certain series of words, lists of figures and formulae. Shereshevskii's behaviour was always the same. He closed his eyes, raised his finger, slowly wagged it around and said: 'Wait ... when you were dressed in a grey suit ... I was sitting opposite you in a chair ... that's it!' – and then and there quite rapidly he reproduced without hesitation the information which had been given to him many years before. The observer got the impression that Shereshevskii was rather 'reading through' the material than 'reproducing' it (for he acted as though the list was present in front of him), and that here there was no more cause for amazement than in the case when a man reads a book lying in front of him without any difficulties as to the number of words to be read and when he is able to read through the same text with equal facility many years later.

Such memory abilities were remarkable enough. But his ways of dealing with the material were more remarkable still. He dealt with the material in terms of vivid imaging. When a digit sequence was dictated to him, he would visualize the digits written down on a blackboard or on paper, mostly in his own legible handwriting: these imaged digits were usually arranged in tabular array, in short lines of four or six figures. When a word sequence was given, he would visually image corresponding shapes and arrange them in a long row so as not to disturb their sequence. He usually did this by taking an imaginary walk, starting from Pushkin Square and going down Gorky Street. As he went along, he 'placed' the corresponding shapes at points along the route. To recall the sequence, he repeated his imaginary walk and read off the patterns he had positioned along the way. In short, he would often translate the material, item by item, into imaged patterns and fix the sequence of these patterns by locating them against the unfolding background of an imaginary imaged route. For the most part, this procedure was highly successful but, on occasion, it would lead to errors and omissions. 'Sometimes in his imagination he "positioned" the object in such a way that it blended with the background (for example, a white "egg" on the background of a white wall) or it was not sufficiently illuminated ("You see" – said Shereshevskii – "it was badly lit by the street lamp and I didn't notice it"), or else it proved to be too small, and then Shereshevskii, in reproducing the series, omitted the corresponding words.'

Here is a further illustration of the kind of memorizing procedure used. In essence, it involves thematic imaging, that is, making up an imaged story whose essential features characterize the successive items being memorized.

Shereshevskii was given a meaningless formula of which we only quote a part:

$$N \cdot \sqrt{d^2 \cdot x \frac{85}{vx}} \cdot \sqrt{\frac{276^2 \cdot 86x}{n^2v \cdot \pi 264}} \cdot n^2b, \text{ etc.}$$

The formula was given in a written form. Shereshevskii looked at it several times, peering closely at the pad with the formula and then lowering it. The memorizing lasted 5–7 minutes. The explanation of the technique of memorizing the formula was given a half-hour later.

'Neiman (N) came out and poked with his stick (.). He looked at a dried-up tree which reminded him of a root ($\sqrt{}$) and he thought: it is no wonder that this tree withered and its roots were laid bare, seeing that it was already standing when I built these houses, these two here (d^2) and again he poked with his stick (.). He said: "The houses are old, a cross (x) should be placed on them." This gives a great return on his original capital, he invested 85 thousand roubles in building them. The roof finishes off the building (–), and down below a man is standing and playing a harmonica (vx). He is standing near the post office and at the corner is a large stone (.) to stop carts bashing the corner of the house. Here is a square, there's a big tree, on it three jackdaws (^{3}). Here I simply put 276, but "in a square", I placed a square cigarette box; on it was written 86. You see, 86 was written on the back of the box, I couldn't see it from the side, and the first time I did not notice it and did not say, did not come near enough to it. x – the unknown man – approached the fence (–), further on there's a girls' school; he wanted to get a date with one of the students; n – a fine young man in a grey suit; he converses, he attempts to break down the poles of the fence first with one foot, then with the other (^{2}), but she is an ugly student, fi! (v) ... Here I travel in my thoughts to Rezhitsa, to the school there ... I see a large blackboard, a piece of chalk is lying there – and I put a dot (.). On the board is written $\pi 264$, then I write (n^2b) after it." etc., etc.

It is interesting that both the first reproduction immediately after memorizing and the second carried out after 15 years were given rapidly without any effort and in a completely identical form.

Schereshevskii's use of imaging was strongly enriched and facilitated by an elaborate system of spontaneous syn-aesthetic imaging. For him, sounds had colour and taste and tactile qualities. Visual forms were experienced as emitting characteristic sounds and as having taste. Music and voices were experienced in terms of twisting lines. The sound a was always white and looked like a flat surface or line: the sound *i* receded into the distance, rather like a spike: the sound *e* looked like a curved convex line. Such synaesthetic imaging was, with him, a spontaneous feature of his everyday experiencing which pervaded his subjective world and clothed his surroundings with strangely unique qualities.

Here he approaches the ice cream seller. 'What would you like – cream or chocolate?' she asks in a sort of dirty voice. And all at once 'it's as if splinters of black coal spread through the ice cream. Can such ice cream exist?!' Or a sudden loud ringing at the door 'and the ringing rolled over and over and my fingers felt something cold and there was a salty taste in my mouth ...' Or lunch in a restaurant, the taste of which varies with the music ('probably they're playing specially to improve the taste'), and then quite suddenly noises on the roof where they are repairing the roofing – 'and, all at once the lunch tasted horrible, completely spoiled ...'

This vivid, elaborate, and spontaneous synaesthesia saturated his everyday experiencing with qualities which would often lead to confusion. For example, his hearing of words was influenced not only by the meaning of the word but also by the synaesthetic qualities it elicited for him. The word 'pig' (*svin'ia*) sounded musical, delicate, elegant, and quite at odds with his visual imaging of the animal. His hearing of words was also affected strongly by the vocal qualities of its utterance. The same word would be experienced very differently if spoken by different voices, and this sometimes made it difficult to recognize the word being spoken. In short, the particulars of the momentary situation elicited constellations of synaesthetic imaging which could obscure what might be regarded as the essential characteristic of the moment, i.e. the meaning of the word. Likewise, he sometimes failed to recognize people because some change in their dress, or manner, or expression would elicit vivid imaging so different from that which he had experienced previously when in the person's presence. The

vivid qualities of his synaesthetic imaging exaggerated these
variable and incidental features of situations which most of
us learn to ignore so effectively. And this often made it
difficult for him to generalize his experiences from one
situation to another, and to deal effectively with problems
of an abstract kind. It seems always to be the case that any
highly developed form of mental specialization impedes the
execution of some activities while, at the same time,
facilitating the execution of others. With Shereshevskii, his
imaging, both conventional and synaesthetic, impeded the
carrying through of activities which give no trouble to most
people. It also facilitated his carrying through memory
tasks which are well beyond the capacities of almost everyone else. Presented material was translated effortlessly into
a succession of vivid and particular imaged experiences and,
later, these imaged experiences were reinstated and translated back to recreate the original material.

However, synaesthesia, having thus helped an accurate reproduction, could in certain circumstances hinder it. If, during the
reading of a series of words or figures, somebody began to cough,
spots appeared in the inner 'visual field' of Shereshevskii which
could shade the shapes and disturb their readability. In the process
of remembering by Shereshevskii it was possible to trace more
clearly than in any other process the role of these 'sounds' which
hindered the production and retention of the shapes. An objective
examination showed that in many cases gaps in the reproduction of
a series were in fact connected with such 'sounds'.

Synaesthesia could appear not only as an external factor
impeding the act of remembering. Sometimes it hampered remembering by virtue of inner causes. One day Shereshevskii did not
remember at once the word 'putamen' a word which had no
meaning for him. 'It is so dark,' he said later. 'I located it on the
wall; it radiated such darkness around itself that I had to take a
lamp in my hand in order to look at it properly.' He often com-
plained of the apparently paradoxical fact that he was bad at
remembering faces: 'There is so much variable and complex in
them: take a man that smiled – he is in a different frame of mind,

and everything has dissolved and altered and I get confused and don't know on what to direct my attention ...' For the same reason we had no success in the attempt to employ Shereshevskii as a dispatcher who had to remember the complex system of traffic on railway lines. 'I remember them badly,' he said. 'I am accustomed to remembering everything not as they actually are but in a modified form. ... I don't mean that the lines don't resound and sing for me – it's just that as soon as I have turned away their voice is different.'

He lived in a complex and changeable world of synaesthesia and this both strengthened and weakened his memory.

One further aspect of Shereshevskii's case should be mentioned because it illustrates a general feature of memory activities; namely: these activities alter to meet the habitual demands made on them. He became a professional performer who undertook public memorizing performances. His audience would give him material of all kinds to memorize, and he would do so. In the course of his career as a performer, he gradually altered his memorizing activities so as to deal both more effectively and more economically with the kinds of task given to him. In part these changes took the form of progressively simplifying his imaging. He simplified the imaged shapes which represented items presented to him, and he simplified the imaged connexions between these shapes.

Previously it used to take me a long time to remember: someone would say 'Kremlin', I saw it, and then 'New York' and I would stretch a rope between Moscow and New York. But now I simply put Uncle Sam on the wall of the Kremlin and I know that it is 'New York'. Formerly when somebody said 'restaurant', I saw the whole picture of the restaurant: its entrance, the people and the orchestra, but now I only see something like the entrance and sometimes something just flashes and I know straight away that it is the 'restaurant'.

In part, these changes in his memory activities took the form of developing new techniques for splitting up and comprehending unfamiliar words in terms of familiar imaged experiences. He could memorize verbatim a poem in an unknown language by translating successive sounds into vivid trains of imaging.

In Shereshevskii, we see an unusual and strongly developed system of functioning in which the predominance of imaging has both advantages and disadvantages. We do not know how or why this unique functional system, this 'mind', developed, but its chief advantage is clear. It enabled him to translate presented material, of whatever kind, into coherent successions of imaged experience. In other words, it enabled him to make the material uniquely meaningful, not in any conventional or logical sense, but in relation to his own individualistic modes of functioning. He was able to retain these 'meaningful' trains of imaging, and thereby recreate the material afresh even years afterwards.

5 The Particularity of Imaging

The case of Shereshevskii illustrates that vivid imaging shares with sensory experience the quality of being particular. That is, imaging concerns specific, concrete details of a relatively non-abstract and non-generalizable kind. For example, a person can clearly image events with distinctive sensory qualities, say, a discrete object or a set of simple spatial relationships. But it is not easy to image clearly a complex set of abstracted, higher-order characteristics such as an argument-form in symbolic logic, or the relationships which mathematicians describe as occupying four-dimensional space. The important characteristics of abstract, generalizable relationships are not sensory in nature, and imaging hardly serves to represent them. Indeed, it is only by ignoring the sensory qualities of events that broadly generalizable relationships can be abstracted from them. It is only a slight over-simplification to say that imaging is useful in dealing with particulars, but not with generalities.

In the case of Shereshevskii, it was seen that the pervasiveness of his imaging impeded his working with abstract relationships but, at the same time, facilitated his memorizing sequences of items with detailed precision. Now, it is no accident that extensive use of imaging is made by men who specialize in memorizing large amounts of relatively meaningless material. These men may be called mnemonists, and their procedures enable them to memorize, at a single presentation, long sequences of words, names, numbers. The performance of a skilled mnemonist is impressive to watch, and many of these men make their livelihood by giving public demonstrations. They owe their success to the development of mnemonic systems, that is, elaborately contrived and practised procedures for memorizing and recalling. And so far as the writer is aware, all accomplished mnemonists use imaging as a central part of their procedures. Whenever a mnemonist talks or writes about his skill, he begins to speak of the importance of imaging. Mnemonic systems will be considered in Chapter Seven; but here we may stress and exemplify the procedures of translating presented material into distinctive imaging and relating successive images unambiguously to each other.

Imaging and Mnemonic Systems. Consider an example of what may be called the Successive-comparison System. This is probably the simplest and least flexible of mnemonic systems, but is one with which all mnemonists seem to be familiar. A sequence of unrelated words is presented and is to be memorized in sequence. SUGAR, DAFFODIL, BOAT, TIGER, NECKLACE, etc. The procedure is as follows. When the first word is heard, visualize sugar as vividly as possible. When the second word is heard, visualize daffodil. Then relate the imaged sugar and the imaged daffodil into one composite image which is as vivid, striking and fantastic as possible. For example, image a really gigantic daffodil, far more than life size, growing out of a mountain of granulated sugar, sucking up the sugar with relish, its trumpet and petals glittering with sugar crystals. This ridiculous, briefly imaged scene deals with the first and second words of the sequence. Now dismiss it from mind and deal similarly with the second and third words. Image daffodil and boat in fantastic conjunction. For example, a boat garlanded with bright yellow daffodils, filled with millions of daffodils, weighted down, groaning, and almost submerged by daffodils. Then dismiss this, and contrive a vivid composite imaging of boat and tiger. In short, the procedure is to deal with only two incoming words at any one time; relate these two words together by translating each into detailed imaging and combining the images together into a composite image which is detailed, far-fetched, exaggerated, and distinctive; when this composite image is achieved, dismiss it from mind and make no subsequent attempt to recall it. When time comes for recalling the sequence of words, the mnemonist must recall the first item of the sequence. He images this, sugar, and finds himself imaging the sugar-daffodil composite. This gives him the second item, daffodil, which prompts recall of the daffodil-boat composite, and so on. The brief but vividly detailed imaging of each fantastic composite suffices to lead him from each word to the next in succession.

Several features of the above procedure are worth noting.

(1) The memorizing task is broken down into a succession of sub-tasks. This succession is of such a kind that, at each moment, the mnemonist knows in outline what he must do next. He does not have to waste time and effort in thinking out his general procedure, since this has been pre-determined at the outset.

(2) Each sub-task is relatively undemanding and is carried through in isolation from every other sub-task.

This means that the mnemonist does not have too much to do at any one time. All he need do is translate each of two presented words into an imaged equivalent, and combine these imagings into a distinctive composite. He is free to create this imaging in whatever detailed way he finds easiest. The more exaggerated and fantastic this composite imaging is, the more distinctive it will be, that is, the less likely he is to confuse it subsequently with any other composite which happens to embody one of the same component items. Confusion between successive composite images is also minimized by creating each composite in isolation from every other. Since he deals with only one composite at a time, he is not likely to relate together, say, sugar and tiger. It is clear that part of the technique which the mnemonist must master is rapidly to create distinctive composite imaging, and resolutely to dismiss from mind any composite on which he is not working at the moment. Ability to keep items out of mind is as important as ability to keep items in mind.

(3) Recalling, like memorizing, is broken down into a succession of pre-determined sub-tasks. And again, each sub-task is relatively undemanding. Each sub-task involves simple redintegrative activity: he recalls an imaged item, thence the composite of which this item has been made a component, thence the next item in the sequence. Notice that, by this procedure, it is as easy for the mnemonist to recall the sequence in reverse order as in the presented order. Notice too that he can recall the sequence, either forwards or backwards, by starting at any given item in the sequence. He can begin his recital as easily from the middle of the sequence as from either end. And of course, it is very easy for him to say which words come on either side of any par-ticular word named. His procedure, then, gives him a very complete and flexible mastery of the sequential relations among words presented. What it does not do is enable him rapidly to recall the exact position of any word in the list.

Imaging

For example, if he is asked to name the tenth word in the list, he cannot do this without recalling the entire sequence and counting off the items until he reaches the tenth. If he is to be able to recall the tenth item directly, he must use another, and more elaborate procedure of the visual-symbol variety. This other mnemonic system will be discussed in Chapter Seven: it makes even more insistent demands on the use of imaging.

The above memorizing task lays emphasis on ability to deal with particular items and to bring these items together in the simple relationship of contiguity. For such a task, the particularity of imaging seems, both in theory and in practice, to provide the memorizer with the most appropriate kind of activity for mastery.

VI Forgetting

The basic questions about forgetting concern what a person remembers at two different times. At one time, he can remember something easily and accurately; but at some later time, he is less able to remember this same thing. For example, he could once recite a certain poem fluently, but now he can only recite fragments of it. Once he could recognize a piece of music, now he fails to do so. Once he could play chess skilfully, now his play is 'rusty'. Once he could recollect a boyhood experience, now he recollects it only vaguely and inaccurately. Once he could recall a certain name, now he can recall it only with great effort. Such differences between two remembering occasions are typical of what is called forgetting. In brief, to say that a person has forgotten something is to say that he is now less able than he once was to remember it. And to ask why we forget is to ask why we are less able than we once were to remember some particular matter. Between the earlier remembering occasion and the later one, something has changed so as to influence our remembering. What are these circumstances which have changed? This is a large question, for many circumstances influence the carrying out of such a complex activity as remembering. Some of these circumstances which cause forgetting derive from alterations in what the person retains from his past. His ongoing experiences and activities modify these cumulative effects of past experience which he carries into the present from an ever-lengthening past. What was retained at one time may no longer be retained and so cannot now be remembered.

Forgetting

Other circumstances which cause forgetting are of a more temporary kind. They derive from the momentary circumstances under which remembering takes place, that is, the context of remembering. Some contexts favour the remembering of a particular event, while other contexts do not. And so forgetting of a temporary kind can occur depending on the circumstances of the moment. Let us start by considering the effects of the context of remembering.

1 The Context of Remembering

The word 'forgetting' often refers to those instances when we fail to remember some particular event at the time we should have liked to remember it. For example, a student writes an answer in an examination and, afterwards, he realizes that he forgot to mention some important point. He is still able to recall this point but he did not bring it to mind at just that moment when it was required. In everyday life, this kind of temporary forgetting often takes the form of failure to carry out some intended activity. We had meant to buy a newspaper on the way home, but forgot to do so. We took a letter with us to post and, later, find it still in our pocket. We are going to meet someone and intend to ask him about a certain matter but, at the actual meeting, we forget to do so. In such cases, we are still able to recall the particular matter – given appropriate circumstances – but somehow the circumstances are not appropriate just when they ought to be. The intended activity is 'driven from our mind' by preoccupation with other matters. In short, the appropriate moment passes without anything happening to prompt our recalling of the intended activity.

Prompts to Remembering. These familiar instances of 'absent-mindedness' illustrate the fact that remembering is an activity which does not arise, so to say, out of the blue. Remembering arises out of a context of circumstances and is, by and large, selectively relevant to the demands of this context. For example, we are often aware that our recalling is prompted by an event in our present environment, and that certain events (a seen object, a perfume, a name) are especially likely to evoke certain 'memories'. Indeed, some people deliberately supply themselves with mementoes and keepsakes whose function is to prompt the recalling of certain events. For the same reason, the medieval clergy built their *memento mori*: these effigies of decomposing bodies are still to be seen in many cathedrals, and their purpose was to prompt their owners to recall the fact of their own mortality. Again, we are often aware that our recalling arises out of the context of our private thinking activities. We must all have experienced those associated sequences of ideas which lead us from one recalled event to another until, at length, we are recalling events that seem quite unrelated to our starting point. In the course of a rambling conversation, we may sometimes ask our companion, 'What made you remember that?' And he may narrate a chain of thinking which led him, through successive promptings, to the finally recalled event.

So, the recalling of any particular event arises out of a context, either perceived or thought: some contexts are appropriate for recalling certain events while other contexts are appropriate for recalling other events. In other words, the remembering of any particular event may be facilitated or impeded by the context in which the remembering activity takes place. This general point is fundamentally important for our considerations of memory. It also suggests a practical step which anyone might take to minimize those instances of 'absent-mindedness' mentioned above. The procedure is this. When we intend to recall some particular event on some particular future occasion, we should anticipate the detailed circumstances of this occasion and mentally relate the intended activity to these imagined circumstances. Later, when the circumstances arise in actuality, they are likely to prompt us to recall the intended activity. Exactly how this procedure is carried out in practice will depend on the circumstances and on the person's ingenuity. But in general terms, the essence of the procedure was expressed by James Mill (1773–1836) as follows.

It frequently happens that there are matters which we desire not to forget. What is the contrivance to which we have recourse for preserving the memory – that is, for making sure that it will be called into existence when it is our wish that it should? All men invariably employ the same expedient. They endeavour to form an association between the idea of the thing to be remembered and some sensation, or some idea, which they know beforehand will occur at or near the time when they wish the remembrance to be in their minds. If this association is formed and the association or idea with which it has been formed occurs, the sensation, or idea, calls up the remembrance, and the object of him who formed the association is attained. To use a vulgar instance: a man receives a commission from his friend, and, that he may not forget it, ties a knot in his handkerchief. How is this fact to be explained? First of all, the idea of the commission is associated with the making of the knot. Next, the handkerchief is a thing which it is known beforehand will be frequently seen and of course at no great distance of time from the occasion on which the memory is desired. The handkerchief being seen, the knot is seen, and this sensation recalls the idea of the commission, between which and itself the association had been purposely formed.

The 'vulgar instance' of the knotted handkerchief has its more sophisticated counterpart in the keeping of an appointments diary. What is to be recalled at some future time is noted in the diary under the entry for that time. When that time arrives (and if the person consults his diary at that time!) the note provides a highly specific prompt for recalling the relevant event.

Environmental Prompts. The importance of environmental prompts to remembering is well known to the amateur actor, to people with a fondness for guessing games, and to teachers. Every teacher knows the value for instruction of arranging such prompts appropriately. A common and effective procedure in guiding a pupil's learning is progressively to reduce the amount of prompting given. For example, when a young child is being taught to write, he may start by being given letters to trace over. Then the letters presented are made progressively more fragmentary until, at length, the child is able to draw the letter on a blank sheet of paper. This procedure of using diminishing prompts is sometimes called the vanishing-technique: it is one aspect of the more general procedure known as training through successive approximations, that is, we start by getting the learner to do what he can already accomplish, and we gradually induce him to extend and modify this accomplishment so that it approximates more and more closely to that new accomplishment which we want him to master. In all this, an important part is played by the giving and witholding of environmental prompts.

However, environmental prompts to recalling may arise incidentally rather than on purpose. The true story is told of the man who lived for several years in China and, by persistent application, managed to learn to speak Chinese. Then he left the Orient and came home for two years. At the end of this time, he had to return to China and, just before setting off, he discovered that he had all but completely forgotten his laboriously acquired Chinese. He naturally expected to have to learn much of it over again. Yet, on arrival, he was surprised to find that, in the Chinese setting once more, he could understand the language perfectly and speak it fairly fluently. He could remember in China what he could not remember at home. Here we have an example of temporary forgetting which is due to altered conditions in the environment. Learning takes place in a concrete setting; it involves a specific task which is carried out in a specific environment such as a particular schoolroom or town. And, although we may not be aware of it, this specific environment becomes a part of what is learned. In general it is true to say that if this environment is greatly altered during the time of attempted remembering then remembering will be impaired. We must all have experienced this phenomenon. We try to recollect what we did in some distant town and fail. Yet, on revisiting the original scene, 'it all comes back to us'. Many instances of this sort of thing have been reported in autobiographies, and psychologists have shown that it can be produced experimentally. When nonsense syllables are presented for learning against a coloured background, it requires more time to re-learn them when presented against a different colour of ground than when the colour remains unchanged. Likewise, the introduction of a small audience produces some forgetting, as will be readily understood by anyone who has experienced 'stage fright'. When the classroom learning of school children is later examined in a different room, the amount recalled is smaller than when the exam takes place in the room where learning originally took place. Having a strange teacher in charge of the exam likewise impairs recall, and this impairment is even greater if both the room and the teacher are changed for the exam.

It should be noticed that, strictly speaking, environmental prompts do not act directly to elicit recall. They act indirectly by influencing the ongoing patterns of activity being carried through by the person at the moment: it is these modified patterns of activity which dispose the person to go on to remember this or that. In Chapter One, reference was made to the matter of preparedness for recognizing. Here we will consider preparedness for recalling.

Preparedness for Recalling. The preparedness of the person for recalling is an important circumstance which influences what and how well he recalls. It is obvious that if the person is in poor general condition, this will affect his recalling activities. For example, a person who is still recovering from concussion is unable to recall many past events, and much of what he does recall is inaccurate; and again, a person who is under the influence of drugs may show marked inability to recall events, especially of a complex kind. Here, however, we will be concerned with states of preparedness which owe nothing to abnormal circumstances. And we may begin our considerations of these states by reference to a kind of task called Continuous Controlled Recalling. In this task, a person is required to recall as many events as he can, all of which have some given characteristic in common. Consider the case where a person is asked to recall personal names (surnames and first-names) which all begin with the letter N. Suppose we ask people to write down as many N-names as they can. What happens? In general terms, people recall names rapidly at first, and then more and more slowly. This progressive slowing down in rate of recall is illustrated in Table 6. The data comes from an experiment done by the writer with a total of 220 university students. Their task was to recall as many N-names as they could in eight minutes. The top row of data show the average number of names produced by each student in each successive minute. The remainder of the table illustrates that some students are

Table 6

Successive One-minute Periods	1	2	3	4	5	6	7	8	Total
All students (N=220)	8·7	3·7	3·0	2·5	2·5	2·1	1·9	1·7	26·3
Top-scorers (N=68)	10·8	4·9	4·3	3·4	3·3	3·1	2·5	2·5	34·8
Low-scorers (N = 61)	6·7	2·5	2·2	1·5	1·8	1·3	1·2	1·1	18·3

much better at this kind of task than others. The 'high scorers' are those sixty-eight students who produce a total of 30 or more names in the eight minutes: the 'low scorers' are those sixty-one students who produce a total of 21 or fewer names in the same time. It can be seen that, on average the 'high scorers' consistently recall names at a faster rate than the 'low scorers'.

When we turn from average results to the performance of an individual student, we find that his rate of recalling is irregular. His recalling is marked by rushes of names and by pauses. Furthermore, the names which he recalls in a rush are often conspicuously similar to each other. If we analyse his performance in various ways and supplement these analyses by his introspective comments, we arrive at the following general description of his recalling.

From the outset, his recalling activities are highly selective and closely relevant to the overall task of recalling only N-names. For example, he does not proceed by recalling just anything and everything he is able to recall and, then, select from this confusion those items which meet the requirements of the task in hand. Rather, he is prepared from the start to recall only relevant or near-relevant names. His activities are dominated by the characteristic of the initial letter; and many students report that names other than N-names do not even 'cross their mind'. In short, the overall preparedness is to recall only N-names; the person adheres to this dominant characteristic that each name must begin with the letter N. He must, of course, supplement this characteristic by others in order to produce names. And he does this be moving among a shifting set of narrower predispositions. Typically, he starts by producing a short rush of N-names which are readily familiar to him, which are, so to speak, on the tip of his tongue. Then he recalls a rush of names, all of a kind; say, boys' names. Then he shifts to a run of, say, girls' names, then perhaps names of novelists, then names all starting with the same syllable, or having the same ending. In other words, his recalling is governed by associations of ideas, by the shifting introduction of supplementary characteristics which enable him to construct relevant names. The dominance of some cluster of characteristics serves as a context within which to construct several names, then this theme 'dries up' and he shifts to another. Even after he feels himself incapable of recalling any further names, he may suddenly 'happen upon' a new and productive cluster of characteristics which enables him to recall a rush of new names. These shifting states of preparedness provide the person with a succession of contexts favouring the recall of this or that kind of name.

Repeated Recall Attempts. When the same person is asked to recall N-names on two different occasions, he does not recall the names in the same order, nor does he even recall the same names. On the second occasion, he recalls many names which he recalled on the first occasion: he also recalls some names not recalled previously: and he does not recall some of the names recalled on the first occasion. On both occasions, the overall requirements of the task are the same: the dominant characteristic is unchanged. But the narrower predispositions are not the same: the supplementary characteristics are different. And so, his recalled list of names differs from one occasion to the next. Now, suppose he makes repeated attempts to recall as many N-names as he can in, say, a five minute period. His list of names tends to lengthen on each attempt. One reason for this is fairly obvious. On his first attempt, he recalls so many names. If his next attempt comes not too long afterwards, he can rapidly recall many of the names from his first list, and, because of his dependence on shifting themes, add some new names to these. On his third attempt, he recalls names from his two previous attempts, and adds yet more. After several such attempts, he can recall, in the time allowed, many more names than he could on his first attempt. In short, repeated attempts at recalling N-names result in his being able to recall more names than he could recall to start with.

This facilitating effect of repeated attempts at recalling is also found under other conditions. For example, there have been studies in which people are asked to recall some poem or speech which they could once quote readily but which, in the meantime, they have almost completely forgotten. At first, they typically recall little except the general atmosphere of the original and perhaps one or two isolated phrases. A few more words may then be recalled and, by the end of some twenty minutes, the person is confident that he can recall no more. But if he is asked to recall on the next day and again on the next, for several days running, it is found that this confession of failure was premature. More and still more of the original is recalled. Sometimes the new words 'just happen' while attempted recall is in progress. Sometimes, new words 'come out of the blue' at a time when the person is relaxing and apparently not thinking about the original at all. At other times, some word which he happens to see or hear during his everyday activities seems to 'stick'; he finds himself thinking about it, and later makes the sudden discovery that it supplies a missing part of the original. In general, we find in such studies that, while people rarely succeed in recalling the entire poem, they can eventually recall at least twice as much of it as they did at that earlier point when they claimed they could recall no more.

The facilitating effects of repeatedly attempted recall are also experienced by people who, for one reason or another, dwell on past events. The person who undertakes to write autobiographical reminiscences, finds that he can gradually recollect more of his early life than he imagined possible. So too with people who meet an acquaintance of long ago and 'go over old times' together. And so too with many elderly people, if they come to dwell on the past. The elderly person may have the leisure to enjoy recalling long-past events and recollecting old times. He may also have the incentive for such recalling. By recounting a bygone era, he may command respect, awe, and interest from younger listeners: or he may compensate for lack of present achievements or, indeed, for impaired ability to keep abreast of current events.

Incidentally, in considering the case of elderly people and their recalling of past events, we should bear in mind an additional consideration. If there is, in the elderly person, an impairment of central nervous functioning, this favours recall of earlier as opposed to more recent events. With progressive impairment of a general neurological kind, recalling activities undergo retrogressive disorganization. That is, recall of recent events is impaired first, then recall of events from the progressively more distant and more long-standing past. This is true whether the person who suffers such deterioration is young or old. In senility, the person typically 'lives in the past'. Current events are forgotten as soon as they have passed, while early events are still recalled. Relatives who have been dead for years are spoken of as though they were still alive and might come in at any moment. This retrogressive tendency is tersely exemplified in the case of the old lady who, in talking about the village where she spent her girlhood, said she could remember it as clearly as if she had seen it yesterday. In fact, she had been taken to visit the village the day before. But this event was now quite forgotten.

As regards repeated attempts at recalling some particular kind of past event, these attempts may lead to fuller recall than was at first thought possible. This is true whether the event is a poem or a personal experience, whether the person is young or elderly. In all this, there is, of course, the danger that the hard-won recall could be illusory. That is, the person may succeed in achieving a fabricated, rather than a faithful, characterization of the event. When the veracity of what is recalled cannot be checked, this possibility of false recall must be borne in mind.

One reason was mentioned above for the facilitating effects of repeated attempts at recall, i.e. on each attempt the person recalls a few more items and adds them progressively to those already recalled in, and remembered from, previous attempts. However, the effects of repeated recall are not quite so simple as this. There are at least two other processes at work. One of these derives from a persisting preparedness for recall, even after the recall attempt is seemingly relinquished. The other is the warming-up effect.

Persisting Preparedness. Suppose a student has been attempting to recall N-names, and is now no longer dealing with this task but with other matters. He may nevertheless continue to be prepared for recalling N-names. Sometimes he is aware that he has not entirely relinquished the task; it remains 'at the back of his mind'. Sometimes, he believes he has completely relinquished the task: and yet, if an N-name should be heard, it 'leaps out' at him as being relevant to the seemingly relinquished task. In other words, he is still alert to recognize the relevance of incidental happenings to the task which is now over. The persistence of such a selective sensitivity to certain kinds of event is often deliberately used by people who have to prepare lectures, speeches, or articles. Many people, in talking about their thinking techniques, report the habitual use of the following procedure. They work on the general theme of their topic and collect what relevant material they can. Then they lay the task aside for some hours or days in that semi-conscious way which leaves them selectively sensitive to any chance happenings which might be relevant to the task. In this way, they find that incidental events, either perceived or thought, are readily recognized as being of the kind required. Such persisting states of preparedness for recalling and recognizing certain kinds of event are known to play an important role in problem-solving activities.

The Warming-up Effect. While a person is immersed in one topic, it may be difficult for him to recall events concerning unrelated topics. For example, if we are immersed in matters concerning chemistry and are suddenly asked a question concerning educational practices in seventeenth-century Germany, we often find that we cannot readily recall the answer (assuming that we know it). It takes time to disengage ourselves from one topic and think ourselves into the other; time to get our bearings, that is, to establish for ourselves a context of activities which enables us to accomplish the required recalling. This familiar experience exemplifies the warming-up effect. When people undertake almost any task, they start 'cold', they require time to 'get into the swing' of the task, to 'pick up the threads'; and the more complex and unaccustomed the task, the more this is so. The need for warming-up is experienced by the typist who returns to the task of typing; by the musician who returns to playing his instrument; by the administrator who returns to his work; by the student who returns to studying some topic. The need for warming-up is typical of the execution of all complex activities. And it is also typical of much remembering. For the most part, warming-up to recalling takes place while the person is actually attempting to recall the particular events required. He 'gathers himself together', establishing more and more of the characteristics which will, eventually, serve to specify the event in question. We are familiar with this in everyday life. The more we try to recall the details of some incident, the more we 'steep ourselves' in the incident, then the more likely we are to recall it vividly and fully. However, warming-up need not take place merely during the recall attempt itself. Warming-up can occur while the person is engaged in recalling different, but related, material. This has often been shown in laboratory investigations of remembering.

For example, students are given the task of recalling as many K-names as they can in a three-minute period. They are urged to make their list as long as possible. In one experiment, a group of students recalled, on average, 11·5 K-names each. Now, a comparable group of students was given this same task. But immediately beforehand, they were given a similar task using a different letter of the alphabet. When these students came to recall K-names, they recalled, on average, 14·3 names each. The preceding task had acted as a warming-up episode. Perhaps it served to disengage students from other preoccupations: perhaps it served to give them practice in the techniques of proceeding through these shifting narrower predispositions which play such an important role in this kind of recalling. Whatever the case, it is to be noted that this warming-up effect is temporary and rapidly lost. If the two recall sessions are separated by twenty minutes or more, then performance on the second shows no improvement over the performance of those students who recall K-names without any preliminary task. When the student finishes the first recall task, he gives himself over to other activities and fairly rapidly loses his preparedness to carry through continuous controlled recalling. So when he returns to this kind of task again, he must re-establish an appropriate context of activity once more; he requires some time to warm up again.

As a general rule, the amount of warming-up required in executing any task increases with the complexity of the task for the person, and with the length of time since he last attempted the task. For example, a skilled typist requires very little time each morning to warm up to the execution of typing activities. But the beginner typist, who is still mastering the skill, takes quite a time to warm up each day. However, even the skilled typist takes time to warm up if he has not used a typewriter for six months: he will take some time to regain his former level of accomplishment. So it is with recalling. If a person has not recalled certain events for a long time, he takes longer to get into the 'mood' for recalling than if he has recalled the events recently. Here, then, is another factor which contributes to the facilitating effect of repeated attempts at recall. With each successive attempt, the person needs less time to warm up to the activities necessary for characterizing the particular kind of event concerned. He more readily establishes the main characteristics of this kind of event. He requires less time to establish an appropriate state of preparedness for recalling.

2 Repressing

The entire emphasis of the previous section can be briefly expressed as follows. Any instance of remembering is an activity which arises out of a context of other activities, and a context which favours recall of certain events rather than others. Examples of this are seen in the effects of environmental prompts and, more basically, in the effects of preparedness for recalling. In this section we will consider an extreme instance of what may be called preparedness not to recall.

It has already been stressed that, from moment to moment, a person may be in a state of preparedness for recalling certain events and, of necessity, for not recalling other events. We all know that there are events which we could recall but which we do not recall at the moment because it would involve us in too much effort and distract us too much from current activities. We all know too that there are some events which we could recall but which we do not because they are distasteful to us: there are past events which we prefer not to recall unless we must. Now, can it happen that a person is prepared not to recall a certain event while, at the same time, he is unaware that he is so prepared against recalling? This can happen, and is known as repressing. As far as memory is concerned, repressing refers to unconscious blocking of the recall of those experiences or activities which have potentiality for causing the person pain. Even when the person gives every indication of trying hard to recall the events in question, he consistently stops or digresses whenever he comes near to recalling these particular events.

Repressing got its name and its first clear recognition from Sigmund Freud (1856–1939) the Viennese psychiatrist-psychologist. Freud himself devised elaborate theories about repressing, but these have not been easy to substantiate, have never gained wide acceptance, and need not concern us here. The main thing is that he drew attention to the existence of repressing and its role in psychiatric disorder. He made his observations on repressing while he was attempting to cure people suffering, in one form or another, from what is called hysteria. Incidentally, the word hysteria should not be confused with the word hysterics which refers to violent and uncontrollable emotional outbursts. Hysteria may involve such outbursts but has a much wider significance. The central feature of the so-called hysterical personality is the tendency to artificial, almost theatrical, modes of conduct. The patient presents himself, both to others and to himself, in the dramatized light of what he would like to be rather than what he is; and he readily engages in elaborate self-deception regarding his 'play-acting'. Indeed, when we encounter a person with marked hysterical tendencies, our first impressions are that he is 'putting on an act'. We then discover that he is genuinely caught up in his own 'play-acting', he sincerely believes in it. (For an overview of hysteria, see *Clinical Psychiatry*, especially pages 131–46, by W. Mayer-Gross, E. Slater and M. Roth, Cassell, 1960.)

'The essence of repression,' said Freud, 'lies simply in the function of rejecting and keeping something out of consciousness.' The process can best be introduced by giving an example. The following quotation is taken from a book, *The Psychology of Abnormal People*, by J. J. B. Morgan and G. D. Lovell. It summarizes a case treated by Pierre Janet, a Parisian psychiatrist and a contemporary of Freud, and illustrates vividly the emotional blocking of recall.

Irene was a girl of twenty years, who was greatly disturbed by the long illness and death of her mother. Her mother had reached the last stage of tuberculosis, and lived alone in abject poverty with her daughter, in an attic. The girl watched her mother during sixty days and nights, working at her sewing machine to earn a few pennies to sustain their lives. When finally her mother did die, Irene became very much disturbed emotionally. She tried to revive the corpse, to call the breath back again. In her attempts at placing the limbs in an upright position, the mother's body fell to the floor, whereupon she went through the strain of lifting her back into bed, alone. Certainly, such experiences could not be forgotten in the ordinary course of things. Yet in a little while Irene seemed to have grown forgetful of her mother's death. She would say, 'I know very well my mother must be dead, since I have been told so several times, since I see her no more, and since I am in mourning; but I really feel astonished at it all. When did she die? What did she die from? Was I not by her to take care of her? There is something I do not understand. Why, loving her as I did, do I not feel more sorrow for her death? I can't grieve; I feel as if her absence was nothing to me, as if she were travelling, and would soon come back.' The same thing happened if you put to her questions about any of the events that happened during those two months before her mother's death. If you asked her about the illness, the mishaps, the nightly staying up, anxieties about money, the quarrels with her drunken father, – all these things seemed to have quite vanished from her mind. What had happened to her? Had something happened to her nervous system to wipe away all traces of the horrible events she had experienced?

Forgetting

Was she simply pretending she did not remember? Or, did she remember without being able to recall, owing to some powerful inhibitions? Some light is thrown on this question by a study of the crises (or fits) which she began to experience some time after her mother's death. These would last for hours at a time, and during them she would lose contact with her immediate surroundings and perform scenes with the skill of an actress. She would re-enact all the events that took place at her mother's death, as well as other unpleasant episodes in her life, all with the greatest detail. She would carry out with words and acts the different events, and when death finally came to her mother would prepare for her own suicide. She would discuss it aloud, seem to speak to her mother, and to receive advice from her. She fancied that she would try to be run over by a locomotive. She acted as though she were on the way, and stretched herself out on the floor of the room, waiting with dread and impatience for death to come. She posed in true dramatic style waiting for the train to come. Finally, when it came she would utter a terrible shriek, and fall back motionless, as if she were dead. Then she would get up and begin acting over again one of the previous scenes. After a time the agitation seemed to die down and she came back to normal consciousness, took up her ordinary business, seemingly quite undisturbed about what had happened and with the concomitant loss of memory for the events she had so faithfully dramatized.

In the above case, we can readily see what is meant by emotional blocking of recall. Irene's experiences had been so harrowing that the recollecting of them was unbearable and could be escaped from only by committing suicide (which she nearly did) or by forming this inhibitory block against recall. When the strong tendency to recall could no longer be inhibited, recall occurred – but at the expense of her waking consciousness so that she went into the 'crises' described. Notice also that it was not only the recollecting of the events of her mother's death which was blocked, but of everything related to these events. The recall of any subsidiary but related event was likewise denied entry into consciousness.

Repressive forgetting can manifest itself in a bewildering variety of ways. But in all cases, there are certain common features which are illustrated in the above account. First, there is no question of the original experience not being adequately impressed on the patient and retained by him. Eventually, recall can occur, either spontaneously or as a result of special treatment (involving drugs, 'free association', or hypnosis). Second, recall cannot occur either in consequence of being questioned or of making a voluntary attempt to remember. However hard the patient may try, he cannot recall. It is this which differentiates repressing from the moderate forgetting which can be brought about by the common techniques of avoidance and distraction. The recall of an unpleasant experience can be, to some extent, checked by avoiding redintegrating circumstances, that is, places and topics which are associated with it and so remind us of it. Recall can also be checked by 'losing ourselves' in pursuits which distract and absorb our attention. But however effective these techniques may be, they are never so successful that we cannot recall the experience when we make an attempt to do so. With repressing, on the other hand, voluntary attempts at recall are of no avail. It is noteworthy, however, that these attempts are often far from strenuous. Although nothing can actually be recalled, the attempt seems to be unpleasant and is often interrupted by such signs of emotion as anxiety, nausea, and the sudden onset of headache. Third, the repressed experiences always turn out to involve deeply disturbing anxiety. They may involve some unresolved and perplexing conflict, or some anticipation of unwelcome punishment, or some strong threat to self-regard. They may arouse the strong emotional reactions of fear, guilt, shame, disgust, sorrow, or feelings of inferiority. But always, without exception, the repressed experiences are such as to arouse, when recalled, some extremely unpleasant emotional reaction. The utility of repression to the patient is, of course, the very avoidance of this emotional upset. Fourth, repression is not only an active process but a continuous one. According to Freud, it is not an act which merely occurs once and disposes of the problem forever: the blocking requires a constant expenditure of energy on the patient's part and may even, in itself, be exhausting. Support is lent to this view by the fact that the repressed experiences can eventually be recollected with surprising vividness and also by the fact that they not infrequently break through the inhibitory block either in a disguised form or at the expense of conscious awareness. This loss of normal consciousness is what happened in Irene's 'crises' (and fiction provides us with the instance of Shakespeare's Lady Macbeth). It is also evident in many cases of soldiers who have forgotten all about some harrowing war-time experience and yet, during sleep, re-enact this same repressed incident. On waking, they are, like Irene, characteristically unaware of their somnambulism. The repressed experiences may have gained overt expression but, again, they have been kept out of consciousness.

Having outlined the main characteristics of repressing, it must now be repeated that what is repressed varies markedly from patient to patient. It may be the recollection of all experiences which occurred over a particular long or short period of time. It may be the recollection of all experiences related to a certain event or sphere of activity. It may be only a name, or a word, or a phrase. And it may not only be the recollection but also the performance of definite motor habits such as how to write, or sew, or drive a car, or make a bed. The patient may even forget how to stand or walk, although he has not lost the ability to use his legs in other ways. In short, repressing may involve the blocking off of any past experience or learned performance, and the resulting loss may be either slight or extensive. Popular interest has, understandably enough, centred round those dramatic cases where the loss has been one of personal identity.

Indeed, the term 'amnesia' – which, strictly speaking, applies to all forms of pathological forgetting whether produced by drugs, brain injury, or repression has been captured by the newspaper press to refer to just this special, and not too common, type of memory disorder. Loss of personal identity is found in the conditions of 'fugue' and 'multiple personality'. Because these conditions have aroused such widespread curiosity and because they further illustrate the emotional blocking of recall, they will now be briefly discussed.

Loss of Personal Identity. The term 'fugue' literally means 'flight'. It is used to refer to an extended episode of acting as a 'different person'. A particularly clear case of this condition was described many years ago by the British psychologist, William McDougall (1871–1938). During active war-service, a colour-sergeant was entrusted with the delivery of a message and was riding his motorcycle through a dangerous sector of the front. All at once – or so it seemed – it was several hours later and he found himself pushing his cycle along the streets of a coastal town nearly a hundred miles away. This town was, incidentally, a port from which soldiers embarked for home. He was startled and bewildered by this and, as often happens in such cases, he gave himself into the hands of the police. He could recall nothing of his long trip but, eventually, under medical treatment, he was able to recollect being thrown down by a shell explosion, picking himself up, getting on to his machine, starting straight for the coastal town, and reading signposts and asking directions in order to reach his destination. As far as he could recollect, he had thought of nothing other than reaching this coastal town: every action and thought had been subordinated to this goal. His condition during the flight had been not unlike that of a normal person who is so absorbed in some task as to be oblivious and 'absent-minded' of his surroundings. What seems to have happened

Forgetting

was that he had been in conflict between fear, suddenly
intensified by his narrow escape, and duty to complete the
dangerous mission. The forgetting of his personal identity
– of who he was and what he was doing – enabled him to
resolve this conflict by giving way to flight while not
exposing himself to the almost equally unbearable anxiety
of being a coward, failing his mission, and undergoing arrest
as a deserter. Once he had gained the safety of the coastal
town, the two sides of his conflict resumed normal proportions and his sense of personal identity returned abruptly
as though he were waking from a dream. With this return of
identity came the characteristic amnesia for the experiences
of the flight itself.

In times of war, there are many cases of fugue which, like
that above, originate under suddenly violent circumstances.
In civilian life, fugue often occurs under conditions which
are seemingly free from any disturbance. Someone goes out
for a walk and is suddenly bewildered to find himself a
complete stranger in strange surroundings: he recognizes
none of the once familiar faces around him, he has no idea
of his name, of his occupation, of whether he is married or
not, of his home. In this amnesic state, he often turns to the
police or to a hospital for help. On examination, he is found
to be quite normal in every respect. His only peculiarity is
that, however hard and genuinely he may try, he can recall
nothing which will enable either the physician or himself to
arrive at his identity. Usually the patient returns, either
spontaneously or with medical assistance, to his normal
state and is surprised to find himself in hospital for, now, he
can recall nothing of the amnesic episode and has no
recollection of how he came to be where he is.

These cases of fugue are not well understood. But where-
ever they have been investigated thoroughly, they have
been found to possess one characteristic in common. The
significant precipitating factor is some intensely unpleasant
conflict amounting to an emotional crisis in the individual's

life. The conflict may be concerned with finance or family, with escape from danger or threatened punishment. And, in the fugue, the patient translates into overt behaviour his need to 'get away from it all'. He blocks off all those innumerable experiences which would bring him back into the conflict situation. Notice, however, that this forgetting is highly selective. He forgets everything which makes him the unique social individual, the Mr X, which he is. But he does not necessarily forget how to speak, how to understand language, write, drive a car, and so on. The consequence of this selective forgetting may well be called fugue. The patient flees, either literally or metaphorically, from his unbearable circumstances. He takes refuge in amnesia from those conflicts which he is incapable of resolving as long as he retains his sense of social identity.

This very brief account of fugue raises one important question. Many people find themselves in a state of acute and unresolved conflict. But not all of them gain relief by repressing their personal identity. Why should one individual 'resort' to fugue, another to suicide, and another to any one of the many forms of so-called nervous breakdown? This, unfortunately, is a question to which there are, as yet, no satisfactory answers. Just what subtle combination of hereditary and environmental influences predisposes an individual to this or that type of mental illness is yet another of those problems which are currently being investigated by psychologists and psychiatrists. It is yet another of those socially important problems on which evidence is beginning to accumulate but which is still far from being solved. Only this much has become apparent: the answer, when and if it does emerge, will be far from simple.

In fugue, the individual becomes, to some extent, a 'different person'. But this 'different person' is lacking in identity, confused, bewildered, agitated, and quite clearly not normal. In multiple personality, on the other hand, the 'different person' has an identity and a self-consistency of expression and behaviour which, superficially at least, makes him an acceptable and balanced social being. Multiple personality refers to that condition where the individual possesses two or more 'personalities' each of which is so well developed and integrated as to have a relatively rich, unified, and stable life of its own. In 1944, two American psychologists, W. S. Taylor and M. F. Martin, undertook to collect and classify all available case records of such multiple personality, and their labours revealed three significant facts. First, there can be no doubt about the genuineness of the condition. It is true that some people may intentionally behave in very different ways at different times. They may even act out an elaborate impersonation. But such intentional deception does not detract from the genuine occurrence of multiple personality any more than the simulated amnesia or bodily illness of the malingerer detracts from the reality of amnesia or illness generally. Skilful examination can usually detect the fraud from the genuine case. Second, multiple personality occurs much less frequently than its literary exploitation would suggest. The extensive search revealed that, out of the thousands upon thousands of recorded cases of behaviour disorder, there were only seventy-six available records of multiple personality. It was estimated that perhaps no more than 150 cases have appeared in the voluminous bulk of the world's medical and psychological case records. Third, the condition manifests itself in such a variety of forms as to defy any brief summing up, since no two cases are quite the same.

Multiple personality clearly differs in degree rather than in kind from the less dramatic dissociation found in day dreaming, play acting, restlessness during sleep, and somnambulism (sleep walking). And many of the cases can be seen as developing out of fugue. After losing his sense of personal identity, the subject does not remain disorientated and neither does he resume his customary orientation. He picks up, as it were, the threads of a new existence. He begins to build up for himself a disparate, protective role. His new phase of existence can be called a role, or even a personality, since it is a way of life which is fairly self-consistent. This role is disparate in that it represents a sharp discontinuity in his living which is more or less opposed to, and separate from, the rest of his personality. And this new role is protective since, in it, the individual can escape from his conflicts and anxieties, and so feel more secure than he could feel otherwise. The new role may be developed gradually or it may already have been built up by fantasy and be ready for him to step into. He may become the sort of person he has often consciously wished to become. He may behave like a baby, or a child, or a peaceful person, or a thief, or a sailor, or like any one real or imagined person. Whatever the role, he learns more and more reactions to augment it until, circumstances permitting, the role becomes sufficiently strong and rich to emerge as a complete way of life. He has a new identity and occupation, new friends and leisure pursuits and, to casual observers, appears quite normal.

While the new role is being developed and maintained, there is, of course, repression of all or many of those recollections which would supply the individual with his former identity. Often after living successfully in this partially amnesic state, sometimes for years, he suddenly and spontaneously returns to his previous condition and, now, may recollect nothing of his second role. He then resumes his former way of living as best he can, and that may be the end of the episode. But, in some cases, there is a later return of the second role and perhaps an alternation between it and the first. Such alternating personalities may be 'mutually amnesic', that is, the different personalities can remember nothing of each other's experiences and activities. It is this type which was so skilfully dramatized by Robert Louis Stevenson in his fictional case of Dr Jekyll and Mr Hyde.

Alternatively, there may be 'one-way' amnesia where personality X recollects none of Y's experiences but Y remembers all of X's. There may even be a 'co-conscious personality' which continues to function subconsciously while the other is dominant and functioning consciously. This 'co-conscious personality' indicates its presence in some roundabout way such as in 'automatic writing' where the patient may be carrying on a normal conversation as X while his hand writes, without his being aware of it, messages of a style and content quite different from both his consciously controlled writing and his present topic of conversation. In these very rare cases (Taylor and Martin discovered records of only twenty-seven) where there are more than two distinct personalities, certain roles may be mutually amnesic while others are one-way amnesic. Thus, different types of organization may be combined within a single case.

The most recently documented case of multiple personality is reported in a book, *The Three Faces of Eve*, by C. H. Thigpen and H. Checkley, 1957. Here, there were two personalities. Eve White was sweet, retiring, dignified, conservative and industrious; and Eve Black was vain, mischievous, irresponsible, and vulgar. Eve White was unaware of Eve Black's existence, but the reverse was not the case. During the course of psychiatric treatment, a third personality suddenly emerged. This was Jane who had a maturity and balance not found in either of the two Eves. Jane was aware of both Eves, and eventually achieved a synthesis of a whole, reasonably coherent, personality. We may conclude our discussion of multiple personality by quoting Taylor and Martin's description of what appears to be the earliest well documented case.

Mary Reynolds was born in England in 1793, and was brought to Pennsylvania by her family when she was four years old. The girl was intelligent. She grew up in a strongly religious atmosphere, and became melancholy, shy, and given to solitary religious devotions and meditations. She was considered normal until she was about eighteen. Then she began to have occasional 'fits', which were evidently hysterical. One of these attacks, when she was about nineteen years old, left her blind and deaf for five or six weeks. Some three months later, she slept eighteen or twenty hours, and awoke seeming to know scarcely anything that she had learned. She soon became acquainted with her surroundings, however, and within a few weeks learned reading, calculating, and writing, though her penmanship was crude compared to what it had been. Now she was buoyant, witty, fond of company and a lover of nature. After five weeks of this new life, she slept long again, and awoke as her 'normal' self, with no memory for what she had experienced since her recent lapse. Thereafter the 'new' or 'second state' and the 'old' or 'first state' ... alternated irregularly. The second state gained over the first, however, and became more rich and stable, until the woman was about thirty-six years old. At that time the second state became permanent and continued until her death in 1854.

Repressing in Normal Behaviour. Does repressing, so dramatically evident in mentally ill people, play any part in the everyday forgetting of normal people? This is a question which is not easy to answer. It is of little avail to seek an answer in our personal introspective experience for, by its nature, repressing is an activity of which we are not aware. We cannot repress our recollecting of an experience and, at the same time, be aware that we are doing so. On the other hand, we would expect that repressing should occur in normal people if it is true, as it usually seems to be, that abnormal activities are exaggerations of normal, everyday processes. Where then should we turn for evidence of repressing in everyday life? Freud would claim that evidence is forthcoming from at least three sources, namely, the results of 'free association', some everyday cases of forgetting names and words, and the facts of 'infantile amnesia'. We may now examine the first two of these sources of evidence, but delay our consideration of the third until later.

Forgetting

Free Association. It was earlier mentioned that we can recall more than we usually imagine ourselves capable of doing. If we persist in trying to recall a poem which we once knew but have since forgotten, we can gradually recall more and more. Now the Freudian technique of free association is, in a sense, an effort which is continued over months, or even years, to recall more and more of our past experiences. For reasons which need not be discussed here, it is one of the aims of psychoanalysis to recover repressed experiences. The manner of doing this was evolved by Freud as a result of much trial and error and is, in outline, simple. Instead of trying to elicit recall by hypnotism or any other form of suggestion, or by urging the patient to recall experiences of a particular kind, the patient is asked to relax and say 'whatever comes into his head'. He must report everything as it occurs to him and make no attempt to hold anything back in the interests of logic or decency. It is perhaps inaccurate to call this a process of 'free' association for, while it is free from many conventional restraints, it is not free in the way that idle reverie is free. In the first place, the patient is suffering from some disturbance and has come to be cured. This circumstance dominates the whole situation and inevitably exerts its influence on the course of the associations. In the second place, the thoughts and recollections must be communicated to a listener, and this at once brings into play our life-long habits of suppressing certain topics and trying to 'put up a good front'. It is by no means easy to express in words every idea that drifts through our head, and it may require weeks or months of practice before we can learn to verbalize these ideas and bring ourselves to do so without reserve. There is a resistance against telling everything, and all sorts of excuses are given for not doing so; for example, there is nothing to tell, or it is too silly or trivial. But this resistance does not go on for ever. The patient is encouraged by the analyst, who points out similarities between this and that recollected experience or thought. He gains confidence in the analyst's sympathy, coming to accept that he will not criticize or be shocked by anything that is said. He accepts that the analyst will comfort him and help him to deal with his anxieties. And he abandons himself to free expression. Sometimes, he reports events and feelings of which he has been aware for some time but has never been willing to express in words. But he is more and more likely to find himself recalling experiences which he had hitherto been unaware of having had. That the recollection of these experiences had been repressed is indicated by the fact that they are recollected not piecemeal but as a whole, not dimly but extremely vividly, and are accompanied by strongly unpleasant emotional reactions. They often, but not always, have the further characteristic of being directly related to some present behaviour disturbance. There seems little doubt that the recollection of these experiences had, until this time, been blocked from consciousness.

Such instances of repression are reported uniformly in the case records of psychoanalysts in such a way that we must accept their authenticity. Granting, then, that free association always reveals repression, this helps us to answer our question, since many of the 'patients' have been normal adults. Psychoanalysis was developed as a method of treating neurotics. But it has also been undergone by people who are, if anything, better adjusted and more stable than the general run of the population. Most of them have been people who wished to become psychoanalysts themselves, and a few have been psychologists who have simply wanted to discover exactly what the technique involves. Now, if these normal people have been found to 'employ' repression, it seems highly likely that we do so too. Thus, the results of free association suggest that repressive forgetting has occurred in the lives of all of us with regard to those experiences the recollection of which would cause us acute anxiety. We all block the recalling of some unpleasant past experiences and our lives are the happier and the better for it.

Everyday Forgetting. In 1914, Freud published an English edition of his *The Psychopathology of Everyday Life*. In this book he endeavours to show that many 'lapses of memory' and 'slips of the tongue' are not inexplicable accidents but can be readily understood if fitted into the personality picture of the individual. The reader is recommended to look at this well-written book for himself and discover the wealth of intriguing anecdotal evidence with which Freud supports and develops his thesis.

Freud is at his best when discussing those seemingly accidental mistakes of speech and writing where one word is substituted for another and, especially, where the substitute word means the opposite of the word intended. A physician is writing out a prescription for an impecunious patient who asks him not to give her big bills because she cannot swallow them – and then says that, of course, she meant pills. An arrogant lecturer says that he could count the number of real authorities on his subject on one finger – he means the fingers of one hand. A President of the Austrian House of Deputies is opening a session from which he fears little good will come and announces that, since such and such a number of gentlemen are present, he declares the session as closed; amid laughter, he corrects his mistake and declares the session as opened. All of these examples perhaps derive from the person saying what he actually thinks without checking himself in time to make his insincere but diplomatic statement. No doubt we have all encountered similar examples in our everyday life. Certainly, writers of fiction have long been aware of this phenomenon, and have exploited it to good dramatic effect by putting such *lapsus linguae* in the mouths of their characters. In Shakespeare's *Merchant of Venice*, for example, Portia has lost her affections to Bassanio but is under a vow not to reveal it. She directs a speech to this welcome suitor in which, throughout, her love for him is thinly disguised and finishes with the words: 'One half of me is yours, the other half yours – Mine own, I would say.' The same expression of our thoughts and wishes is seen in some erroneously carried-out actions. Thus, one physician reports that he is quite often disturbed in the midst of engrossing work at home by having to go to hospital to carry out some routine duty. When this happens, he is apt to find himself trying to open the door of his laboratory with the key of his desk at home. The two keys are quite unlike each other and the mistake does not occur under normal circumstances but only under conditions where he would rather be at home. His error seems to express this wish.

When Freud begins to discuss 'lapses of memory' in terms of repression, he seems to move on to less firm ground. He does not, of course, claim that all lapses are due to repression. His concern is to show that at least some are and, to this end, he gives examples in which a name or word is unexpectedly forgotten, and proceeds to demonstrate that the forgotten item is associated either directly or indirectly with unpleasant circumstances. Here we may cite two of his most convincing examples. The first concerns a man (X) who repeatedly forgot the name of an old acquaintance and business associate (Y). When he required to correspond with Y, he had to ask other people for his name. It transpired that Y had recently married a young woman whom X himself had hoped to marry. Thus, X had good reason to dislike his happy rival and want to forget all about him. The second example concerns a man who set out to recite a poem, got so far, and then could recall no more although he knew the poem well. The line on which he blocked was descriptive of a pine-tree which is covered 'with the white sheet'. Why should this phrase have been forgotten? Asked to relate what came to mind when he thought of this phrase, it was found that it immediately reminded him of the white

sheet which covers a dead body, and of the recent death of
his brother from a heart condition which was common in
his family and from which he feared he too might die. The
phrase referring to the white sheet appears to have been
forgotten because it was associated with circumstances
which the man did not wish to recall. In Freud's other
examples, the link between the forgotten item and some
unpleasant circumstance is not so easily demonstrated. The
'subject' (often Freud himself) considers the item, keeps on
telling what it suggests to him and, sooner or later, reports
some unpleasant association. This, says Freud, is the explanation. The item was 'deliberately' forgotten because it
was associated with this unpleasant experience, the conscious
recollection of which would have been painful. Now
Freud's analysis of these examples may be correct. They
may, on the other hand, be more ingenious than veridical.
And there seems to be no definite way of deciding. His
whole case seems to rest on an often tortuous association
between the forgotten item and a painful experience. Any
critic could start with any word whatever and trace a link,
no less indirect than those traced by Freud, to an unpleasant
experience. It would be possible for him to match each of
Freud's examples with a case in which he takes a word
which is not forgotten by an individual, traces it to some
unpleasant experience which that individual has had, and
so explains why (although the word was recalled) it ought
really to have been forgotten. In short, the great bulk of
Freud's examples, while ingenious and suggestive, are un-
convincing when we realize the highly selective nature of
the argument he invokes. It may, in fact, be that a temporary inability to recall a word is due to our not really
wanting to recall it. It may be that an object is misplaced
because we really want to lose it. But, at the moment,
there is no evidence to suggest that this is anything more
than a plausible hypothesis.

Overview of Repressing. In summary of this whole section, it may be said that repressing is an extreme exaggeration of the normal selectivity of remembering. In repressing, there is failure to remember certain events because the person undertakes remembering in the context of a strong preparedness not to remember. What he fails to remember is not forgotten in any absolute sense but is typically something which he still retains and is of great importance to him. Perhaps the main peculiarities of repressing are its effectiveness and the fact that the person is unaware that he is blocking remembering. There is evidence to suggest that repressing is not an activity confined to the mentally ill but, rather, occurs in the behaviour of most, perhaps all, normal people. However, we must be extremely cautious over this issue. We must not be over-ready to interpret any particular instance of forgetting in terms of repressing. Each instance must be considered on its own merits and in the wider context of what is known about the person as a whole. It is a misplaced enthusiasm to see signs of repressing in every instance of forgetting, every slip of the tongue, and every mistake made. Such an enthusiasm merely serves to impede rather than advance our understanding of human functioning and, also, it tends to rob the concept of repressing of its utility.

3 Is Anything Permanently Forgotten?

A person may, at any particular time, remember less than he is capable of remembering. This is because he is adversely affected by the context of the moment. The many instances of temporary forgetting prompt us to ask whether it is true that nothing is ever 'really' forgotten. This question might be interpreted as follows. Is a person potentially

Forgetting

able to recall every momentary experience he ever had?
The answer to this question is clear. No, he is not. The
facts of immediate-forgetting show that the greater part of
ongoing experience cannot be recalled beyond the moment
of its occurrence. There is, however, another version of the
question. Granted that a person could, at one time, remember a specific event; and granted also that he cannot now
remember this past event; then, can we be sure that he will
never be able to remember it? In other words, without re-
learning the event, might he not, at some future time, be
able to remember it? The short answer to this question is
that we cannot be absolutely certain that the person will
never be able to recall some particular event which he
seems to have forgotten completely. Let us be more specific.
At the age of six, a person learned a particular poem until
he could recite it without error. At the age of sixty, this
same person is asked to recite the poem again. If, in the
years between, he has had frequent occasion to recall this
poem, then he will still be able to recite it. But if he has not
kept the poem alive by repetition, he may well be unable to
recite it. However hard he tries, he cannot recall the word
sequence of the poem: it is forgotten, gone. Our question is
this. Will he ever be able to recite the poem, assuming he
does not memorize it afresh? The answer is that we can be
reasonably certain that he will not be able to recall this
poem. We could gamble on his inability with only slight
risk. But there would be a risk, however small. It has
already been mentioned that when people make repeated
attempts to recall some long-past event, they usually
succeed in recalling more than they thought possible. Such
observations make us hesitant to assert dogmatically that
any particular event could never be recalled.

There are yet other observations which reinforce this
hesitance. These are the well authenticated reports of
people who are surprised to find themselves recalling events
about which they have not 'thought for years'. Especially

under conditions of illness, emotional excitement, or hypnosis, people have sometimes been found to remember childhood events or a native language which, to the best of their belief, they have not maintained by periodic recall. Now such instances in which people recall long-forgotten events are uncannily dramatic; and the personal experience of even one such instance is certainly sufficient to loosen a person's conviction in the general rule that frequently repeated recall is necessary for the continued retaining of past events. However, two points should be made about these uncanny instances. The first is that they do not warrant the generalization that *every* recalled event will be potentially recallable for always. One or two such instances do not prove the indestructability of *all* 'memories'. The second point is that the impressiveness of such instances is due to the claim that the particular event has not been recalled for years. Is this claim to be believed, even if made in all sincerity? In fact, there are good reasons to doubt the ability of people to know what they have *not* recalled. These reasons were first brought forward by Galton in the course of experiments which may now be outlined briefly.

The Galton Experiment. In his book, *Inquiries into Human Faculty*, Galton reported the results of introspective experiments. Like his contemporary, Ebbinghaus, he conducted these experiments on himself, and under conditions which demanded a high degree of self-discipline. And like the experiments of Ebbinghaus, these pioneer studies laid the foundation of a whole tradition of inquiry: in this case into 'word-association' and 'idea-association'. Galton started with the question: what prompts recall of what? His procedure consisted in presenting himself with a word, written on a piece of paper and unknown to him in advance, 'allowing the mind to play freely for a very brief period, until a couple or so of ideas have passed through it, and then, while the traces or echoes of those ideas are still lingering in the brain, to turn the attention upon them with a sudden and complete awakening; to arrest, to scrutinize them, and to record their exact appearance'. He repeated his experiments several times, carefully recording the experiencing prompted by seeing each word. He tabulated his results and examined their trends. This showed him the relative frequency of occurrence of different modes of imaging. It also showed that most of his prompted experiences dated from the distant rather than the recent past: 39 per cent from boyhood and youth, 46 per cent from subsequent manhood, and only 15 per cent from quite recent events. His results also showed that the same word, when presented at different times weeks apart, tended to prompt the same experiencing.

Perhaps the strongest of the impressions left by these experiments regards the multifariousness of the work done by the mind in a state of half-unconsciousness, and the valid reason they afford for believing in the existence of still deeper strata of mental operations, sunk wholly below the level of consciousness, which may account for such mental phenomena as cannot otherwise be explained. We gain an insight by these experiments into the marvellous number and nimbleness of our mental associations, and we also learn that they are very far indeed from being infinite in their variety. We find that our working stock of ideas is narrowly limited and that the mind continually recurs to the same instruments in conducting its operations, therefore its tracks necessarily become more defined and its flexibility diminishes as age advances.

These general conclusions have been amply confirmed by studies conducted since Galton's time.

The part of Galton's findings which is most relevant to our present question is the occurrence of experiences concerning events which he had thought were long forgotten. He expressed these findings in the following words.

The instances, according to my personal experience, are very rare, and even these are not very satisfactory, in which some event recalls a memory that had lain *absolutely* dormant for many years.

Is Anything Permanently Forgotten?

In this very series of experiments a recollection which I thought had entirely lapsed appeared under no less than three different aspects on different occasions. It was this; when I was a boy, my father, who was anxious that I should learn something of physical science, which was then never taught at school, arranged with the owner of a large chemist's shop to let me dabble at chemistry for a few days in his laboratory. I had not thought of this fact, so far as I was aware, for many years; but in scrutinizing the fleeting associations called up by the various words, I traced two mental images (an alembic and a particular arrangement of tables and light), and one mental sense of smell (chlorine gas) to that very laboratory. I recognised that these images appeared familiar to me, but I had not thought of their origin. No doubt if some strange conjunction of circumstances had suddenly recalled those three associations at the same time, with perhaps two or three other collateral matters which may be still living in my memory, but which I do not as yet identify, a mental perception of startling vividness would be the result, and I should have falsely imagined that it had supernaturally, as it were, started into life from an entire oblivion extending over many years. Probably many persons would have registered such a case as evidence that things once perceived can never wholly vanish from the recollection, but that in the hour of death, or under some excitement, every event of a past life may reappear. To this view I entirely dissent. Forgetfulness appears absolute in the majority of cases. . . . I strongly suspect that ideas which have long since ceased to fleet through the brain, owing to the absence of current associations to call them up, disappear wholly. A comparison of old memories with a newly-met friend of one's boyhood, about the events we then witnessed together, show how much we had each of us forgotten. Our recollections do not tally. Actors and incidents that seem to have been of primary importance in those events to the one have been utterly forgotten by the other. The recollection of our earlier years are, in truth, very scanty, as anyone will find who tries to enumerate them.

This quotation makes clear that, in Galton's case, there was an event which he believed he had not recalled in years. Yet he had done so, with such fragmentary and momentary fleetingness that it did not survive immediate-forgetting. At the very least, this finding casts doubt on people's ability to report that they have not recalled some particular event for a long time. It stresses the need for caution over accepting the dramatic recall of seemingly long-forgotten events as evidence that nothing is ever really forgotten.

In summary, we can give this answer to the question about whether anything is ever 'really' forgotten. It is wise to admit the small likelihood that some apparently forgotten event may be recalled at some future time. But it is an unwarranted generalization to assert that everything which could once be recalled may be recalled still. Indeed, so far as the writer knows, no serious student of human functioning has ever made this sweeping claim; not even Freud, who is often misrepresented on this issue. So, our question is a complex one to which no clear and general answer can be given. The best that can be done is to appreciate the difficulties raised by this question, and avoid two extreme assumptions. One extreme is that everything which a person could once recall is still, potentially, recallable by him. The other is that a person will never be able to recall some particular event more fully and faithfully than he can at his present attempt. The second extreme may lie nearer the truth than does the first. But both of these extreme assumptions are, like most sweeping generalizations about human functioning, demonstrably false. There seems little doubt that many events which we could once remember cannot now be remembered, and that much that we can remember will be forgotten in the future.

Loss of Retaining. What a person remembers is influenced by each of the three main phases of memory. First, his remembering of an event depends on his activities at the time of the original event: how he perceived the event, what he observed and did not observe, how he interpreted the event, the characteristics he abstracted, how these characteristics modified the retained effects of his cumulative past experience. Second, his remembering of an event depends on his activities at the time of remembering: what the present circumstances are, his states of preparedness for remembering, his need to make what he remembers relevant to the demands of the present situation as he interprets it. Third, his remembering of an event depends on the cumulative effects of his past experience to date: on what he has retained of the event, and what he has not. The first two of these phases have already been discussed. The third phase is the chief concern of the remainder of this chapter.

The retaining phase of memory occupies the interval between the taking in of an event and the remembering of this event. It should be said straight away that this phase is rather a mystery. There can be little question that retaining is carried out by the nervous system and involves persisting changes in the brain, that vast complex of living cells which, like all living matter, requires nutriment and freedom from physical injury for its proper functioning. Those patterns of brain changes which retain the effects of past experience are called memory-traces. But these changes cannot, as yet, be examined by direct physiological means, and very little is known about their exact nature. This means that what a person retains or does not retain must, in the last analysis, be inferred from what he can or cannot remember. The scarcity of physiological techniques for examining memory-traces directly means that detailed inferences about retaining are difficult to make. They can only be made under rather special experimental conditions which cannot be considered here. There are, however, two general inferences about which there is no dispute.

The first general inference is that the retained effects of past experience must form an organized and interrelated system. This much is evident from even a brief consideration of human remembering. One of the most impressive features of human remembering is its selectivity. The person is not confined to recalling past events in the order in which he encountered these events. He can recall events which were taken in at widely separated times in the past, and he can do this without having to recall the events which intervened between these times. For example, continuous controlled recalling of N-names would be impossible if human beings stored information in the way that a cine-film does, that is, if information were retained solely according to the time sequence in which it was taken in. The astonishing selectivity of human remembering indicates that the retained effects of past experience are organized into elaborately inter-related systems and sub-systems. The second general inference is that the retained effects of past experience must undergo continual selective modifications. From a biological point of view, a person is a self-modifying system which is neither simple nor static. That is, the person changes under the influence of his ongoing activities and experiences: his cumulative past is, today, different from his cumulative past of a year ago. There is mutual interaction between the retained effects of his past experience and his current activities. Thus, the past influences the present: the circumstances of the present moment are reacted to in terms of the relevant aspects of his cumulative past experience: the retained effects of the past are selectively brought to bear upon the present. Likewise, the present influences the past. In so far as the circumstances of the present moment are retained for future use, this is accomplished by their producing modifications in the person's cumulative past experience: the present selectively changes the retained effects of the past. All this mutual interaction between past and present means that the cumulative effects of past experience are forever undergoing complex and selective changes. The kinds of interaction which occur may be classified into four broad categories. These categories oversimplify the intricate interactions between a person's present activities and the retained effects of his previous activities. But they have the merits of convenience.

Categories of Interaction. (*a*) The retained effects of past experience can facilitate the learning and retaining of current events. This general effect has already been referred to in discussing the ease with which people can learn events of a kind which is already familiar to them. In situations where the learning of one lesson makes it easier for the person to master a second lesson, the overall effect is called pro-active facilitation (or sometimes, positive transfer of learning). (*b*) The retained effects of past experience can impede, interfere with, the learning and retaining of current events. For example, a typist who has mastered the use of one keyboard finds difficulty in mastering a keyboard in which the positions of all the letters are different. The old patterns of activity are no longer appropriate, and the typist must not merely learn the new keyboard but also unlearn the old. Any long-established and well-practiced mode of activity, whether simple or complex, may impede the learning of new and conflicting modes of activity. In situations where the learning of one lesson makes it more difficult for the person to master a second lesson, the overall effect is called pro-active interference (or negative transfer of learning).

The two categories just mentioned refer to the influences of the past on the present. The next two categories refer to the influences of the present on the past. (*c*) The learning and retaining of current events can facilitate the retaining of previously learned events. The most obvious example of this is learning through repetition. Repetition of the same lesson facilitates the retaining of what has been learned already. Likewise, the continued learning of a foreign language facilitates the retaining of what has already been learned about the language. Continued learning occasions the periodic recall of previously learned items, and also occasions the relating of these items into a wider and more coherent system of items: all this facilitates the retaining of the items in question. In situations where the learning of a second lesson makes it easier for the person, subsequently, to remember a first lesson, the overall effect is called retro-active facilitation. (*d*) The learning and retaining of current events can impede, interfere with, the retaining of past events. It was mentioned above that, in the case of the typist learning a new keyboard, this learning disrupts what has already been learned about the old keyboard. Everyday recollecting also provides examples of the interfering effects of new experience on retaining old experiences. Suppose, for example, a person pays his first visit to the dissecting-room of a medical school. If this is his one and only visit, it will very likely be a memorable event for him, one which he does not readily forget. But if he is a medical student who subsequently spends many hours in this dissecting-room, then after a time, he is unlikely to be able to recollect much about his first visit. Likewise, a person who attends only one or two university lectures is likely to be able to recollect these particular occasions. But how many graduates can recall, say, the circumstances of their first university lecture? In general, the repeated experience of somewhat similar events tends to make us unable to remember the individual characteristics of any one of these events. The day on which lovers meet and war breaks out is memorable. But not so the humdrum, uneventful periods of routine whose very lack of individuality ensures their being forgotten as unique events. Subsequent experiences can, clearly, interfere with our retaining of previous experiences. In situations where the learning of a second lesson makes it more difficult for the person, subsequently, to remember a first lesson, the overall effect is called retroactive interference. Since many, and perhaps all, instances of normal, permanent forgetting conform to the pattern of retroactive interference, the next section is devoted to this kind of forgetting.

4 Retroactive Interference

Retroactive interference refers to a decrement in remembering which is brought about by the interpolation of some particular activity between the time of the original learning and of the remembering. This effect is perhaps the most potent single factor in everyday forgetting. In order to demonstrate it clearly, an experimental procedure must be adopted which, at its simplest, can be schematized as follows:

	Time 1	Time 2	Time 3
Subject 1	Learn A	Activity x	Remember A
Subject 11	Learn A	Activity y	Remember A

Subjects 1 and 11 represent two people, or more usually two groups of people, who are 'matched', that is, who are selected so as to be of the same age, sex, educational level, and, most important, of the same ability to learn the lesson being employed. This matching procedure involves a number of technical difficulties, but it can be achieved, if not always beforehand then certainly afterwards, when we need consider only those people who have learned the same amount in the same time. Subjects 1 and 11 both follow exactly the same procedure of learning some lesson (represented by A) and remembering it after a specific lapse of time. They differ, however, in the activity they pursue during the interval between Time 1 and Time 3. Activity x is usually a learning activity of some sort while Activity y is ordinarily rather non-strenuous and may merely involve describing photographs or reading light literature. What we are eventually interested in is how much better Subject 11 remembers than does Subject 1. And since the two subjects are matched and have been treated in exactly the same way, any difference in their remembering performances can be attributed to the difference between the interpolated activities x and y.

The sort of results which emerge from the above type of experiment may be indicated by citing a study published in 1931 by J. A. McGeoch and W. T. McDonald. Their subjects were university students; their lesson A was a list of adjectives to be memorized; their activity x was the learning of a list of items which were more or less similar to the original adjectives; and their activity y simply involved reading jokes. The results were as follows:

Interpolated activity	Per cent of adjectives recalled
Reading jokes	45
Learning 3-place numbers	37
Learning nonsense syllables	26
Learning adjectives unrelated to originals	22
Learning adjectives antonymous with originals	18
Learning adjectives synonymous with originals	12

These results leave us in no doubt as to the influence of interpolated activity on recall performance. They show, too, an increasing impairment in recall with increasing similarity between the interpolated activity and the original learning. Like findings occur in many other investigations and, from such studies, three significant relationships have emerged. First, the amount of interference is an increasing function of the similarity between the original and the interpolated activity. Second, the amount of interference is an increasing function of the amount of the interpolated activity, i.e. the more active we are in the interval, the more likely we are to forget. And third, the greater the degree of original learning, the less susceptible it is to interference, i.e. the better we learn the original task, the more likely we are to remember it despite interpolated activities.

The above results indicate that forgetting is not so much a matter of the fading away of old impressions as of their being 'crowded out' by new impressions. The learning of a new list of adjectives involves, to some extent, the unlearning of an old list and will also give rise to errors in remembering because of confusions between the new and the old.

Forgetting During Sleep. Since forgetting can occur from the interpolation of certain activities between learning and remembering, the interesting question arises: if there were no intervening activities whatever, would any forgetting occur? What would happen if it were possible to place someone in, so to speak, a functional vacuum between the time of learning and the time of remembering? If retroactive interference were the sole cause of forgetting, then no forgetting should occur. This question cannot, as yet, be answered because any living being is, to some degree, always active. In particular, the nervous system, like the heart, remains active even during the deepest sleep. However, we can ask whether forgetting takes place when normal waking activities are at their lowest ebb, that is, during sleep. It is feasible to find out how rapidly forgetting occurs during sleep as contrasted with the rate of forgetting during workaday waking activity. Of the experiments which have investigated rate of forgetting under these two conditions, the earliest and most famous is that of two American psychologists, J. G. Jenkins and K. M. Dallenbach. Their investigation, reported in 1924, employed two senior university students as subjects. It took two months to perform and, during this time, each subject underwent over sixty different tests. Each test consisted of the learning and the later recall of a list of ten nonsense syllables. Under the waking condition, the list was memorized in the morning to a criterion of one errorless recitation, and the subject then went about his routine affairs to be called back, after a specified interval, for recall. Under the sleep condition, the list was learned at night after the subject was undressed and ready for bed: he then retired immediately to an improvised bedroom adjoining the experimental room and was awakened later for his recall. Under both conditions, four different time intervals were employed between learning and recalling, namely, 1 hour, 2 hours, 4 hours, and 8 hours.

The results of the Jenkins and Dallenbach experiment were almost identical for both subjects. After the different intervals, the average number of syllables recalled by both was as follows:

Number of hours since learning

	0	1	2	4	8
After sleeping	10	7·0	5·4	5·5	5·6
After waking	10	4·6	3·1	2·2	0·9

Results of the waking condition follow the usual course, namely, a sharp initial drop in recall followed by a progressively slower decline. In contrast, results for the sleeping condition show a slight initial drop followed, after the 2-hour interval, by no further forgetting. (The rise from 5·4 to 5·6 is too small to be accepted as indicating a genuine increase.) It is to be stressed that, at each interval other than zero, there is a real difference in the amount of forgetting which has occurred during sleep and during waking activity, that these differences are not due to any flaw in the conduct of the experiment and, moreover, that similar differences have been found by later investigators using both nonsense material and meaningful prose passages. There can be no doubt that the ordinary activities of daily life bring about a substantial degree of forgetting. In the words of Jenkins and Dallenbach, 'forgetting is not so much a matter of the decay of old impressions and associations as it is a matter of the interference, inhibition, or obliteration of the old by the new.'

It should be realized that, while the Jenkins and Dallenbach type of study demonstrates the presence of retroactive interference, it by no means proves that other forgetting processes are absent. It is possible, for example, that there may be some decay of memory-traces, since there is impairment of remembering even after sleep. However, this forgetting might also be due to retroactive interference, since the sleep condition is not such as to eliminate all activity between the time of learning and recall. Before sleep, the subject leaves the room, gets into bed, and may remain mentally active for as long as ten minutes: after sleep, he must waken again and make his way back to the experimental room: even during sleep, he is not totally inactive. It can never be settled as to whether or not the interfering effects of these activities are sufficient to account for all the forgetting which occurs during sleep – not, at least, until the unlikely event of obtaining a control condition in which there would be no activity of any sort between the moment of reaching the learning criterion and the moment of beginning recall. Only if there were no forgetting during this psychological vacuum would it be possible to conclude that atrophy of the memory traces had been absent.

A practical question which arises out of the above type of investigation is: Would it be advantageous to study just before going to sleep rather than through the day? The most likely answer seems to be that there would be no advantage one way or the other unless the material were to be remembered fairly soon after waking. If a lesson is learned at night, it will probably, in the first place, require more effort than in the relative freshness of morning. In the second place, retroactive interference will occur on the following day anyhow. Wherever night study did happen to be profitable it would be because little forgetting would occur during sleep and, on waking, the learner could return to the task refreshed and with renewed vigour.

Qualitative Changes in Remembering. Retroactive interference

Forgetting

affects not only how much is remembered but can give rise to qualitative distortions in remembering. This effect is familiar in everyday life and has also been studied experimentally. One such study may be mentioned briefly. It was reported in 1950 by D. R. Davis and D. Sinha, both of Cambridge University. In part of this study, adults were given a story, some 750 words long, which dwelt on a Dutch wedding feast. The story told of two families between whom there has been a long-standing feud: a daughter of one family is now marrying a son of the other family: and the wedding feast is disturbed by several incidents which threaten to rekindle the old feud. Three days after reading this story, the subjects were shown a reproduction of a painting by Brueghel. This painting, 'The Peasant Wedding', also deals with a Dutch wedding feast, but one of good-natured conviviality. From one to four weeks later, the subjects were asked to recall the story. It was found that their recall included details which derived from the picture: these details were absent in the recall of other subjects who had not seen the picture. So there was, in recall, some confluence between the story and the picture. This same confluence took place in the recall of people who were first shown the picture, then given the story, and then asked to recall the picture. For example, innocent musicians in the picture were recalled as 'servants threatening with weapons', a background cluster of celebrating peasants was recalled as 'an unruly mob'. In short, studies such as these confirm everyday experience. Experience of one event may later influence the way we interpret a second, somewhat similar event; and this second event may influence our later recalling of the first. Incidentally, it should be mentioned that the purpose of experiments such as the above is not merely to confirm that recalling may involve confusion between separate experiences; the main purpose is to study these confusions more closely and determine the conditions under which they occur.

Retroactive interference can, then, arise from encounters with environmental events. It can also arise from the person's own thinking, from his recalling and imagining. It seems likely that, in the course of our private thinking, we recall past events more frequently than most of us imagine. Galton may be quoted on this point. 'I conclude from the proved number of faint and barely conscious thoughts, and from the proved iteration of them, that the mind is perpetually travelling over familiar ways without our memory retaining any impression of its excursions. Its footsteps are so light and fleeting that it is only by such experiments as I have described that we can learn anything about them. It is apparently always engaged in mumbling over its old stores.' So, without assistance from the external environment, the person can provide his own interpolated activities, often without being aware of it. When the person recalls an event, he may introduce distortions: and these distortions may persist to occur again in his subsequent recall of the event. A specific example of this distorting effect of recalling may be given.

In 1955, the writer had, and made a note of, an interesting experience. This experience fell naturally into four parts and a shortened account of it is as follows.

(a) In the week beginning 23 October, I encountered in the Psychology Department of the University a male student of very conspicuously Scandinavian appearance. He was accompanied by a smallish, dark-haired companion and, as they seemed to be lost, I asked if I could help. The dark-haired student replied that his friend came from such-and-such a Scandinavian country and that he was looking for a certain lecturer. I then had the two men directed to this lecturer's room, and that was the end of the incident. I recall being very forcibly impressed by the Scandinavian man's nordic, Viking-like appearance – his fair hair, his blue eyes, and long bones. This nordic appearance was made all the more noticeable by the contrast between him and his companion. (b) About two hours later, I was leaving for lunch and met the Scandinavian student once more. I recognized him immediately and conversed with him as we walked out of the University together. Next day, I was speaking with the lecturer for whom he had been looking and discovered that his name was, we shall say, X. (c) About two weeks later, without having seen X again, I found and recognized his name among those of some students whom I was to meet one day for tea. I wrote to X asking him to tea on 23 November. On several occasions, as well as at the time of writing to him, I recalled his appearance in connexion with a Scandinavian correspondence I was then conducting and thought of him as the 'perfect Viking', visualizing him at the helm of a long-ship crossing the North Sea in quest of adventure. On 18 November, I even gave this fanciful description of him to someone who was also coming to tea on the 23rd. (d) When X arrived on the 23rd, I did not recognize him and he had to introduce himself. It was not that I had forgotten what he looked like but that his appearance, as I recalled it, had become grossly distorted. Two things struck me. The first was that he was very different from my recollection of him. His hair was darker, his eyes less blue, his build less muscular, and he was wearing spectacles (as he always does). The second was that I had seen him twice in the interval since our first two encounters without recognizing him. On each occasion it had been at a meeting where there was no opportunity to speak but, each time, I had been struck by his Scandinavian looks and had speculated as to where his home might be and whether he might know any of my Scandinavian acquaintances.

The above sequence of events clearly illustrates that retroactive interference may stem from the individual's own recalling. It was not that the writer's original perceiving of X was at fault, for if it had been he would not have recognized X on the second encounter two hours later. It was that in subsequently recalling X, the writer had also recalled his personal stereotype of a Viking, and this latter recalled experience had moulded his subsequent recall of X to such an extent that X was not recognized when actually present. As recalled, X now resembled a 'perfect Viking' more than he did himself. Apart from this example, the writer has observed not a few instances of the interfering effect of recalling in his own activities. Buildings, objects, and people have been recalled in terms of those characteristics originally noticed as dominant, and these characteristics (of size, gloominess, colourfulness, etc.) have become sharpened and accentuated in being recalled until the building, object, or person – as recalled – is but a caricature which is much larger, more gloomy, or more colourful than the original ever was. On being seen again, the original is now almost or completely unrecognizable.

That recalling of an experience may interfere with the later recognition of it is not a phenomenon which is unique to the writer. It is, for example, well demonstrated in an experiment reported by Dr Eunice Belbin of Cambridge in 1950. She had thirty-two subjects in all (comprising ten naval ratings, eight 14-year-old children, and fourteen university students). At the beginning of the experiment, each subject was left sitting in a waiting-room for two minutes. On the wall facing him was a large road-safety poster, but the subject was given no instructions of any kind regarding it. As far as he was concerned, it had nothing to do with the experiment, and he was simply waiting until the experimenter was ready for him. At the end of the two minutes, each subject was called into the experimenter's room and, after a short while, shown an identical poster and asked if this was the same as the poster in the waiting-room. The ingenious turn in the experiment came in the interval between being in the waiting-room and being asked to identify the poster. Half of the subjects (the recall group) were asked to describe as much as they could of the poster, and their recalling was prompted by standardized questions. The remaining half of the subjects (the non-recall group) were occupied with an unrelated task during an equivalent period of time. Given the poster to identify, fourteen out of the sixteen non-recall subjects did so correctly without hesitation. But only four subjects in the recall group identified it as being the same. The difference between the two groups is significant and cannot be attributed to individual differences of any sort, especially in view of Dr Belbin's similar findings in other experiments of the same basic type. What happened was that the recall group constructed their recalling around the dominant features of the picture and thereby made these features more outstanding than in the original; they also invented one or two details, such as Belisha beacons or an additional car, which they accepted as having been genuinely recalled. In short, the constructive character of their recalling introduced distortions, omissions, and additions into the poster as recalled so that the poster, as later seen, appeared to be substantially different and was not recognized as being the same as the original. The non-recall group, on the other hand, were not hindered in their recognition by any distorted recall of the poster.

To conclude our discussion of retroactive interference, it is the decrement in remembering which is due to activities and experiences interpolated between original learning and later remembering. It is by far the most potent factor in bringing about forgetting, and is often responsible not only for quantitative but also qualitative changes in what is remembered. The effects of interference increase with the amount of interpolated activity and with the similarity of this activity to the original; these effects show themselves most potent in the case of material which has not been well learned to start off with. At a practical level, this means that the original learning should be as thorough as possible and that if one period of study must be followed immediately by another, we should arrange to switch to that form of learning which is the least similar to the one in which we have just been engaged.

5 Recollecting Childhood Experiences

We can recollect remarkably little of our early childhood experiences. Why should this be so? Freud's suggestion is that the recollection of these early experiences is repressed because they are so intimately associated with the primitive, selfish, pleasure-seeking tendencies of early childhood; tendencies which were initially repressed because they met with punishment and parental disaffection; tendencies which are denied present expression because they would be so painfully inconsistent with our socially-derived notions of the sort of person we are and the way we should behave. Freud and others have accumulated much evidence to show that infants and pre-school children have many strong (and sometimes 'sexual') behaviour tendencies which are, somehow or other, eliminated in the lengthy process of learning to be socially acceptable beings. It may be that much of this elimination is achieved by repressing. If this were so, then early childhood would be the time, above all others, for repression, and it would not be surprising that we should have forgotten all about our early non-conforming tendencies and the experiences associated with them. In the face of present-day knowledge about child development, this suggestion of Freud's is by no means as fantastic as it might appear at first sight. It is a hypothesis which must be considered seriously. Let us now try to see how it squares with the facts of 'infantile amnesia'.

In setting out to investigate the recollection of childhood experiences, our greatest difficulty lies in obtaining authentic recollection. Recall of events is, as we have seen, susceptible to considerable distortion, particularly events which occurred a long time before. There is also the possibility that the recollection may not be genuine and that the account is based on stories of his own past which the individual has heard so often that he has come to believe erroneously that he can actually recollect the event concerned. It may be said at the outset that there is no way of guaranteeing the authenticity of the recalled events, although there are some methods of eliciting recall which are more likely to be free from errors than others. For example, a particularly unsatisfactory method would be to send out mailed questionnaires and so obtain details of the earliest experiences which can be recollected by respondents whose identity and sincerity may not always be known. Obviously, it is much better to elicit recall by direct (but non-suggestive) questioning and, if possible, check the accounts with relations, friends, teachers, or other witnesses of the original event. Bearing in mind, then, this inherent difficulty in the investigation of childhood memory, we may now cite a study conducted in America by S. Waldfogel in 1948, and briefly summarize the main findings as they apply to university students.

After securing the cooperation of 124 students and stressing the importance of careful and candid reporting, Waldfogel gave these young men and women eighty-five minutes in which to write down all the experiences they could recollect from their first eight years of life. They had to date each experience as accurately as possible and also state if it was one which they felt sure they had recollected spontaneously, if it was one which they had not been able to recollect but had been told about, or if they were uncertain whether or not they had recollected it. The great majority of students found that the eighty-five minute period was long enough to complete this task to their satisfaction. At the end of the period, the students were asked to re-read each event reported, consider it carefully, and indicate whether it had been very pleasant, pleasant, neutral, unpleasant, or very unpleasant. They were also asked to indicate their emotional reaction at the time of the original event. Some forty days later, this whole procedure was repeated without warning. The outcome of this second session was substantially the same as that of the first, with the notable exception that almost half as many new experiences were reported in addition to those reported before. This illustrates, once more, the important point that, in any one attempt at recall, we recall less than we are, in fact, capable of recalling. This also means that we cannot speak in absolute terms about the number of events which can be recalled: we can only say that, under such and such conditions, so many experiences are recalled. In both sessions, each student was known to the experimenter only as a number in the hope that, if his identity were unknown, he would be less tempted to hold back any possibly embarrassing experiences.

Of the total number of experiences reported, some 90 per cent were indicated as having been recollected. The average number of such recollections for each student was as follows:

	Age at time of event (in years)							
	0–1	1–2	2–3	3–4	4–5	5–6	6–7	7–8
Average number of events recollected	0·0	0·1	0·7	2·8	6·8	11·3	14·0	16·5

We can see from these figures that recollections from the first three years of life are very rare and that the *average* age of the earliest experience is in the fourth year of life. Most investigators agree that, while the earliest memory may be as early as the first year or as late as the seventh, the average individual has, as his earliest recollection, an experience which occurred between the ages of three and four. The above figures also show that the number of recollected experiences increases rapidly with increasing age.

Forgetting

When the memories were studied in terms of their affect, it was found that the emotions which the subjects recalled as having prevailed at the time were numerous and varied. Most commonly experienced had been joy which constituted about 30 per cent of the total. Next in frequency had been fear, about 15 per cent, followed by pleasure, anger, grief, and excitement, all between 5 and 10 per cent. The recall of pleasant events was more frequent than of unpleasant or neutral events. In round numbers, pleasant memories constituted about 50 per cent of the total, unpleasant memories about 30 per cent, and neutral memories about 20 per cent.

Now there is nothing in the above findings which runs directly contrary to Freud's hypothesis. On the quantitative side, we find the small number of recollected experiences consistent with the assumption that there has been a great deal of repressing in the early years. On the qualitative side, we find the preponderance of pleasant or neutral experiences consistent with the suggestion that there has been a selective forgetting of the unpleasant. Thus, in face of the facts, Freud's repression explanation of 'infantile amnesia' holds its ground. However, before accepting Freud's explanation, we ought to consider whether the above findings might not be accounted for in terms of those more prosaic processes which have already become familiar to us in this book.

Turning first to the quantitative findings regarding the number of memories from each age level, the explanation which immediately suggests itself is that of retroactive interference. If we take the average age of Waldfogel's subjects as being twenty years, many experiences must have occurred in the twelve to twenty years between the original experiences and their recall. This might well account for the obliteration of many of those early experiences, but it seems unlikely that it would account altogether for the different number of memories from the different ages. The number of memories from fifteen years ago is more than twice that from sixteen years ago and more than nine times the number from seventeen years ago. Suppose a man of 40 were recalling his past experiences of fifteen, sixteen, and seventeen years ago, would there be an equally large difference in the number of experiences recalled? There is no definite information on this question but, on the grounds of general observation, it seems most unlikely that there would be. The years of intervening experiences would, it is true, progressively reduce the quantity recollected but, out of fifteen to seventeen years, a year here or there would probably make little difference. We would certainly not expect that our man of 40 (like these students of 20) would be able to recall anything at all of his experiences from twenty years back. In short, retroactive interference undoubtedly plays some part in producing forgetting; but some part must also be played by the age of the individual at the time of the original experience.

It is well known that intellectual abilities in general strengthen rapidly during the childhood years. In the learning of any task, the older child, on the average, is more efficient than the younger or, to say the same thing in another way, the experiences of the younger child do not have such lasting effects. (This is not, incidentally, to deny the importance of early experience as a major determinant of the lines along which later development will occur, for this importance is due less to any individual experience than to a sequence of similar experiences.) Consider the performance of children of different ages in the testimony type of experiment. In one typical study, a picture was shown, and it was found that the average number of details later reported by three, four, five, and six year olds, respectively, was 11, 22, 35, and 44. Thus, shortly after the event, the younger children could recall less than the older children. Now, in the adult's recollecting of childhood experiences, the situation is essentially the same as in the testimony experiment (with the important difference that recall is delayed for a very much longer time), and exactly the same relation holds between age at the time of the experience and ability to recall this experience. It looks as though the younger child cannot retain his unique experiences and that this is a major factor in 'infantile amnesia'. We cannot recollect our very early experiences because they left no adequate impression to begin with.

The quantitative facts of early memories can, then, be explained by the combined effects of retroactive interference and of poor initial learning ability. But what of the qualitative findings? How can we account for the recollecting of this or that particular experience and for the predominance of pleasant and neutral memories? As regards the disproportionately small number of unpleasant memories, a simple explanation would exist if it could be shown that, in the child's life, there were, in fact, more pleasant and neutral experiences than unpleasant ones. And there are one or two pieces of evidence which indicate strongly that this is the case. Thus, it has been found that smiling and laughing are displayed considerably more frequently in normal children of pre-school age than is crying as a symptom of anger or grief. To the extent that such outward signs may be trusted, it would appear that pleasant and neutral tones predominate greatly over unpleasant states in normal children. The conclusion seems clear that the proportion of pleasant to unpleasant memories may well reflect directly the proportion of originally pleasant and unpleasant experience. In addition to this, there is the effect which different amounts of rehearsal have on the retaining of past experiences. In our conversation and probably also in our private reveries, we tend to recall (and so rehearse) our pleasant experiences and avoid the unpleasant, just as we tend to use pleasant or neutral words in speech and neglect unpleasant words. The tendency of children to avoid words with unpleasant connotations was shown impressively by one psychologist, who made an analysis of the remarks of children aged between five and nine years and found that the ratio of pleasant to unpleasant words was no less than 1,057 to 80. If we do indeed, as seems likely, recall (and so keep alive) our pleasant experiences more often than our unpleasant ones, this would further increase the preponderance of pleasant memories in a way which is selective but has nothing to do with repression. The unpleasant is not actively inhibited but merely loses out in competition with the pleasant. And, of course, an experience which was originally disagreeable may, in being recounted to others, lose its unpleasant tone and even seem pleasant on recall as, for example, when we laugh about our discomfitures in a previously embarrassing situation.

In conclusion of this section on the recollecting of childhood experiences: explanations exist both in terms of repression and also in more conventional terms. The writer would prefer to accept the latter type of explanation as being more consistent with general findings in the field of memory and with the facts of childhood memory as outlined in Chapter One. But it should be realized that there is no specific evidence against Freud's explanation. Present knowledge is not such that we can easily decide between the alternative theories. Even our conventional explanation is not altogether satisfactory in that it contains too many untested assumptions. In this respect, it reflects the present condition of psychology itself, which contains too few facts and too many question marks.

Qualitative Changes. When we revisit places we have once known, these places often fail to come up to our expectations. Sometimes this is because the place itself has changed. Sometimes it is because we have changed. Sometimes it is because the place, as we recall it, has become distorted. The question is this. Assuming that the place itself has not changed, why should there be discrepancy between the place, as we recall it, and this place as we now perceive it?

Forgetting

Such discrepancy may occur when we revisit places we last visited only months ago. But it is especially striking when we revisit places we have not seen since our childhood. When we revisit such a place, we are often struck not merely by how much we have forgotten but also by the shrunken appearance of the place. A house, a room, a building, a street, a toy: each may be found to be much smaller in size than we had remembered it. As an illustration of this familiar effect, here is an account of a personal experience of the writer.

I was motoring through a town which I had last visited twenty-three years before at the age of four. On that previous occasion, I had been taken through a certain school in this town by a relative who was a teacher there. And on several occasions since, I had vividly recollected this tour of inspection, largely in terms of visual imagery. I had recalled the large cement-covered playground in front of the school, the high iron railings, the grey stone façade of the building itself, the class-room on the left of the vast main doorway, and the enormous gymnasium at the end of the lengthy corridor. I still recall being impressed, as a child, with the vastness of the whole building. On seeing the school again, it seemed to have shrunk to such an alarming extent that I had to be reassured by someone else that this was, in fact, the same school. The railings were small, the playground tiny, and the building itself, although moderately sized, diminutive compared with my recollection of it.

Why this shrunken appearance of the building? Why should this building, as now perceived, be smaller than the building as recalled? In an attempt to answer this question, we must consider all of the three main phases of memory. We must consider the original perceiving of the building, the present recalling of the building, and the events which intervene between original perceiving and present recalling, e.g. how often and in what ways the building has been remembered in the interval. We must also consider the present perceiving of the building. Let us start with the matter of perceiving. The main point here is that the same building is likely to be perceived differently by the child and by the adult. One reason for this is the different physical sizes of child and adult. Another reason is that perceiving is profoundly modified by the cumulative effects of the person's past experiences: a person perceives an object against his background experiences of similar objects; and as this background experience, this frame of reference, alters, so too does his perceiving of the object. (For a readable overview of perception, see *The Psychology of Perception*, by M. D. Vernon, Penguin Books, 1962).

The same building is likely to appear larger to the child than to the adult because the child is physically smaller. The corridor appears longer because the child has to take more steps in traversing it; and it appears higher because he must tilt his head more sharply in order to view the roof. The doors are heavier because he must push harder to open them; the door-handles are higher because he must reach up to them, and they are larger because he cannot close his fingers around them. The railings are higher because they tower above his head, whereas they only reach the adult's shoulder. The building may also appear larger to the child because of his limited previous experiences of buildings. He has probably had less experience of large buildings, classrooms, halls, and long corridors than the adult has had. His frame of reference for buildings is likely to have been acquired in terms of his own home and the houses of friends rather than in terms of the larger spaces of public buildings such as schools, theatres, museums, hospitals. In visiting a school at the age of four, the writer was probably coming into contact for the first time with a building which was more commodious than a domestic dwelling house; so in comparison with his past experiences, the school would appear truly enormous. Indeed, the most vivid aspects of the writer's recollecting is that he was impressed by the immense size of the school; and it may have been this very

Forgetting

impressiveness which made the experience as memorable as it was. In short, the same building is likely to be perceived differently by child and adult. In part, this difference may be due to the altered physical size of the person. In part, it may be due to the person's altered modes of perceiving against a different background of past experience.

So child and adult are likely to perceive the same building differently. Now this, of itself, could account for the present discrepancy between the building as recalled and as now perceived. Suppose the person accurately recollected his original experiences of the building. This recollecting would be relative to his size and his mode of perceiving at that time. But both his size and his mode of perceiving have altered in the interval. And so, his accurate recollecting will be relative to a frame of reference (himself) which has altered meanwhile. In such a case, then, the discrepancy between current perceiving and recalling is not due to distorted recall, but to recall which is accurate in terms of a frame of reference that no longer applies. This point may be further illustrated by quoting an experience reported to the writer by a colleague. This colleague met a boy, then aged fifteen years, whom he had not seen for two years; and when he met this boy, he had the strong and persisting impression that the boy had shrunk in height from the time of the previous meeting. Why this strange impression? In brief, what had happened was as follows. At the first meeting, the colleague has seen this boy as being the same height as his own son, and this was how he recalled the boy's height, that is, in relation to the height of his own son as a standard of reference. However, between the first meeting and the second, his son had a growth spurt and increased in height considerably, whereas the other boy grew hardly at all. Now, in anticipation of the second meeting with the boy, the colleague recalled the boy's height as being equal to that of his own son, without realizing that this standard of reference had altered in the meantime. His standard of reference (his son's height) had been appropriate at the time of the first meeting with the boy, but was appropriate no longer. Hence the impression that the boy had grown shorter.

It can happen, then, that when we revisit a childhood scene, the shrunken appearance of the scene is due to changes between our perceiving during childhood and our perceiving now. But the shrunken appearance may also be due to distorted recalling. In recalling any event, we are liable to accentuate any characteristic of this object which had especially impressed us at the time of perceiving. If the object's largeness impressed us, we tend to recall the object as being larger than it really is: so too with objects which impress us as being especially small, or colourful, or fragile, and so on. In short, a recalled object tends to be accentuated in regard to whatever characteristics the person abstracted as being dominant; and with repeated recalling there is a tendency towards greater and greater accentuation of these dominant characteristics. So, if a building impressed a child by its size, he might, over the years, recall a progressively larger caricature of this building. In addition to this tendency for recalling to caricature what is being recalled, there is another slight effect for which experimental evidence has been obtained. This is a tendency for people to recall a highly valued object as being larger than it really is. For example, if children are shown coins of different value and subsequently asked, in one way or another, to characterize the sizes of these coins, then some children over-estimate the size of the more valuable coins, that is, the recalled size of the coin is influenced by the value of the coin to the child. It could be that this accentuating effect of value plays some part in distorting a 'treasured memory'.

In summary: why should there be qualitative discrepancy between a place, as we remember it from childhood, and this place as we now perceive it? The only general answer which can be given is that one or all of three effects may be at work. One is a change in the way the person perceives the place, as a child and as an adult. Another is distortion in recall due to accentuating those characteristics of the place which were originally dominant for the person. A third, and probably much less important, effect is a tendency to exaggerate the size of recalled objects which are of value to the person. The relative vagueness of this answer serves to stress a point of importance. There is no one cause of forgetting. In this chapter, we have considered what seem to be the main conditions responsible for forgetting, but in most real life situations it is by no means easy to discover whether any particular instance of forgetting is due to this condition or that. To ask the reason for any specific instance of forgetting is often to ask for the impossible. Usually, the best that can be done is to give a number of likely reasons, any or all of which may be valid for this particular instance.

VII Improving Memory

1 The Practical Problem

Can memory be improved? The answer to this question depends on what is meant by the words 'memory' and 'improvement'. But since the answer is, with reservations, that memory can be improved, the critical question is this: How can memory be improved? A broad answer was given to this question by William James in 1891. 'All improvement of memory consists in the improvement of one's habitual methods of recording facts.' To the present day, this answer cannot be bettered; unless by adding the obvious rider that the continued retaining of recorded facts can be ensured by their being brought into repeated use. So, granted that a person is in a normal state of health, it seems certain that we must direct our efforts at improving the first of memory's three main phases. Repetition apart, there seems little that we can do about improving, as such, the phases of retaining and remembering. In other words, the basic practical problem is to ensure that learning is appropriate in the first place: if some event passes without leaving any effects within the person, there is nothing which can subsequently be done to make the person either retain or remember this event. For all practical purposes, our question is this. How can learning procedures be improved? But even this question must be made more precise before it can be answered. It must be rephrased in specific terms so as to specify the kinds of events which are to be remembered, the circumstances under which future remembering is to take place, and the kind of person who is to do the remembering. We can only begin to answer the question once we have specified what is to be remembered, when, and who by. Once we have done this, the question can, at least in principle, be answered.

The main point is that our starting question is, as it stands, too vague to be answered in any helpful way. As with so many practical problems, we must first consider in detail what state of affairs we eventually want to produce, then what state of affairs we have to start with, and only then begin to work on the problem of modifying what we have so as to bring about what we want to achieve. Furthermore, it is important to realize that the best possible solution will vary according to detailed circumstances. The solution will vary from one person to another, e.g. a procedure which enables a professional chemist to remember the main content of an article about chemistry is not, in detail, appropriate for a novice who wants to remember the article's contents. The solution will vary from one kind of material to another, e.g. a procedure which enables a person to recall verbatim a list of nonsense syllables is not, in detail, appropriate when this same person wants to be able to recall the main points made by a book he is reading. The solution will vary from one kind of remembering to another, e.g. a procedure which enables a student to answer a recognition-type exam is not necessarily appropriate when he wants to be able to answer a recall-type exam on the same material. The solution will vary according to the circumstances under which remembering will be required, e.g. a procedure which enables a student to recall facts when prompted by specific questions is not necessarily appropriate if he wants to be able to recall these facts in problem-solving situations where they might be relevant. The solution will vary according to how far hence the remembering will be required; so a procedure which enables a person to recall a short digit sequence immediately after hearing it will not usually suffice if he wants to be able to recall this sequence a week hence.

It should be clear that the question as to how memory can be improved cannot be given any general, all-purpose answer. To be useful, an answer must be tailored to fit the details of the problem, that is, what is to be remembered, when, and who by. And the answer will vary according to these details. This means that if a person asks how he can improve his memory, he may well be disappointed on two counts. First, he cannot be given any answer of practical worth until he makes his question more specific. He must say what kinds of events he would like to be able to remember, in what ways he would want to remember them and under what circumstances. We must discover what it is that makes it difficult for him, as an individual, to learn these events appropriately. Only then can we begin to try to answer his question by suggesting procedures which may enable him to learn in such a way that he can achieve the kind of remembering he wants. Second, he cannot be given any answer of practical worth which does not involve effort on his part. Learning procedures which can be suggested to him must, to become effective, be implemented by him. He must undertake to modify his own activities, learn what to do and when. The acquisition of improved learning techniques is like the acquisition of improved techniques in golf, or swimming, or musicianship: it can only be brought about by selectively directed effort on the person's part.

So there is no all-purpose, effortless recipe for improving memory. This point must be stressed because most people who ask about 'improving their memory' assume, or at least hope, that there is some all-purpose recipe which demands little or no effort on their behalf. In face of the fact that such a recipe does not exist, a person may well decide to make do with his 'memory' as it is. Changes could be effected, but the cost of these changes does not, the person feels, justify their gains. Belief in an all-purpose recipe for 'improved memory' seems to die hard. As recently as the seventeenth century, some people claimed that 'improved memory' could be effected by some recipe which varied all the way from magic spells, through herbal mixtures (cinnamon was supposed to be a great help), to rituals such as suspending an animal's left foot. One recipe which would enable a person to remember everything he read was as follows: wear a cap made of beaver skin, anoint the head and spine monthly with drops of castor oil, and take a pound of castor oil internally each year. In more recent times, the all-purpose recipe has become more sophisticated and, at first sight, more directly relevant to the activities of memory. One form of all-purpose recipe is repeated practice in memorizing. The person is advised to memorize, say, poetry, or prose, or the names above the shops in a street, or objects displayed briefly on a tray. Another form of all-purpose recipe is that the person should master the use of mnemonic systems which enable him to memorize verbatim long sequences of relatively meaningless material. These two all-purpose recipes will be considered later in more detail; but it may be said briefly that, while each can effect some improvement in some memory activities, neither is guaranteed to do so.

In summary, the problem of memory improvement cannot be tackled in general terms. It can only be solved by specific consideration of the kind of memory task which is to be accomplished, that is, what is to be remembered, who by, and when. In the light of these detailed considerations, the next step is to devise learning techniques which are appropriate for the accomplishment of the task. The final step is mastery of these learning techniques by the person himself. In short, the practical problem is one of developing learning techniques which are appropriate to the detailed requirements of a particular kind of memory task. In the next section, we will consider the fitting of techniques to a task of a kind favoured by mnemonists.

2 Tasks and Techniques

A person is given a single presentation of a sequence of randomly selected words. His task is to learn the presented sequence so that he can, afterwards, remember in the following ways. He must be able to recall every word correctly and in its correct sequence. He must readily be able to recall the sequence in reverse order; recall which word occupies any given position in the sequence, say, the twentieth word presented; and recall the particular position in which any word came. This, then, is the task. It is a task which professional mnemonists can accomplish with word sequences of fifty or a hundred items. It is not a task which most people could, off-hand, accomplish – or indeed want to be able to accomplish. But there are two reasons why it is worth considering what learning techniques are necessary for such a task. Such consideration exemplifies the solving of a specific problem in fitting the techniques to the task, and indicates some general principles to be borne in mind whenever we undertake any problem of fitting techniques to memory tasks.

The writer has used the above kind of memory task for purposes of classroom demonstration with university students acting as subjects. In order to keep the task within reasonable proportions, he uses a sequence of only ten words and also simplifies the task by giving the sequence number of each word before reading it out. Let us consider first what happens when this task is presented to students who are given no instructions regarding the learning procedures they might use. Let us call these students the Uninstructed Group.

Improving Memory

The Uninstructed Group. Students are told to write down, in their notebooks, the numbers from one to ten. They are told that a list of ten unrelated words will be read out and that the number of each word will be given before the word itself is read out. They are told that, after the list has been presented, they are to write down as many of the words as they can, writing each word opposite its appropriate number. Their final recall score will be assessed by giving one mark for each word correctly written against its correct number, i.e. the word itself must be correct and so must its position in the sequence. One list actually used is as follows; each item (whether number or word) being read out at a steady rate of one item every two seconds. ONE – SUGAR, TWO – DAFFODIL, THREE – BOAT, FOUR – TIGER, FIVE – NECKLACE, SIX – TABLE, SEVEN – FEATHER, EIGHT – CUP, NINE – MOUNTAIN, TEN – BLACKBIRD. In one such Uninstructed Group, there were thirty-two students. Table 7 below shows the number of students who made each score. Two students score full marks, two score 9, and so on. It can be seen that, although some students do better than others, this task is too much for most of them. Half of the students fail to get as many as seven of the ten words correct.

What are the difficulties of this task, and how do the students deal with them? One source of difficulty is the relatively large number of words: with a three-word list, every student would score full marks. Another difficulty is the unrelatedness of the words to each other: if the words made a meaningful sequence, most students would score full marks. Another difficulty is the relatively rapid pace at which the words are presented: if there were a gap of, say, ten seconds between successive items, most students would score full marks. Yet another difficulty is that the list is presented once only: if the list were presented six times, most students would score full marks. Now, by what procedures do these students attempt to deal with these

difficulties? When they are questioned about their procedures, it is found that, in detail, each student proceeds in
his own unique way. But certain general procedures are
used more often than others. A few students count off the
words on their fingers. Rather more students use thematic
chaining, that is, they cumulatively elaborate a story whose
key features represent successive words presented. The
majority use cumulative rehearsal: they repeat the first
word, then the first and second, then the first three words,
and so on. However, after taking in some five or six words,
there is too little time for such cumulative rehearsal; before
he can run through the list given to date, another word is
being read out. At this point, he is uncertain how to
continue. Some students start a fresh chain of cumulative
rehearsal; some decide to ignore new words and simply
keep rehearsing the chain they already have; some adopt a
compromise procedure and try to rehearse the early words
while, at the same time, listening to new words in the hope
that they might 'stick'. In general then, despite individual
differences between one student and the next, each student
adopts a procedure which is inadequate to the demands of
this rather unfamiliar task. He finds himself with too much
to do in too short a time. He finds himself losing some words
and losing the correct sequence of others.

When each student comes to recall the word sequence,
he proceeds in a way which closely reflects his learning
procedure. Some students look at their fingers; some try to
reconstruct the story they made up about the words; some
recall the cumulative chain of words they started rehearsing.
All this underlines an important general feature of remembering, namely: remembering is an activity which proceeds
along lines that reflect the original learning procedure. The
person's remembering procedures are dominated by the
procedures he adopted during original learning. Most
students correctly recall the early words in the presented
list, and the last one or two words; but they either cannot

recall the middle words, or they recall them in the wrong
position. When these uninstructed students are asked to
recall the list in reverse order, they find great difficulty.
They can only recall a forward sequence and, in attempting
to reverse this, they often forget some of the words. It is
noteworthy that those few students who learned by thematic
chaining are especially likely to recall words which were not
in the list presented to them.

The Instructed Group. Students in this group are given
exactly the same memory task. But they are instructed
beforehand in learning procedures which are designed to
make the task manageable. They are taught a mnemonic
system which is a version of the visual-symbol system to
be discussed later. The particular system used is, itself,
designed to be mastered in under five minutes. The instructions are as follows.

'We start with a rhyme. One is a bun; two is a shoe;
three is a tree; four is a door; five is a hive; six is sticks;
seven is heaven; eight is a gate; nine is wine; ten is a hen.
I want you to learn this rhyme, but one thing is important.
Think, for example, not of '*bun*' in general, but of a very
particular bun. Visualize the bun if you can. Is it large or
small? Brown or yellow? Has it raisins? Has it icing? One
is a bun.' The instructor continues through the rhyme in
this way, encouraging students to think about each rhyming
word as a detailed, vividly imaged object. 'Now, I want to
tell you how to use this rhyme in learning the word list.
When you hear the number, think of the rhyming object.
And when you hear the word, relate this to the object as
strikingly and as vividly as you can. Suppose the first word
is PETROL. See your particular bun covered in petrol,
reeking petrol, swimming in a can of petrol, belching
flames like a petrol-bun. The more outrageously odd the
relation, the better. Do this sort of thing with each number-
word pair you hear. The next point is that, once you have

related each pair, forget it, dismiss it from mind, attend fully to the next pair. The rule is: compare only two things at a time, and never attempt to go back and remember what a previous part of the list was.'

In one such Instructed Group there were thirty-two students. Their recall scores are shown in Table 7. It can be

Table 7

Recall Score	4 or less	5	6	7	8	9	10
Uninstructed Group (N=32)	0	5	11	9	3	2	2
Instructed Group (N=32)	0	0	1	2	4	8	17

seen that this group does markedly better than the uninstructed group. More than half of this group score full marks. It is also found that this group can readily recall the words in backward sequence, and readily recall which particular word occurs in any position mentioned. It might be added that the writer has used this mnemonic system with more than eight hundred students in all. He has also presented different lists of words to these students. And the use of the system never fails to improve the recall performance of the majority, often to the great surprise of the students themselves. A small minority of students fails to benefit from the system: in such cases, it seems always to be the case that the student decided privately not to use the system, or that he could not resist recalling earlier items while later items were still being presented to him. However for most students, the mnemonic system provides adequate, predetermined procedures for both learning and recalling. In essence, the merits of these learning and remembering procedures are the same as those outlined for the successive-comparison system discussed in the final section of Chapter Five. The main distinguishing features of the present system are twofold. First, it enables its user directly to recall which word occupies which particular position in the presented list: this is because each word is learned in relation to its position rather than in relation to its neighbouring words. Secondly, the system requires the initial mastery of a code which represents each number (position) by an imagined object. In the above demonstration, the mastery of this code was facilitated by the use of a rhyme. The code comprises the number sequence from one to ten (a sequence which is already well learned) and each number is represented by an object-word which sounds almost the same as the number-word. What is the code-word for FIVE? A familiar object-word which sounds almost the same. This severely delimits the number of possible code-words; the word HIVE is, so to speak, heavily signposted. The further translation of HIVE into a detailed imaged object is, for most people, easy; especially since the person is free to construct that particular image which comes most readily to him. In short, the activities involved in learning and remembering the code are related together in such a close-knit way that a few repetitions suffice for mastery of the whole.

Extending the Technique. It is clear that the learning and recalling procedures just outlined could be extended to deal with lists of words far in excess of ten. To extend the procedures thus, the person would have to devise and master a longer code. He would also have to gain facility in the use of this code and, to do this, he would have to practice using the code. But notice that he would have to undertake this practice in a self-critical way. That is, he would have to employ the code in memorizing lists, and examine his own activities carefully for strong and weak points. He would have to note errors and falterings, and use the system again with particular reference to modifying and improving this or that facet of his activity. In short, his practice would not be a mere repeated use of the system. It would be an active, self-critical, self-modifying undertaking in which the person is constantly alert for ways of improving and short-cutting his learning and remembering efforts. In the course of this self-critical practice, he would gain facility in a variety of necessary techniques. For example, techniques of translating presented words into distinctive and unambiguous imaging; techniques of rapidly forming distinctive composite images; techniques of abstracting from the presented sequence only those characteristics which are relevant to the use of his system, even at the clear risk of not noting any conventional meaning in the presented material; techniques of concentrating on the task of each successive moment and not being distracted either by incidental circumstances in his environment or by trying to recall what he did a moment ago. In this way, he would gain expertise in the task of memorizing long sequences of unrelated words. However, it is altogether another question whether he would gain techniques which could be transferred to other kinds of memory tasks.

Some General Implications. The above considerations suggest some general implications for 'memory improvement'.

(1) Memory, in a restricted sense, can be improved by developing learning techniques which are adequate to the kind of memory task in hand.

(2) The first step in developing such techniques is to survey the nature of the task and diagnose its requirements. What is to be remembered, and what ignored? What are the main difficulties about carrying through this selective learning? How far is the person already equipped to undertake the required learning? How far is he not already equipped, and so what learning techniques must he acquire, and how? In short, the first necessity is to diagnose the task, try to understand the particular difficulties of this task for the particular person, and try to discover how either the task or the person can be modified so as to surmount these difficulties.

(3) Modifying the task is chiefly a matter of translating the material into terms which are familiarly meaningful to the learner. How can new items be related to items that are already familiar? How can new items be related to each other in terms of familiar relationships? How, in short, can the person's cumulative past experience be employed so as to minimize the novelty of the learning he must undertake?

(4) Modifying the person's learning techniques is chiefly a matter of getting him to adopt a self-critical attitude to his own learning activities. The person should realize that each learning situation presents him with a problem to be solved by diagnosing the sort of demands it makes on him. He should realize that a large part of 'memory improvement' consists in being able to diagnose the requirements of the memory task in hand. He should adopt a self-critical attitude to his own diagnosis and learning techniques in order to discover which diagnosis and techniques are most effective for him in this or that learning situation. In short, the person should explicitly undertake, not mere practice in learning, but the enterprise of learning from his own learning experiences the requirements of different tasks and the nature of his own capabilities.

3 Mnemonic Systems

Mnemonic systems have been called 'memoria technica' or 'artificial memory'. They were known to the ancient Greeks and, in medieval times, were included among the magic arts. In the present day, they are sometimes used as the basis of courses which claim to 'improve your memory'. Their chief use is by stage performers. Up to the present day, so-called memory experts have packed halls with audiences eager to witness their feats of memory. These experts are of two kinds. There is the 'memory-man' who specializes in answering factual questions relating to some fairly circum-scribed field such as historical dates or sport. He owes his talent to a vast store of knowledge which has been built up over the years not by supernormal means or by the use of mnemonic systems but by the prolonged study of some subject in which, for some reason or other, he is profoundly interested. It is noteworthy that the memory-man facing his audience is comparable to the well-prepared university student taking his final examination, and that he may actually be inferior to the latter in the range and spon-taneity of his answers. This is not to belittle either the memory-man or the student, but merely to emphasize that the memory-man is someone who can readily recall from an extensive and well-organized body of past learning. As such, he is not so rare as might be imagined. There are many professional and business men and 'enthusiasts' of various sorts who, allowed their own field of specialization and appropriate conditions of publicity and theatricality, could emulate the professional memory-man and not suffer in comparison. The second form of memory expert specializes in memorizing, on the spot, lists of new and unrelated material presented to him by his audience. These are the 'mnemonists', and it is they who have evolved and practised mnemonic systems. They do not stop at laying down general principles for memorizing but elaborate highly specific rules. The efficacy of these rules is attested by the mnemonist's amazing performance, for he can memorize, at a single hearing, a series of objects or numbers which, without his system, he would require to study for some considerable time.

A great deal is known about mnemonic systems because many practitioners of this art have written in detail about their procedures. (A recent and informative example is: *Develop a Super-Power Memory*, by Mr Harry Lorayne, The New English Library, 1963. This book is written by a skilled

293

mnemonist who is reporting his own procedures. He describes these procedures in detail, so that anyone wanting to accomplish various specialized memorizing feats would be able to do so. His book has the merit of not exaggerating the utility of such procedures, and of making clear that their acquisition involves much work and practice.) When we examine what mnemonists have to say about their art, we find that there are as many different mnemonic systems as there are people who employ them: each individual carries through his skilled activities in his own special way. However, it is feasible to place each system into one of three general categories, namely: the visual-symbol type, the successive-comparison type, and the digit-letter type.

Visual-symbol Systems. This type of system was exemplified in the preceding section. It is the most widely used of systems and is also the oldest on record. It is supposed to have been devised by the Greek poet Simonides around the year 500 B.C. According to Cicero, the outline of this system occurred to Simonides under dramatic circumstances. A certain Greek had won a wrestling victory at the Olympic Games and was giving a banquet at his house by way of celebration. After the fashion of the times, he invited a poet – Simonides – to provide a recitation as part of the entertainment. After delivering his eulogy, Simonides was called away to speak with two men who were waiting outside, and scarcely had he left than the floor of the banquet room collapsed, killing the host and all his guests. Naturally, relatives wished to sort out the bodies, but these were so mutilated as to be unrecognizable. However, Simonides had observed, during his recital, the positions occupied by the guests in the room and, by searching in the appropriate places, he was able to identify the bodies. He could recall who was present by recalling where they were. This incident set Simonides thinking. If such were the case with places and people, surely names, objects, and even ideas could be better memorized by assigning them fixed positions in space. He would imagine, as vividly and with as much detail as possible, a room. And each item he wished to learn he would visualize as being placed in a certain part of this room. The first item would always be placed, say, on the middle of the far wall, the second on the top left-hand corner of the window, and so on. Then, when he wanted to recall these items, he would systematically peruse this imaginary room and find each item located in its particular position. Simonides found that a technique of this sort was, indeed, of considerable assistance in memorizing. He reduced his technique to a system and appears to have taught it to others, since both Quintilian and Cicero confess themselves indebted to it. These orators used to prepare their speeches by thinking of each division in connexion with a specific, visualized locality. Since the order of these localities was well known, the speaker had only to imagine each in turn to recall or redintegrate the divisions in their correct sequence.

For obvious reasons, this type of system was called the 'locality' or 'topical' system. (The word 'topical' comes from the Greek word for 'place'. It is of interest that we still speak of 'topics' in connexion with discourses, and that Simonides' system is believed by some to have furnished the origin of such expressions as 'in the first place'.) Since the time of Simonides, many mnemonists have employed variations of the locality system. Rooms, houses, public buildings, the human body, the back and palm of the hand – all of these have been broken up into distinctly visualized localities so that items to be learned in sequence can be associated with them.

In the mid seventeenth century, a Cambridge man, Henry Herdson, devised what might be regarded as a logical development of the locality system. Up to this time, mnemonists had represented sequence by standard visual images occupying different parts of an imagined spatial whole. What Herdson did was simply to dispense with the spatial aspect of the model and employ merely the images themselves. He represented each numeral by one of a variety of objects as follows: 1 = candle, or any elongated object; 2 = swan, or any 2-shaped object; 3 = trident, or any tripartite object; 4 = dice, or any object with four parts; 5 = hand, or any object with five parts; 6 = tobacco pipe, or any 6-shaped object; 7 = open razor, or any 7-shaped object; 8 = spectacles, or any object involving two round shapes; 9 = burning glass, or any 9-shaped object; and 0 = orange, or any round object. An intending mnemonist would decide for himself which particular object would represent each numeral. He would, incidentally, be likely to represent each numeral by only one object: Herdson's system is atypical in using more than one object for each digit. Having made his choice, he would then familiarize himself thoroughly with his code. At this point, he would be in a position to employ his system in exactly the same way as a locality system proper. He need not, of course, limit himself to the first ten numbers. He could extend his code indefinitely. In practice, most mnemonists seem to extend their systems to cover numbers up to thirty and often up to a hundred. Neither need he be bound to any particular code. He is free to represent any number by any visual image he cares to select. The very variety of images used by different mnemonists argues that there is nothing magical about Herdson's selection. One symbol seems to be as appropriate as any other, and it matters little which is used. What is important is that one definite code should be decided upon and should be made completely familiar before being put into use.

In the practical application of the visual-symbol system, mnemonists do not seem to rely exclusively on visual relationships. The examples which they give of their associations reveal that the key object is often related to the given object in verbal terms as well. Consider the task of

associating 'Tokyo' with 'three-legged stool'. In addition
to visual relations, the Japanese might be thought of as
wearing toques, as having a toe stuck in a bottle of Tokay
wine, and as crying 'Oh my toe is stuck in the Tokay, oh!'.
Here the two items are related together in an imaginary
situation which has verbal as well as visual characteristics.
Examples employing both means of relating are not at all
infrequent in the literature, and it seems that mnemonists
are shrewd enough to pass over any helpful device in the
interests of preserving the purity of their chosen system. A
system dictates, as it were, the strategy. The tactics it leaves
to the individual mnemonist.

Successive-comparison Systems. This type of system was exemplified in the final section of Chapter Five. It is extremely
simple, does not require the preliminary learning of any
code, and indeed hardly merits the name 'system'. It does
nothing more than exploit an elementary but astonishing
feature of memory activity. The feature is this: if two simple
events are brought into vivid relationship with each other,
then the subsequent occurrence of one of these events will
lead to the recall of the other. This is the feature which was
named 'redintegration' by Sir William Hamilton in 1836,
the feature which is extensively used by mnemonists, and
the feature involved in the successive-comparison type of
system. This system is nothing more than the use of redintegration to master a sequence of simple items. For example,
in learning a sequence of words, the mnemonist compares
the first word with the second, bringing them together into
some related whole. He then dismisses this whole from
awareness and attends to comparing the second and third
words. This done, he relates the third word with the fourth,
and so on. The important thing is that at no point is he
concerned with more than two words: he relates each pair
successively. The first word in the series must, of course, be
learned as it stands. But, in recall, this word redintegrates

the second which, in its turn, is recalled as linked with the third. The actual method of relating any two words together is highly variable. They may be brought together by any of the myriad relationships which used to be described so minutely by philosophers of the British Associationist School. The objects for which the words stand may be visualized together: the words may rhyme; they may suggest some causal sequence of events, either mundane or absurd; they may be related through one or more intermediate words or 'secondary associations'. These are but a few of the ways in which associations might be forged. As with other systems, the mnemonist becomes, with practice, increasingly skilful in relating one item with another. The basic rule may be expressed as follows. Never compare more than two items at a time, and bring these items into inter-relation as vividly and distinctively as possible. If this is done, even for less than a second, the mnemonist can rely on being able to recall the one item whenever he has the other.

Digit-letter Systems. This type of system is designed to assist the memorizing of digit sequences by translating digits into code items which can easily be related together. It was in the year 1684 that von Winckelmann, a German, published his 'most fertile secret' of symbolizing digits by letters of the alphabet. These letters were then built up into easily learned words or sentences. In the following century, variations on von Winckelmann's system appeared, including a version by the philosopher Leibniz. But the system seems to have gained its greatest popularity in the nineteenth century. By way of illustration, one of these systems of a century ago may be cited in detail. It is that devised by an English clergyman and schoolmaster called Brayshaw. His code was as follows.

1	2	3	4	5	6	7	8	9	0	00
B	D	G	J	L	M	P	R	T	W	St
C	F	H	K		N	Q		V	X	
			S			Z				

Applying his system to education rather than to theatrical entertainment Brayshaw published, in 1849, his *Metrical Mnemonics*, which contained a collection of rhymes embodying over 2,000 dates and numerical facts drawn from history, geography, physics, astronomy, etc. These rhymes were clearly intended for use in schools and were, presumably, learned by the pupils of Keighley Grammar School where Brayshaw was headmaster. The method of this facile rhymester is apparent in the following typical example which gives the 'dates' of English sovereigns.

1066 By *men*, near Hastings, William gains the crown:
1087 A *rap* in Forest New brings Rufus down.
1100 Gaul's *coast* first Henry hates, whose son is drowned:
1135 Like *beagle*, Stephen fights with Maude renoun'd.
1154 A *cloak*, at Becket's tomb, sec'nd Henry wears:
1189 And *brave* first Richard oft Saladin dares.
1199 John's *act* at Runnymede England pleased avows:
1216 His *face*, *in* Parliament, weak third Henry shows.

The verse continues in this way up to the last line which gives the date of Queen Victoria's accession.

1837 Lastly, *our hope* rests on Victoria's will.

Thus, Brayshaw inserts in each line the sovereign's name, some outstanding fact about him, and the date of his accession to the throne. This date is embodied in the second word or in the second and third words combined, it being understood that the dates begin at the year 1000.

None of the other versions of the digit-letter system differ from Brayshaw's in more than three minor respects. First, they may use a different code, e.g. 'one' may be represented by P or W or any other letter of the alphabet. Second, the letters may not be formed into words but may be used initially to construct a phrase in which each successive word begins with the appropriate letter. Thus, 1855, the date of Lord Raglan's death, is represented by the letters

C–R–L–L. Instead of embodying these letters in a word such as 'carol-l', they may be embodied in a phrase such as 'Courageous Raglan Lamented Lies'. The third variation concerns, again, the code itself; phonic elements may be used in place of letters. Here each number is represented by a sequence of sounds. Such a system would obviously be preferred by those mnemonists who possess strong auditory imagery.

It should be apparent that these digit-letter systems would, like visual-symbol systems, gain greatly in efficiency by being practised. It is, however, noteworthy that they have played no appreciable role in the stage performances of mnemonists. This is doubtless due, in part, to the lesser interest shown by audiences in an ability to recall numbers as opposed to sequences of objects. But chiefly it may be attributed to the greater difficulty of fitting the letters together into words or phrases. It is impossible to compare only two items at a time: four or five letters at least must be related together simultaneously. Accordingly, this type of system lends itself but poorly to the rapid-fire conditions of the stage. It has, instead, been employed by educators who could take leisure to devise the happy phrase which others could learn and 'decode' as occasion demands. This raises the question of whether Brayshaw was correct in assuming that his was the most effective method of teaching a large body of numerical data. It must be borne in mind that his educational programme involved vast amounts of rote memorizing. His unfortunate pupils had to learn hundreds of dates and distances, to say nothing of the areas and populations of countries. Faced by such an undertaking, pupils may well have found their metrical mnemonics of assistance. The modern pupil, however, would not find it worth while to master a digit-letter system since, for good or ill, the educational emphasis has swung away from rote memorizing. School history, for example, is no longer synonymous with lengthy lists of dates.

Mnemonic Systems

The Uses of Mnemonic Systems. It has been seen that mnemonic systems are, in essence, procedural techniques which are explicitly designed to meet the learning requirements of certain types of memory task. The tasks typically require rapid memorizing of long, and usually haphazard, sequences of items such as words, playing-cards, digits, objects. There is no question that, for such tasks, these systems are not only effective but, for the great majority of people, essential. They enable the person to translate the presented items into other items (usually imaged) which he can readily relate together in distinctively appropriate ways. The skilled mnemonist is a person who has built up, through prolonged constructive efforts, a large repertoire of such procedural techniques, along with various individualistic short-cuts and devices. In practice, he deploys these procedures with flexible ingenuity: he knows just what he can do and what he cannot do: he shows great deftness in selecting just that particular procedure which is, for him, most fitting to the particular task in hand. Having acquired his learning techniques, he can, of course apply them to memorizing everyday material, e.g. the names of people he meets, addresses, telephone numbers, historical dates, formulae. He can readily learn, and retain, large quantities of detailed factual information. This being so, two questions arise.

The first question is this. Is it worthwhile mastering mnemonic systems, not for their own sake, but for the sake of being able to apply their techniques in learning everyday matters? This question cannot be given a straight, general answer since much depends on the amount and kind of memorizing the person wants to accomplish in everyday life. In general terms, however, the writer's guess would be that few people would find it worthwhile to master a repertoire of mnemonic systems for the sole purpose of the contribution they would make to his everyday learning requirements. Incidentally, this general assertion should be tempered by one consideration. The mastery of some simple mnemonic system may lead some people to realize, for the first time, that they can control and modify their own mental activities. And this realization may encourage them to undertake that self-critical experimentation with their own learning and remembering procedures which is such an important part of intellectual development. Bearing in mind the value of this incidental effect for some few people, it is probably true to say that most people could get their best practical results by directly considering the requirements of those memory tasks which most trouble them in their daily life.

The second question is this. Since mnemonic systems are so effective, why should their use be so often criticized adversely in, say, the work of the university student? The main point of this criticism does not concern the efficacy of mnemonic systems as such but, rather, their inappropriateness to the kinds of learning and remembering tasks which the student is expected to undertake. The material which a student encounters in lectures, articles, books, is not, for the most part, to be learned for verbatim recall. He is not expected to characterize the material in ways which most readily enable him to learn it as a meaningless, rote sequence. He is, rather, expected to abstract higher-order characteristics of a generalizable kind. That is, he is expected to 'understand' rather than 'memorize' (to use these two words in the colloquial sense discussed in Chapter Three). Even when factual material is to be memorized with detailed precision, it is expected that he will relate this material to a variety of other kinds of material. This is so that he will be able to recall the fact not only when explicitly asked for by some specific question but also under a variety of circumstances where the fact might be of use. The aim is that he should make the fact part of an inter-related system of facts, make it available for ready and flexible use in problem-solving situations. Consider an extreme example of what is meant here. A medical student who could recall verbatim the words of a textbook would not, by this accomplishment alone, be of much assistance to someone requiring medical attention: the student would also have to be able selectively to recall what is relevant to the case confronting him, and selectively inter-relate what he could recall so as to meet the particular requirements of the situation. In short, the important thing is not what or how much a person can remember but the selective relevance of his remembering to present circumstances. The criticism of mnemonic systems is that they do not, of themselves, contribute to such flexible understanding. Indeed, the habitual use of these systems may impede such understanding if the person becomes accustomed to abstracting from material only those characteristics which are relevant for rote memorizing. It will be remembered that Shereshevskii, despite his outstanding ability to memorize meaningless material, was sometimes unable to deal appropriately with, or even remember, meaningful material. However effective a learning procedure may be for some tasks, it is not effective if it does not fit the requirements of the particular task in hand.

4 The Effects of Practice

Suppose a person memorizes a lesson, say a poem. Does he learn anything beyond the poem itself, anything which will enable him to learn another lesson more easily? There are two main ways in which the learning of one lesson may facilitate the learning of a second. One way is through the common content of the two lessons. Different lessons may involve the same content, albeit arranged in different ways. If, for example, in learning the first poem, the person becomes familiar with a new word, then he will learn this same word more easily when it occurs in the context of a second poem. Thus, one lesson may involve material or relationships which will arise in subsequent lessons. And to this extent, the learning of the first lesson can make it easier to learn subsequent lessons: in a sense, some parts of the subsequent lessons have been learned already. The other kind of facilitation lies in the acquisition of learning techniques which can be generalized to the mastery of subsequent lessons. In learning one lesson, the person may learn something about his own learning techniques, their merits and disadvantages, where they are appropriate and where they are not. For example, with poetry, he might learn the merits of getting an overview of the whole before proceeding to detailed consideration of the parts, or he might learn something about how to use anticipatory recall as an aid to memorizing. The main point is that a person can, through practice in learning, acquire techniques which he can use to facilitate his mastery of subsequent learning tasks. In short, through the undertaking of learning, he can learn how to learn. There is no question that this learning to learn can happen. The question is: under what circumstances does it happen?

The earliest attempts to answer this question seem to have been the experiments done by William James and his colleagues. These men selected two 'test pieces' of poetry or prose. The two pieces were similar to each other in difficulty, and were usually excerpts from the same work. One 'test piece' would be memorized, and a note made of the time required. Subsequently, the second 'test piece' would be memorized under the same conditions as the first, and again the time required was recorded. But between the first and second learning episodes, the man would spend some weeks regularly memorizing poetry or prose. The question was: would all this practice in memorizing make the second 'test piece' easier to master than the first? The clear and consistent answer was that it did not. Memorizing ability was neither improved nor impaired by practice in memorizing. The results of these experiments were unambiguous. However, we must be careful how we interpret them. The men who acted as subjects in these experiments were all intellectually accomplished to a high degree. They were all products of an educational system which heavily stressed the memorizing of poetry. Furthermore, many of these men were psychologists with an interest in the study of learning activities. So it may well be that these men were, at the outset of the experiments, fully accomplished memorizers who had but little scope for further improvement. Their ability to learn poetry and prose may have been fully developed before the start of practice: and it may have been for this reason that practice had no effect. The results of the experiment might be very different if practice were undertaken by people whose learning abilities are clearly underdeveloped.

Since the time of William James, there have been several investigations into the effects which practice has on various kinds of people who learn various kinds of task. The general finding of these investigations may be expressed, with some over-simplification, as follows. Practice in memorizing does not, of itself, improve ability to learn; even ability to learn the kind of material on which practice was expended. But practice can be effective if it is taken as an opportunity to explore, discover, and modify the activeness of learning. That is, if the person doing the practice is encouraged to consider and experiment with his own learning activities; in short, to learn something about the nature of his own capabilities. So if practice in learning is made, so to speak, an exercise in self-discovery, it can often lead to the development of more effective learning techniques. The directing of practice as an exercise in self-discovery may be effected by the instructor who draws attention to this or that way of proceeding; or it may be effected by the person himself, as in the case of the mnemonist who develops expertise by self-critical use of various learning procedures. It is noteworthy that, when adults undertake to modify their learning procedures, this usually involves a great deal of deliberate and self-conscious activity; but as the person gains in experience, his selecting and using of appropriate learning procedures undergoes automatization until, at a highly developed level of proficiency, he carries through strikingly effective learning without any great awareness of what he is doing. Broadly speaking, then, the general finding is that, while practice is necessary for the development of learning techniques, practice does not, of itself, guarantee the development of generalizable learning techniques. Indeed, practice may serve to strengthen inadequate procedures rather than give rise to improved skills. In short, it is not practice itself which is important, but what the person is doing during practice.

The general remarks just made may be illustrated by outlining two investigations. The first gave practice to school children, but with no direction towards consideration of learning techniques. The second gave practice to university students, and drew attention to techniques of learning.

Sleight's Experiment. This experiment was reported by W. G. Sleight in the *British Journal of Psychology* in 1911. His subjects were eighty-four school girls whose average age was 12 years and 8 months. At the start of the experiment, each girl was given ten different learning tests. These tests involved: memorizing dates of historical events, lists of nonsense syllables, stanzas of poetry, passages of prose, and lists of names; immediately reproducing the gist of a factual prose passage, the positions of towns and rivers on a map, a dictation passage, an array of visual forms, and a list of letters of the alphabet. The performance of each girl on these 'fore-tests' was scored. On the basis of this score, she was allocated to one of four groups, so that each group, as a whole, had done equally well on the fore-tests. Three of those four groups were then given practice in memorizing. This practice was continued for thirty minutes daily on each of four days per week and for a total of six weeks, that is, for an actual practice time of twelve hours in all. Group 1 practised memorizing poetry. Group 2 practised memorizing quantitative facts such as numerical conversion tables, scientific formulae, and geographical distances. Group 3 was given selections of scientific, geographical, and historical prose passages and required to write out the gist of these immediately afterwards. The fourth group – the Control – had no special practice of any kind.

At the end of the six weeks, each of the four groups was given 'after-tests' comprising the same ten tests as originally given. The actual content of these tests was, of course, different, but they had the same general form, and each test was so constructed as to be equivalent in difficulty to the corresponding test given at the start of the experiment. The interest of the investigation lay in discovering whether the girls would, as a consequence of practice, do better on the after-tests of learning than on the fore-tests. Would they learn more quickly? But there was the possibility that, quite independently of their training, their learning abilities might have improved as a result of all the other activities in which they had engaged over the six weeks. It was for this reason that the Control Group was included, being given the fore- and after-tests without any memorizing practice in between. In assessing the effects of practice on, say, Group 1, Sleight could not simply compare this group's performance on the after-tests with its performances on the fore-tests. These two sets of performances may have differed in consequence of innumerable factors which had nothing whatever to do with the intervening practice as such. It was necessary to compare the performances of

Group 1 on the after-tests with those of the Control Group on the same after-tests. Since the two groups were equated for learning abilities to start off with, and since the major difference between them lay in the presence or absence of practice, any difference in their final learning performances could then be attributed to the effects of practice. The inclusion of a control group was, incidentally, only one of the many careful precautions which had to be taken in order that such a complex study as this should yield completely unambiguous results.

The outcome of Sleight's experiment was a complete absence of any general improvement in learning as a result of any of the three forms of practice. Some of the tests showed a very slight improvement and others showed a slight impairment but, in all tests, the effects were small and not statistically significant. This was true even for the memorizing of poetry in Group 1. After six weeks of practice, these children, relative to the Control Group which had had no such practice, showed no improvement whatever in the poetry after-test. The only exception was that the groups which had practised memorizing poetry and 'tables' showed a significant improvement in the memorizing of nonsense syllables – an improvement which was due to the technique, acquired during training, of organizing the material into rhythmical units.

Woodrow's Experiment. This experiment was reported by the American psychologist, H. Woodrow, in 1927. The design of Woodrow's investigation followed closely on that of Sleight. He divided 182 university students into three groups and gave each group a set of fore-tests and after-tests. These tests involved memorizing stanzas of poetry and passages of prose, reproducing the gist of factual prose selections, learning the English meaning of Turkish words, learning the dates of historical events, and finally, a test of auditory memory span for consonants. The Control Group did only the fore- and after-tests. The Practice Group devoted a total of three hours (in eight periods spaced over four weeks) to memorizing poems and nonsense syllables. The Training Group divided this same time of three hours between exercises in memorizing poems and syllables and the receiving of instructions in methods of efficient memorizing. For a total of 76 minutes, they listened to an exposition of the techniques of memorizing, including rules and illustrations of how these rules should be applied. They spent the remaining 104 minutes in memorizing poetry and nonsense syllables with the explicit purpose of attempting, as far as possible, to apply the rules they had been given. In the after-tests, the Practice Group was no better than the Control: their learning abilities had not improved as a result of their practice. The Training Group, on the other hand, definitely surpassed the other two groups in every single test – even although it had spent less time in actual memorizing activity than had the Practice Group.

The rules taught to the Training Group were as follows: be alert, concentrate on learning, and have confidence in your ability to memorize; learn by wholes rather than by parts; use recitation; organize the material in terms of its rhythm and its meaning and, with nonsense syllables, of elaborating 'secondary associations'. (The use of repetition was not emphasized because the practice conditions were such that the student had no opportunity for varying the number of repetitions.) These methods were explained, illustrated by reference to examples of poetry and nonsense syllables, and the students urged to use them in their memorizing practice. Notice that the students had no direct practice in applying these methods to the learning of Turkish–English vocabularies, dates of historical events, lists of consonants, or the substance of factual passages. Yet, in the after-tests, the students successfully applied the methods to these unpractised forms of learning. As the

Practice Group showed, mere routine practice in memorizing is insufficient to establish techniques which can be used in new learning situations. It is necessary that the students be aware of these techniques in terms of general principles or rules. It has also been found in other investigations that the mere knowledge of rules is, by itself, of no value unless the individual exerts the effort of putting them into practice. He must learn not only that rules can be used but also how to use them. This latter aspect of improvement is, of course, something which only the individual can achieve for himself. However skilfully rules may be taught, it is, in the last analysis, the individual himself who must learn to apply them through his own intellectual efforts.

This section can be summarized as follows. Opportunity to carry out learning is essential for the development of learning, and practice in learning can be effective in developing generalizable learning procedures – provided such practice is treated as an opportunity to discover the properties of learning procedures and to gain experience in their use. Of itself, practice in learning by no means guarantees development of improved learning techniques, even in people whose learning abilities are underdeveloped. Nor is improvement guaranteed by the mere giving of 'rules' for learning. The person must come to understand such rules, not as verbal formulae but in terms of his own learning activities; and he can only do this by applying these rules in practice.

5 Organizing the Task

Learning does not happen passively. It is an activity which a person does. It is a task which can be attempted in various ways, some of which are more appropriate than others. When the material to be learned is of a brief and simple kind which is familiar to the person and of intense interest to him, effective learning usually proceeds automatically. In the first place, the person at once relates the material to other material which is already securely learned. Subsequently, the relevance of the newly learned material to his interests ensures its being recalled on many occasions; and this repetition minimizes the likelihood of forgetting. Furthermore, the subsequent use of the new material is likely to take place in a variety of contexts and, so, the material becomes related to a wider range of other material. Because of all this, the material is rapidly learned, long retained, and recalled with increasing readiness in an increasing variety of contexts. Without really trying, the person has fulfilled several important conditions of effective learning, conditions expressed by William James as follows. 'Briefly, then, of two men with the same outward experiences and the same amount of mere native tenacity, *the one who* THINKS *over his experiences most,* and weaves them into systematic relations with each other, *will be the one with the best memory.*' However, learning does not proceed automatically when the material to be learned is not brief, not simple, not of a kind which is already familiar to the person, and not perhaps of much interest to him. In this situation, effective learning does not go forward with unthinking ease. Learning becomes a problem to be solved, a task to be organized by deliberately considering the learning requirements of the task.

The exact factors to be taken into account in organizing any particular learning task depend on the details of the task. They concern the objectives of learning: what is subsequently to be remembered, in what ways, under what circumstances, and how far ahead. They concern the nature and amount of the material, and which characteristics of it are to be learned. They concern the present abilities of the individual learner; what he has learned already, what kinds of material are familiar to him, how experienced he is in selectively directing his own learning efforts. They concern the amount of time available for this learning task in relation to all the other activities which the person is to carry out. In brief, there are many detailed factors to be considered in deciding the optimal organization of any particular learning task. These details cannot be discussed here. (Many of them have been mentioned in earlier parts of this book. The following books consider some factors of importance to the learning tasks of university students. *The Psychology of Study*, by C. A. Mace, Penguin Books, 1962; *How to Study*, by H. Maddox, Pan Books, 1963; *How to Study*, by C. T. Morgan and J. Deese, McGraw-Hill, 1957.) However, we may outline three general aspects of organizing any learning task, whatever its precise nature.

Three Aspects. Perhaps the first step in organizing the task is to be aware that organizing is required, that learning cannot usually be left to chance, and that different ways of proceeding can lead to different kinds of learning. Granted this, the factors to be considered might be gathered under three broad headings.

(1) *Surveying the task.* This involves overviewing the learning requirements of the task, the nature of the material in relation to the kind of learning which is to be accom-

plished. What characteristics of the material are to be remembered, and for what purposes? How much effort is likely to be needed for such learning? Should this effort be expended all in one learning episode, or distributed across several learning episodes at different times?

(2) *Organizing the material*. This involves considering the material as a whole, and perhaps a rearrangement of the material, so as to gain an overview that coherently serves to inter-relate the component parts together. It also involves relating the material, in whole and in its parts, to material which is already familiar; discovering the similarities and differences between the material and what is known already.

(3) *Repeating what has been learned*. This involves subsequent periodic review and use of the learned material so as to minimize its being forgotten, and to increase the variety of other material to which this material is related. In short, this final phase continues the essential activities of weaving the details of experience into systematic relations with each other.

Bearing these three broad aspects in mind, we may consider a simple and familiar kind of learning task which exemplifies them. This is the task of learning and remembering the names of people we meet. When we are introduced to a person, many of us find that we cannot recall his name subsequently. Usually, this is because we do not, at the time of the introduction, make any attempt to learn the name in relation to its owner. Often we do not even hear the name clearly; it is just a mumble against a diffuse background of noise. Or if we do hear it, we forget it immediately amid the distractions of other matters. Subsequently, we cannot remember the name for the simple reason that we never learned it in the first place. So, the first necessity is to remind ourselves that, if we want to be able to recall the person's name later, we must do something about learning it now. We are faced by a simple learning task which requires us to relate two items together, the person and his name, and do this in such a way that either item can be recalled when one is given. So we must consider the distinctive characteristics of these two items. Regarding the name, this must be heard correctly, even if we must ask for its being said again. Is it a name we know already? Is it the name of someone we already know? Is it an unusual name? If so, what does it suggest to us? In short, we must examine the name in relation to our prior experience with names. As with the name, so with the other item, the person. What are the outstanding characteristics of his manner or appearance? Does he resemble someone or something we already know? Once we have abstracted what seem to be the distinctive characteristics of the two items, we must then relate them clearly to each other. Does the person look like his name? How different is the person from other people we know with the same name? In short, we must bring the two items into distinctive relation, even if this means creating a bizarre and unflattering name–person composite. With a little practice, this entire procedure takes much less time to perform than it has taken to describe. The last necessity is that the relation between the person and his name should be given the advantage of repetition, either privately or openly by addressing the person by name as often as conversational convention permits. This, then, is the technique: survey the task, make the material meaningful, and repeat it. If the reader is not already familiar with this general procedure, he should try it. He will be surprised at how effective it is, and with what automatized ease it can be carried through if practised habitually.

Organizing the Material. The above task of learning and remembering people's names illustrates, in one setting, the three broad aspects to be considered in organizing any memory task. Surveying the task requirements, organizing the material, and repeating what has been learned. Of these three aspects, the second requires some special mention.

Organizing the material lies very much at the heart of learning activity. It involves abstracting from the material those characteristics which are most useful to remember, relative to the objectives of the task. It involves relating those characteristics to each other in ways which are both familiar and coherent. It involves relating the material to what has been learned already so as, in short, to weave the material into systematic inter-relation with the person's cumulative past experience.

Consider the organizing of material from the point of view of someone who is presenting the material;. a teacher, a lecturer, indeed anyone whose task is to 'put over' material to others. He does not mention items of information in the order in which he happens to recall them at the moment. Rather, he goes over his material beforehand and arranges it. He groups together those parts which have something in common: he groups and sub-groups those items which are, in some important respect, similar. He relates these parts in ordered sequence: he develops a sequence of themes which lead coherently into each other. He evolves an overall structure for his material, one which serves to hold together the component parts and emphasize those features which he regards as most important. He is especially likely to adopt group-labelling methods of organizing which encompass large amounts of information within a brief set of relationships – a general principle, or rule, or law. The merits of such group-labelling have been discussed already but, here, one obvious example may be given. Suppose we want to remember how far an object has fallen through space after it has been falling freely for a given time. We could memorize all the individual distances: after one second, the object has fallen 16 feet; after two seconds, 64 feet; after three seconds, 144 feet; and so on. However, this is a cumbersome and, as it happens, unnecessary undertaking. We are ignoring the fact that these values are not independent of each other, that these values can be related together so as to abstract a common characteristic. The distance fallen at the end of t seconds is $gt^2/2$ feet; and since the value of g is approximately 32, all we need abstract, learn, and remember is the formula $16t^2$. This simple example illustrates the powerful economy of relating specific items of information together in such a way as to abstract a compact characteristic which serves to specify the common features of all the items. This is the economy basic to the rules, laws, principles, and generalizations of science and scholarship. This is the kind of economy at which the person aims when he is trying to organize his material for most effective presentation. In short, when the person is presenting material, he attempts to weave his items of information into systematic relationships with each other, and to do this in ways which will be evident to and readily learned by his audience. It is both fascinating and instructive to observe the accomplished expositor organizing his material so as to make it most comprehensible to his audience, so as to 'predigest it for easy consumption'. These efforts of the expositor reflect the fact that, if people are to learn and remember the material he presents, then they must take in this material in organized ways which are as familiar and as coherent to them as possible.

Now consider the organizing of material from the point of view of someone who is attempting to learn and remember the material. More specifically, consider a simple task of relating a name to an item. In arithmetic, a fraction, say $\frac{1}{2}$, has one number on top and another below. One is called denominator, and one numerator. The writer has often asked students how they remember which number is called by which name. Some students 'just know'. Others do not know. But between these extremes, different students recall in different ways, and at different speeds and with different degrees of certainty. Here are three examples. Denominator is on the bottom since it is the longer word and sinks below the other. Denominator begins with the same letter as the word 'down'. Numerator is 'up' because it contains the letter 'u'. Notice that these relations are all of an artificial kind involving rather incidental characteristics of the material. But notice also that these relations work effectively for the students who use them: and this, after all, is the important issue. Here is another example. Denominator denominates, names, the size of the portion, and numerator enumerates, numbers, how many portions there are in the fraction. These relations hold the items and names together in a meaningful, reliable way. They involve the central, distinctive characteristics both of fractions and of the words used to describe them. The material is inter-related in ways which are consistent with and shared by other features of the student's knowledge about arithmetic and language. The material is, in short, made part of a wider and coherent system of relationships. Should the student forget which number is called by which name, he can work it out by means of this wider system of relations. By contrast, one student could not recall whether denominator came on the bottom because its initial letter is the same as that of 'down', or on top because 'd' comes before 'n' in the alphabet. He could recall that one or other of those relations applied, but could not specify which. And when a person forgets such isolated and artificial relations, there is no supporting context of relations enabling him to work out the answer.

To say that a person relates material in a meaningful way is usually to say that the material is dealt with in terms of its distinctively important characteristics; and also that these characteristics are related in unambiguous ways which make them part of a larger, systematically organized complex of learned material. Such meaningful ways of relating material are clearly more effective than ways which stress incidental characteristics and relate them together in isolated ways which neither fit with previous experience nor facilitate subsequent learning of new material. In short, there are good reasons to disparage, in general, the use of artificial mnemonic relations and to stress the merits of understanding the meaning of the material in relation to a wider system of cumulative past experience. However, it must be granted that meaningful relations are not always available to the learner. Sometimes this is because the material is essentially arbitrary. Sometimes it is because the meaningful relations lie beyond the comprehension of the learner. In such cases, the material can only be organized by artificial relations and by repetition. Many of us know from our own experience that artificial, fanciful mnemonic relations can facilitate learning, and that, if we often repeat what we have learned, these contrived relations become increasingly unnecessary for remembering, and tend to be forgotten. Some examples of these artificial mnemonic relations may now be given.

If there is difficulty in learning the difference between stalactite and stalagmite, this difference can be specified by noting that stala*c*tites grow from the *c*eiling and stala*g*mites from the *g*round. If there is difficulty in learning which 'arm' of a graph, the vertical or the horizontal, is called abscissa and ordinate, this can be specified as follows. When we say 'ordinate' we part our lips wide, almost mouthing the vertical direction: when we pronounce 'abscissa' we mouth the horizontal direction. In these two examples – and the reader can doubtless think of many more – one item is related to another by some characteristic which they share. However, the two items sometimes have no such common characteristic, and in this case use can be made of a third intermediate item. This device of using an intermediate is often used in learning the vocabulary of a foreign language. Thus, the German words, *Stuhl*, *Blume* and *Koffer* can obviously be related to their English equivalents of chair, flower, and suitcase through the intermediates of stool, bloom and coffer. It is, of course, possible to use more than one intermediate mnemonic relation.

When it is more than two items which have to be related together, further reorganizing devices emerge. A common trick is to reorganize the items so that they are embodied in a poem or jingle of some sort. We are probably all familiar with the rhyme which starts off: 'Thirty days hath September, April, June, and November.' It is by means of this verse that many of us learned, and still recall, the number of days in each month of the year. This device exploits all the organizational advantages of rhyme and rhythm, and its success is attested by the myriad verses (including Brayshaw's) which have been composed to help us learn the more cumbersome facts of history, foreign languages, and so on. An advantage is often to be gained not only by recasting the material into verse form but also by arranging the lines of the verse in such a way that the first or last letters or words of each line constitute, when taken in sequence, a familiar letter or word combination such as a name or a sentence. This is the time-honoured device of the acrostic, and it is at least as old as the 119th Psalm. This ancient composition consists of twenty-two eight-verse sections corresponding to the twenty-two letters of the Hebrew alphabet. The first word of every verse in each section always begins with the same letter: the letter for the first section is 'aleph', for the second section 'beth', and so on. As most frequently employed, however, the acrostic is not usually in verse form but simply relates the different items altogether in a whole which is either a word of a phrase. An example of this is that we must be '*careful*' to pronounce the letters *c, r, f* and *l* at the end of French words. Other examples of this acrostic device are known to medical students who are learning anatomical names. For example, recalling the names given to the branches of the external carotid artery may be prompted by the following phrase: *S*weet *L*ittle *F*lappers *O*ccupy *P*ositions *A*s *S*tenographers *M*ainly. The initial letter of each word in this phrase is, in order, the same as the initial letter of the branch whose name is to be recalled.

In summary, the organizing of the material is a critical aspect of learning. It may be difficult, and the form of organization sought will vary with the material to be learned, with the individual's past experience, and with his present interests. But when the parts of the material can be woven into systematic relations with each other and with what the person has already learned, then the learning of this material is strongly facilitated. The material then fits readily into the person's cumulative past experience and, in subsequent remembering, is supported by this cumulative experience. The organizing of the material also modifies past experience in such a way as to facilitate later learning of new and related material. Where compact and meaningful organization of the material is not feasible, for one reason or another, the person must have recourse to artificial mnemonic relations and to rote repetition.

Studying a Book. The activities of studying a book suffice as a final setting in which to consider the three broad aspects of organizing a learning task. The first step is to survey the book together with our objective in reading it. On the one hand, we want to get some preliminary impression of the sort of book it is. Is it meant to be a popular book, or a technical work requiring specialized prior knowledge? Which parts are relevant to our interests, and which are not? On the other hand, we want to get some preliminary impression of our objective in reading the book, of what we want to learn from it. Do we want to savour the background atmosphere of a historical period? Or find details about a particular viewpoint such as a philosophical school? Or answer questions requiring factual information? Or learn about a technique in, say, surgery, or engineering, or logic? In general, the reader gains most from his reading when he starts by surveying the book in relation to what he wants to learn from it. In relation to his purposes, not all books have the same value. This fact was expressed by Francis

Bacon (1561–1626) as follows: 'Some books are to be tasted, others to be swallowed, and some few to be chewed and digested: that is, some books are to be read only in parts; others to be read, but not curiously; and some few to be read wholly, and with diligence and attention.' The reader may find that he wants to learn a variety of different things from the same book, and that he may have to read the same material several times with a different objective in mind each time.

Having made this preliminary survey of the book in relation to what we want to learn from it, and assuming that the book is of a kind which is to be 'chewed and digested', the next step is to survey the whole book more closely. The general procedure is to glance at the table of contents, the arrangement of headings and sub-headings, summaries, the index, and thereby get an overview of the book as a whole and the relations of its various parts to this whole. As with the actor mastering his role, the reader best masters his book by proceeding from an overview of the whole towards progressively more detailed parts. This is the case not only for the entire book and its constituent chapters, but also for a chapter and its constituent sections, and for a section and its constituent paragraphs. The understanding of a part is facilitated by being studied in a larger context.

The study of a book, then, usually requires that we devote some time to surveying the nature of the learning task. Such surveying takes us some way into the second broad aspect of organizing the task, namely, organizing the material in the book. Here, it is perhaps our most frequent fault that we read too passively. Reading involves much more than darting the eyes across lines of print. It involves us in attempting to relate what we read to what we have already learned, to rearrange what we read so as to make it most meaningful to us. So we ought constantly to be evaluating what we read. And this means that the greater part of our reading time may not be spent in viewing the print but in thinking about the meaning 'behind' the print, and perhaps even in writing out our own précis of what we have read.

Throughout this evaluating of the material, the question-answer sequence of activity plays an important part. The asking of questions ensures that we deal with the material in a selectively active way. Furthermore, it seems to be pervasively the case that information is best learned when it is taken in as an answer to a question being asked. Even at pre-linguistic levels of activity, this is seen in classical Pavlovian conditioning. A dog hears a bell and 'questions' it by showing what Pavlov called the 'What is it?' reaction. Subsequently, his 'question' is answered by discovering that the bell signifies the arrival of food. Also at a pre-linguistic level, the question-answer sequence is evident in the exploratory activities of the young child. He 'questions' events by experimenting with them to see what happens and, thereby, he learns much about the characteristics of the world in which he lives. At a linguistic level, the asking of verbal questions is a conspicuous part of the older child's activities: he may spend much time eliciting verbal answers to a host of questions which he puts to people in words. And in higher-level adult learning, questions, whether verbal or non-verbal, play an important role in determining what is selectively learned and what is not. So, it is typically the case that information is best learned by a person when it supplies the answer to some question he is asking. Now, in reading, we may exploit this question-answer sequence by habitually asking ourselves questions such as the following. Does this material make sense? Does it relate to anything I know already? Can I think of other examples of this generalization? Can I rephrase this passage in my own words? What is the essential point here? Our reading profits from being conducted as a kind of active conversation between ourselves and the book. We should constantly remind ourselves that our purpose in reading is to understand and remember what we read; and this can be achieved by actively asking questions about what we are reading. These questions may arise from the book itself, or from our previous knowledge about the subject-matter of the book. But throughout, we should attempt to interpret our reading, translate it, and transform it so as to bring it into relation with what we already know and what we want still to know.

The third broad aspect of organizing the task is to repeat what has been learned from reading. This repetition may take the form of synoptic review, or of using what has been read in our writing, and conversation, and thinking. During reading, it is often helpful to stop at the end of a section or paragraph and review the gist of what has just been read. This lets us know what we have understood and what we have not understood: it lets us know how much we have already forgotten: it maintains our interest in reading: it reminds us that our objective is to be able to remember what we read; and it reduces the likelihood of subsequent forgetting. Synoptic review at the conclusion of the whole reading session serves similar functions. And after reading is over, the periodic use of what we have learned serves not merely to maintain our learning but also to bring it into relation with our other learning, to make it readily and flexibly available for selective use in an ever-increasing variety of contexts.

Conclusion. Throughout recorded history, men have asked questions about memory. Around 1880, the answers to these questions began to be sought by systematic empirical inquiry into memory activities as they actually take place in this or that setting. And such inquiries have continued into the present day for, although much has been discovered, a very great deal remains obscure. For the most part, these inquiries have not been undertaken for the sake of any immediate practical value. Rather, they have been pursued as part of a long enterprise which seeks to understand the rich and marvellous functioning of human beings. In the course of this continuing enterprise, discoveries have been made which can be used in practical affairs. More specifically, we know more than we did about the problems and complexities of effectively organizing the activities of learning. However, most of these advances have been made at a detailed level, have concerned the particular merits and demerits of this or that particular set of circumstances. For this reason, it is not possible to give a brief summary of these advances. At the level of tersely general practical advice, it can only be said that 'memory improvement' is the problem of organizing the learning task with special regard to three aspects, namely, surveying the requirements of the task, organizing the material, and repeating what has been learned. These three broad aspects of organizing the task are well expressed in a poem written in 1562 by an Englishman, William Fulwood. In the not inept metaphor of his day, he compares memory to a castle of strategic importance in the battle of life, and gives directions by which this coveted fortress may be taken into possession. 'Memorie' he writes 'sayeth:

> To him that would me gladly gaine
> These three precepts shall not be vaine.
> The first is well to understand
> The thing that he doth take in hand.
> The second is the same to place
> In order good and formed race.
> The thirde is often to repeat
> The thing that he would not forgeat.
> Adioning to this castell strong,
> Great virtue comes er it be long.'

Recommended for Further Reading

References for further reading have already been given at appropriate places in the text. The following selection of relatively non-technical books is presented here for the convenience of the general reader.

1. Allport, G. W., and Postman, L. *The Psychology of Rumor.* New York: Henry Holt & Co., 1947. A blend of experimental work with findings in the field of social psychology. It discusses the how and why of the spread of rumour.

2. Barlow, F. *Mental Prodigies.* London: Hutchinson's Scientific and Technical Publications, 1951. A non-psychologist describes mental prodigies including famous memory-men and mnemonists.

3. Fraisse, P. *The Psychology of Time.* London and New York: Harper & Row, 1963. Presents an interesting variety of evidence about the issues of time-perception and recollection.

4. Freud, S. *Psychopathology of Everyday Life.* London: T. Fisher Unwin, 1914. Contains Freud's ingenious application of psychoanalytic concepts to everyday remembering and forgetting.

5. McKellar, P. *Imagination and Thinking.* London: Cohen & West, 1957. An interesting book containing excellent discussions of imaging.

6. Morgan, J. J. B., and Lovell, G. D. *The Psychology of Abnormal People.* London: Longmans, 1928. A general survey of abnormal psychology. Chapter 8 is devoted to disorders of memory.

7. Russell, W. R. *Brain, Memory, Learning.* Oxford University Press, 1959. A neurologist discusses some problems of memory and presents evidence about the effects of brain damage.

8. Stern, W. *Psychology of Early Childhood*. London: Allen & Unwin, 1924. Part V outlines the development of memory in the young child. The book is especially rich in observational description.

9. Wooldridge, D. E. *The Machinery of the Brain*. London and New York: McGraw-Hill, 1963. A general account of brain functioning which incorporates recent work in biology, psychology, and cybernetics.

Index of Main References

Index of Main References

More about Penguins
and Pelicans

Penguinews, which appears every month, contains details of all the new books issued by Penguins as they are published. From time to time it is supplemented by *Penguins in Print*, which is a complete list of all titles available. (There are some five thousand of these.)

A specimen copy of *Penguinews* will be sent to you free on request. For a year's issues (including the complete lists) please send 50p if you live in the British Isles, or 75p if you live elsewhere. Just write to Dept EP, Penguin Books Ltd, Harmondsworth, Middlesex, enclosing a cheque or postal order, and your name will be added to the mailing list.

In the U.S.A.: For a complete list of books available from Penguin in the United States write to Dept CS, Penguin Books Inc., 7110 Ambassador Road, Baltimore, Maryland 21207.

In Canada: For a complete list of books available from Penguin in Canada write to Penguin Books Canada Ltd, 41 Steelcase Road West, Markham, Ontario.

A Dictionary of Psychology

James Drever

The technical vocabulary of psychology is not in itself an unduly large one, but several other sciences border upon the psychological field and some knowledge of their terms is also necessary. The stimuli which act upon our sense organs are described in physical terms; what happens in the nervous system is relevant and has to be expressed in physiological terms; abnormal behaviour and the clinical description of it and its causes require medical terms. Thus the technical vocabulary actually used by psychologists tends to be rather extensive.

It is the aim of this dictionary to give some help, not merely to the layman, but also to the student, in what has now become an important branch of contemporary science.

'It is commended with confidence as a document relevant not merely to the experimental psychology of former days, but to recent developments in psychometrics, social psychology, psychopathology and industrial psychology' – *Higher Education Journal.*

Uses and Abuses of Psychology

H. J. Eysenck

Psychology occupies a somewhat ambiguous place in the world today. Its findings are being widely applied in clinics, in industry, in education, and in the armed forces. At the same time, many intelligent people are critical of the alleged laws of human behaviour discovered by psychologists, psychiatrists, and psychoanalysts, and doubtful about the applicability of scientific methods to the study of human beings. In this book, a well-known psychologist has tried to strike a balance, to indicate to what extent the claims made for his science are justified, and to what extent they fail to have any factual basis. Topics dealt with are the testing of intelligence, selection procedures in schools and universities, vocational guidance and occupational selection, psychotherapy and its effects, national differences, racial intolerance, Gallup surveys, industrial productivity, and many others. In each case, psychological findings are submitted to a searching criticism, and a clear distinction made between those uses of psychology where enough is known to support social action, and those abuses where personal opinions rather than experimentally demonstrated fact seem to be involved.

Sense and Nonsense in Psychology

H. J. Eysenck

There are many topics in modern psychology about which speculation
has been rife for hundreds of years. Much has been written on the powers
and dangers of the hypnotic trance, the wonders of telepathy and clair-
voyance, the possibility of the interpretation of dreams, the nature and
assessment of personality, and the psychology of beauty. These early
views, while often amusing, have little value because they are not based
on scientific facts. In recent years, much experimental evidence has been
collected regarding all these topics, but few reliable accounts have
appeared which would acquaint the interested layman with these facts
and their possible interpretations and implications. This is what the
author has attempted to do in this book, by carefully reviewing and
sifting the evidence, by frankly, boldly putting forward a definite point
of view where the evidence appears to justify it. Throughout the book
emphasis is laid particularly on the detailed discussion of the facts,
leaving to the reader the decision as to whether the conclusions drawn
are justified.

Also available

FACT AND FICTION IN PSYCHOLOGY

Hypnosis : Fact and Fiction

F. L. Marcuse

This book attempts to offer a broad view of the field of hypnosis. It answers questions frequently asked by students and non-students alike, and to both classes of readers presents new material of interest and importance. In addition to discussing some of the general problems of hypnosis, it is also concerned with applications (clinical, medical, dental, and so on), techniques, dangers (real and imagined), theories (sleep, conditioning, etc.), and attitudes (academic, religious, medical). The book's main purpose is to separate fact from fiction in this highly controversial field.

The viewpoint of the author is not that hypnosis offers a panacea or a magical solution of the problems of psychopathology, but rather that it is a technique which is often of value and that its study can add important new data to our knowledge of human behaviour.